To Retire or Not?

To Retire or Not?

Retirement Policy and Practice
in Higher Education

Edited by
Robert L. Clark and P. Brett Hammond

Pension Research Council
The Wharton School of the University of Pennsylvania

PENN

University of Pennsylvania Press

Philadelphia

Pension Research Council Publications

A complete list of books in the series appears at the back of this volume

Published by
University of Pennsylvania Press
Philadelphia, Pennsylvania 19104–4011

Library of Congress Cataloging-in-Publication Data

To retire or not? : retirement policy and practice in higher
education / edited by Robert L. Clark and P. Brett Hammond.
   p. cm.
   "Pension Research Council publications"—T.p. verso.
   Includes bibliographical references and index.
   ISBN 0-8122-3572-X (cloth : alk. paper)
   1. College teachers—Pensions—United States—Congresses.
I. Clark, Robert Louis, 1949–   II. Hammond, P. Brett.
III. Wharton School. Pension Research Council.
LB2334 .T6   2001
331.25′2913781′20973—dc21   00-055218

Contents

Preface   vii

1. Introduction: Changing Retirement Policies and Patterns
in Higher Education   1
Robert L. Clark and P. Brett Hammond

2. Faculty Retirement at Three North Carolina Universities   21
Robert L. Clark, Linda S. Ghent, and Juanita Kreps

3. Age-Based Retirement Incentives for Tenured Faculty Members:
Satisfying the Legal Requirements   39
David L. Raish

4. Survey of Early Retirement Practices in Higher Education   65
John Keefe

5. Cornell Confronts the End of Mandatory Retirement   81
Ronald G. Ehrenberg, Michael W. Matier, and David Fontanella

6. The University of California Voluntary Early Retirement
Incentive Programs   106
Ellen Switkes

7. Ending Mandatory Retirement in Two State Universities   122
Robert M. O'Neil

8. Intangible and Tangible Retirement Incentives   128
John Keefe

9. Faculty Retirement: Reflections on Experience in an
Uncapped Environment   138
Sharon P. Smith

10. Reflections on an Earlier Study of Mandatory Retirement:
What Came True and What We Can Still Learn   148
Karen C. Holden and W. Lee Hansen

List of Contributors   167

Index   171

Preface

This book examines the impact of the ending of mandatory retirement, the aging of faculties in higher education, and the human resource policies universities employ to influence the retirement decisions made by older faculty. We began to study these issues in response to interest and concern expressed by John Biggs of TIAA-CREF and Juanita Kreps of Duke University about, first, the impact of faculty aging and delayed retirement on the academy and, second, government policies regulating university retirement policies, early retirement windows, and phased retirement programs.

The insightful questions and critical comments posed by Kreps and Biggs inspired the editors to assess what was currently known about these issues and to develop new research ideas for evaluating the academic labor market in the twenty-first century. With their encouragement and support, the editors commissioned papers from some of the leading scholars and administrators on the legal, behavioral, and administrative policy issues associated with faculty retirement. These papers were presented at a national conference on faculty retirement in Washington in May 1998. Funding and organizational support from what is now the TIAA-CREF Institute, as well as from North Carolina State University's College of Management, enabled the editors to bring together an outstanding group of scholars, policy analysts, and academic administrators to discuss the effects of the elimination of mandatory retirement and the ensuing change in faculty retirement patterns. This book contains the best assessment of the leading authorities on these important issues.

Special thanks go to Juanita Kreps, John Biggs, TIAA-CREF, and North Carolina State University. Without their support, this project would not have been undertaken and completed. In addition, we would like to thank Diane Oakley and Mark Warshawsky, who helped conceptualize and design the project, as well David Breneman, Richard Burkhauser, David Card, Jay Chronister, Clare Cotton, Joyce Fecske, Ruth Flower, Frederick Ford, Jim Kane, Harriet Morgan, and Jack Schuster, all of whom commented on, debated, and thereby improved the analysis presented in these chapters. Finally, we would like to thank Clare Burnett for her organizational acumen, Cynthia Alvarez for the logistical and administrative support she provided, and Gladys Bolella for preparing the final manuscript.

Chapter 1
Introduction: Changing Retirement Policies and Patterns in Higher Education

Robert L. Clark and P. Brett Hammond

As the new century begins, the tectonics of the faculty labor market are shifting rapidly. The aftershocks of these movements are challenging colleges and universities to confront a wide range of faculty resource and compensation policies. This book focuses on retirement and retirement policies—the back end of the labor market, but it is this end that drives or deeply affects such issues as new faculty hiring, the ability of colleges and universities to change the direction of teaching and research, and the age structure of the faculty. The reason for such a focus is that we are now gaining experience with what to do about a fundamental shift in the retirement rules: the end of mandatory retirement.

Until 1994, mandatory retirement was an integral component of human resource policy for academic personnel at most of the nation's colleges and universities, especially research institutions. On January 1, 1994, at the end of a seven-year exemption, an amendment to the U.S. Age Discrimination in Employment Act (ADEA) took effect, ending mandatory retirement for tenured faculty.[1] At that moment, most colleges and universities confronted a significantly altered academic labor market, one in which tenured faculty could not be required to retire at any specified age.

Higher education already faced some significant academic personnel issues based on widespread concerns about three perceived trends: (1) a faculty "bulge"—a disproportionate number of faculty hired in the 1960s and early 1970s to teach the baby boomers and who are now approaching age 60; (2) a "surplus army"—a large number of people who received doctoral degrees in the past ten years compared to the number of academic job openings during that period; and (3) modest or no increases in higher education budgets (Bowen and Sosa 1989; Finkelstein, Seal, and Schuster 1998; National Research Council 1993; Brewer, Gates, and Goldman 1998). To make matters worse, these trends in the higher education labor market were thought to be concentrated in some fields—physics and English, for instance—more than others—for example, in computer sciences (National Research Council 1998).

Therefore, on top of possible negative effects of limited budget increases, a faculty bulge, and a surplus doctorate army, elimination of mandatory retirement as a personnel policy raised several additional concerns among academic administrators. First, many feared a decline in academic quality if senior professors remained on the job past the traditional retirement age. Second, these administrators anticipated a reduced ability to renew and enrich their faculties by hiring either newly trained assistant professors or senior professors with established reputations. Third, they expected a loss in flexibility to reallocate faculty positions to emerging areas of interest and in response to shifts in student demand. Finally, they pondered the possibility of higher costs associated with retaining senior professors instead of hiring newer, entry-level professors.

These management concerns contrast with the legitimate interest of faculty members in obtaining an employment right granted by Congress to almost all other American workers. This new right bestowed on individual faculty members an economic benefit that they could exercise by choosing to continue working past age 70 or by "selling" the benefit back to the university in exchange for their earlier retirement. In comparison to earlier years, universities could not force older faculty to retire, but they could continue to offer financial incentives to encourage retirement at younger ages.

Before 1994, two major studies, by Hammond and Morgan (National Research Council 1991) and by Rees and Smith (1991), respectively, assessed the likely impact of ending mandatory retirement in higher education. These studies reached five major conclusions.

Retirement ages in higher education. Most faculty retired before reaching the age of 70. Faculty at the majority of colleges and universities—institutions where tenured faculty teach a relatively large number of courses each year and have relatively less access to research funds, graduate students, and opportunities for publication—traditionally chose to retire well before age 70. Through the 1980s, most faculty followed the trend in the American workforce toward voluntary retirement at earlier ages.

Retirement ages in research universities. A bunching of faculty retirement at the required retirement age of 70 occurred primarily at the major research universities. Faculty at research universities—institutions where tenured faculty teach relatively few courses per year and have greater access to research funds, graduate students, and opportunities for publication—chose to retire later than their colleagues elsewhere. At private research universities with mandatory retirement, about 35 percent of the faculty who retired did so at the mandatory retirement age, while at public universities with mandatory retirement policies, about 18 percent retired at age 70. At a very small number of universities, more than 50 percent of faculty retired right at age 70. These studies anticipated that the proportion of faculty who continue to work past age 70 in a post-mandatory retirement world will be related to the proportion who worked right up to age 70 prior to 1994.

Faculty performance and aging. These studies found no evidence that age predicts professional vitality in college teaching or research. Instead, studies on aging and performance show that variations in ability and competence are greater within age groups than between age groups. Special studies of higher education faculty teaching and research failed to show strong age effects among faculty who chose to keep working. Instead, there was evidence that negative feedback on research and teaching, at some institutions, led to faculty self-selection (i.e., exit from employment).

Tenure and faculty dismissals. Despite having tenure, faculty could be, but rarely are, dismissed for poor performance. The legal status of tenure doesn't prevent faculty dismissals for poor performance. Appropriate post-tenure review programs can be used to provide incentives for faculty to maintain a record of good performance, to encourage poor performers to improve or leave the institution, and to dismiss poor performers who neither improve or leave on their own. Some institutions have instituted serious posttenure review. The obstacles for those who haven't are more often anthropological than legal.

Retirement incentive programs. Retirement incentive programs could induce faculty to retire earlier. Designed well, phased or early retirement incentive programs have affected faculty retirement in the past. Specific tools include cash payments, pension credits, part-time teaching, and continuing access to campus facilities (e.g., library card, parking, office space, and other perquisites). Costs of specific programs vary widely; high-cost incentive programs can be a significant portion of an institution's faculty compensation budget. But in the past, the uncertain legal status of retirement incentive programs—particularly upper age limits in what are called "window plans"—have dampened their use.

In summary, the studies reported that the effects of ending mandatory retirement would impose significant costs on the nation's research universities and to a lesser extent on other colleges and universities. They also noted that retirement incentive programs and related programs were effective tools to deal with issues affecting the broadest swath of institutions, including limited budgets and labor market trends. Consequently, these studies recommended that mandatory retirement should be allowed to lapse, as long as Congress legally enabled all colleges and universities to use tools, such as age-based retirement incentive programs, that would enable institutions to provide positive incentives for faculty to elect early retirement.

Since these reports were issued, there has been no systematic follow-up. Based on individual campus-level experience, but without the opportunity to compare across campuses or to obtain national data, some academic administrators have become increasingly concerned that older professors are in fact remaining on the job too long. Many are worried that delayed retirement is already adversely affecting the academic quality and financial condition of their institutions. And these concerns are compounded by what administrators report to be an increasing age structure at many colleges and universities as well as uncertainty about future institutional revenues and costs.

Some institutions, particularly private colleges and universities, have found that benefits and age discrimination laws have tied their hands by inhibiting them from instituting age-based retirement incentives. In September 1998, as part of the Higher Education Act reauthorization, Congress passed legislation allowing all higher education institutions to use certain types of age-based retirement incentives, specifically incentives that expire when a faculty members reaches a certain age, but there has been as yet little attention given to this new law.

Thus, there is a strong and growing need for a national discussion of these concerns, an examination of new evidence that might bear on them, and a consideration of newly available practical options for colleges and universities. This book addresses these important issues. The analysis outlines the critical issues associated with ending mandatory retirement in higher education and examines reasons for changes in age-specific patterns of faculty retirement. Research presented in this volume shows what the effects of these changes are, how they interact with other trends in higher education, and where they have been most severe. Several chapters analyze appropriate use of retirement incentive programs and other methods of increasing faculty turnover. Throughout this examination of the changing academic labor market, the discussion reflects the current thinking of key academic administrators, faculty groups, and other expert policymakers and practitioners— all of whom share an interest in determining the extent of any problems that have been caused by changes in retirement behavior and what new policies, if any, are needed. This debate is shown through a series of chapters by leading thinkers on retirement patterns, policies, and programs in higher education.[2]

Employment Rights and Retirement in Higher Education

Until the passage of the Age Discrimination in Employment Act and its amendments, human resources policy in most institutions of higher education had two basic elements: the tenure system, which provided faculty members considerable protection against loss of employment, and mandatory retirement, which required professors to relinquish tenure along with their job rights at a predetermined age.

Compensation systems and retirement programs were developed around these two basic features of the academic labor market. At many institutions, regular increases in salary with years of service implied that older professors would be paid more than younger faculty. The design of retirement plans reflected the assumption that retirement would occur at or before the mandatory retirement age.

One implication of a system based on tenure and mandatory retirement was that at many institutions, while pretenure review was quite rigorous, posttenure review was less so. Tenured faculty members were (and are) only rarely dismissed for lack of professional productivity. Prior to 1994, mandatory retirement could serve as a relatively uncontroversial means to ensure an endpoint for an academic career that had been less than fully successful.[3]

An important, unresolved question is whether less rigorous posttenure review was in fact a result of mandatory retirement policies. If the existence of mandatory retirement was the primary explanation for less rigorous posttenure review, then the elimination of mandatory retirement rules should lead to changes in the review process on many campuses. Alternatively, less rigorous posttenure review might also be consequence of other aspects of the "culture" of higher education, including collegial governance. If the academic culture is the stronger explanatory factor, then the end of mandatory retirement might not be accompanied by any changes in posttenure review processes.

The end of mandatory retirement essentially awarded the current cohort of older professors an unanticipated new property right—albeit one that was already enjoyed by almost all other American workers—the right to remain on the job until they decided to retire, regardless of their age. To the extent that professors exercise this new right, their behavior will directly affect the faculty age structure and labor costs at their institutions.

A review of the current size and age structure of the academic labor force indicates the key importance of retirement policy (Bowen and Sosa 1989; Atkinson 1990; Finkelstein, Seal, and Schuster 1998). Because most colleges and universities are long past the growth years of the 1960s and early 1970s, employment opportunities for newly trained Ph.D.s in most fields are created when older faculty retire and vacate their academic positions. If older faculty remain on the job, fewer vacancies occur, and thus fewer new assistant professors are hired.

Examination of the current age structure of the academic labor force indicates that retirement policy will become a more important issue in the next ten to fifteen years. During this period, the relatively large number of faculty hired in the late 1960s and early 1970s will begin reaching the traditional retirement ages. To date, any decline in age-specific retirement rates has resulted in only a few additional faculty members remaining on the job, because a relatively small number of professors are currently in their 60s and 70s. However, a much larger number of professors will attain these ages within the next two decades. As a result, any future decline in retirement rates will have a more significant effect on new employment opportunities at many universities.

Many academic administrators fear that a decline in retirement rates will adversely affect the cost or academic quality of their institutions. Institutions can elect to counter declines in retirement rates with the use of early and phased retirement programs that offer a financial incentive for older professors to retire. In effect, such programs allow the institution to buy back the new employment right from older professors. When designing such early retirement programs, administrators must decide whether the gain to the institution of having older professors retire is outweighed by the added financial cost of the early retirement option.

Is the Age of Retirement Increasing?

National-level information about the length of faculty careers is indicative, but far from definitive. The National Research Council has been collecting sample survey information about the oldest Ph.D. holders for less than a decade, but a separate analysis of faculty is not available. Similarly, TIAA-CREF data indicate that today's higher education and research institution employees exhibit a bifurcated pattern; some begin receiving retirement income much earlier while others do so much later than their predecessors, but an analysis of the faculty is not available. Developments like these have caused concern among administrators that a large number of professors might work well past age 70 in response to the end of mandatory retirement.

To examine changing retirement patterns in depth, Orley Ashenfelter and David Card (1998) conducted a preliminary study that focuses on faculty retirement decisions using employment records from a national sample of colleges and universities. They compiled employment records from thirty-seven institutions, consisting of eleven research universities, three degree-granting institutions, thirteen comprehensive colleges, and ten liberal arts colleges for the years 1986–1995.[4] They used these data to examine the work and retirement decisions of a sample of 5,035 faculty members employed at these thirty-seven institutions who are age 50 or older. In addition to the employment records of this sample of faculty members, the researchers obtained the value of retirement funds for those persons who were TIAA-CREF participants.[5] They offered a preliminary report from an ongoing project that includes an effort to expand the number of colleges and universities in the sample to over one hundred.

Ashenfelter and Card use these data to estimate parameters in a model of an individual's decision to retire at any specific age, both before and after the ending of mandatory retirement. They reached the following conclusions:

End of mandatory retirement. In the mandatory retirement era, about 20 percent of faculty who reached age 70 were forced to retire and 40 percent vol-

TABLE 1. Tenure Track Faculty Retirement Rates at Age 70 by Cause:
Preliminary Results for Sample of 37 Institutions

Period	Number of observations	Voluntary retirement (%)	Mandatory retirement (%)	Other reasons (%)
All institutions				
Mandatory (1986–93)	510	40.8	22.0	2.4
Post-mandatory (1994–95)	140	29.7	2.0	2.0
Change	—	–11.1	–19.9	–0.3
Research institutions only				
Mandatory (1986–93)	413	42.6	22.0	1.9
Post-mandatory (1994–95)	110	25.5	2.7	2.7
Change	—	17.2	–19.3	–0.8

Source: Ashenfelter and Card (1998), Table 6.
Those not retired at age 70 in the mandatory retirement period were retired the next year.

untarily retired at age 70. After the elimination of mandatory retirement, the fraction of faculty retiring at age 70 declined sharply. The retirement rate at age 70 is now similar to the retirement rates at ages 68 and 69.

Research universities. Faculty at research universities have significantly lower retirement rates than faculty at other types of institutions. Faculty with higher salaries are less likely to retire; a 10 percent higher salary results in a 0.6 percentage point reduction in the probability of retirement. Retirement rates didn't vary significantly by gender or race.

Pension wealth. Among faculty covered by TIAA-CREF, a 10 percent increase in the value of the individual's total TIAA-CREF account balance at age 67 increased the likelihood of retirement by 0.1 percentage points from 12.0 percent to 12.1 percent. During the 1990s, the retirement rate of faculty in their 60s rose. This might be due to the unanticipated increase in the values of TIAA-CREF retirement accounts associated with relatively high rates of returns during this period.

Table 1 is drawn from Ashenfelter and Card and shows the national decline in retirement rates of faculty who work until age 70. Before elimination of mandatory retirement, about 65 percent of faculty turning age 70 retired that year (virtually all of those that did not retire then were forced to retire the next year by the mandatory retirement rules). Following elimination of mandatory retirement in 1994, only 34 percent of faculty reaching age 70 at all institutions (about 31 percent at research universities) retired.

In Chapter 2 of this volume, Robert Clark, Linda Ghent, and Juanita Kreps present their estimates of how age-specific retirement rates have changed at three North Carolina universities. They examine data on faculty retirement decisions, specifically the 1988–97 employment records of Duke University, the University of North Carolina (UNC), and North Carolina (NC) State University. They reached conclusions that are consistent with the findings of Ashenfelter and Card:

Retirement age. Between 1988 and 1997, the average age of faculty members at each of these universities increased by over 2 years with the mean overall age for the faculties increasing from 46.5 years to 49 years. The proportion of the faculty less than 40 years of age decreased from 27 percent to 18 percent between 1988 and 1997, while the proportion aged 55 years and older rose from 24 percent to 29 percent. This aging was the result of both an increase in the average age of new faculty, as well as a decline in retirement rates among existing faculty at all ages.

End of mandatory retirement. Retirement rates for persons reaching the mandatory retirement age declined sharply following the end of mandatory retirement. Retirement rates for persons age 69 at the beginning of the academic year fell from 61 percent to 38 percent after the elimination of mandatory retirement. The retirement rate for those age 70 at the beginning of the academic year dropped from 77 percent before 1994 to 13 percent after 1994. These figures are even more dramatic than the national-level data reported by Ashenfelter and Card.

Pension plan. Faculty who participated in the Teachers and State Employees Retirement Plan (a defined benefit plan available only to faculty at NC State and UNC) were 10 percentage points more likely to retire at any age than participants in one of the defined contributions (including TIAA-CREF) offered by the three universities. After the elimination of mandatory retirement, predicted retirement rates declined for persons in the state retirement plan but increased for those in one of the defined contribution plans. This finding is consistent with the observation of Ashenfelter and Card that participants in TIAA-CREF were more likely to retire during the 1990s and this might be associated with unanticipated increases in account balances.

Based on both of these preliminary studies, ending mandatory retirement has had an observable effect on the retirement decisions of faculty, especially at research universities, where professors who reach age 70 are less likely to retire now than before 1994. This effect is tempered by an recent increase in the retirement rate for all faculty in their 60s, so that fewer faculty reach age 70 than in the past.

Legal Status of Retirement Incentive Programs

Since colleges and universities can no longer rely on mandatory retirement policies to force retirement, they must now look to voluntary retirement incentive programs if they wish to affect faculty retirement decisions. One of the most critical issues affecting colleges and universities with defined contribution pension plans, especially those in the private sector, is the changing legal status of retirement incentive programs. In Chapter 3, David Raish analyzes the legal issues associated with retirement and retirement incentive programs in higher education.

In conjunction with defined benefit pensions, retirement incentive programs are clearly legal and have been used frequently by public sector colleges and universities to provide inducements to increase faculty retirement rates. In this setting, formal retirement incentive programs are most often part of a public-sector pension plan and therefore not subject to Employee Retirement Income Security Act (ERISA) requirements. Such programs can also take advantage of age-based formulas already built into defined benefit plans, which can also be modified to accommodate increased retirement incentives.

Since most (though certainly not all) defined contribution plans are offered by private colleges and universities, until recently they were often subject to ERISA and ADEA rules and regulations effectively limiting the use of certain policies, such as those associated with upper age limits. In addition, because of the way in which defined contribution benefits are structured, these pensions do not typically or explicitly link benefit payout streams to age.[6]

The nature of most defined contribution plans—namely, that there is no age-related benefit that can be altered to provide a retirement incentive—presents additional challenges for an employer who wishes to target retirement incentives at a key group of professors within a specific age bracket. For example, a promise to provide faculty of any age an incentive payment would allow recipients to wait until they would have retired anyway and still receive the payment. Thus, for these professors it would no longer act as an incentive to retire early.

Therefore, in order to be effective as well as economical, retirement incentive programs must induce a sufficient number of faculty to retire before they might otherwise do so, thus freeing up salary dollars to be used for replacement hiring. Consequently, retirement incentive programs offering a lump sum payment are thought to work well when faculty can be offered an age window during which they are eligible to apply for the retirement incentive.

Until recently, the legal status of including an upper age limit in such a program was cloudy. In the past, some experts argued that the Age Discrimination in Employment Act prohibited offering retirement incentives to younger employees and not to older employees. ADEA clearly permits offering retirement incentives to older employees but not to younger employees. Therefore, some believed that a defined contribution window program could have a lower age limit, but not an upper one, thus effectively keeping the window of opportunity open forever for faculty who are over the initial age threshold. Others believed that an upper age limit is permissible for a retirement incentive program used with a defined contribution pension. Without clarification of this issue, many colleges and universities believed that they would have to offer retirement incentive payments to all faculty over a certain age and further believe that this outcome would be ineffective, costly, and self-defeating.

Compromise legislation intended to address these issues was proposed several times during the 1990s and received support from most of the private and public interest groups concerned with higher education and aging, as well as from the appropriate congressional committees. This legislation, which finally passed in September 1998, provides a safe harbor allowing colleges and universities to offer, with certain significant restrictions, retirement incentive programs with an upper age limit. Such a limit would enable all college or university employees who reach an initial threshold, for example age 60, to pass through a window of opportunity during which they could choose to apply for retirement incentives. However, once they pass beyond the upper limit, for example age 65, they would no longer be eligible for the program. The new legislation also requires that any retirement incentive program be offered for a sufficient time period so that all employees can become aware of the program's details and have the opportunity to consider their options carefully.

In January 2000, the Supreme Court somewhat limited court protection for the safe harbor for retirement incentive programs as they apply to public employees. Public colleges and universities may still offer such incentives, especially in connection with defined benefit plans. Public sector defined contribution-based retirement incentive plans with upper age limits may still enjoy safe harbor protection through the Equal Employment Opportunity Commission.

Raish outlines current ADEA, ERISA, and state laws that pertain to the safe harbor provision, an important tool that has been available to other U.S. employers and employees and is now available to private colleges, universities, and faculty. Such a change enables college and universities that find they are suffering or will suffer negative consequences from the end of retirement to offer clearly legal, cost-effective programs focused on the problems they have encountered.

Design and Use of Retirement Incentive Programs

Individual campus experience with retirement incentive programs reflects each college and university's unique circumstances as well as factors that are common to many institutions. In Chapter 4, John Keefe evaluates the current understanding and use of retirement incentive programs in higher education. Keefe surveyed private and public institutions, with special attention given to research universities and liberal arts colleges. The survey focused on plans in which faculty receive severance payments as an incentive to retire as well as on phased retirement plans in which senior faculty are offered part-time work at prorated salaries in exchange for giving up tenure and retiring. Keefe approached 125 institutions and received responses from sixty-six institutions on seventy-seven different plans. Eighty percent of the responding institutions currently offer an early retirement or have done so within the past few years.

Under the incentive plans, the amount of the severance payments at private institutions vary from 40 percent of final salary to 200 percent of final salary with most of these institutions offering between 100 and 200 percent of final salary. Payments by public institutions were smaller, ranging from 12 percent to 100 percent of final salary. Most plans provided for a single lump sum payment.

Phased retirement plans vary considerably across institutions, based on the duration of the contract, the amount of work, and the relationship between workload reduction and salary reduction. Both incentive and phased retirement plans can be either formal (offered through a documented process whose details are well known to the faculty) and informal (often undocumented and offered by administrators to selected individual faculty members with details that vary according to each case).

Retirement incentive plans can be ongoing programs or they can be offered only for a specified time period. Legally, an ongoing program is subject to being declared an employment benefit like the basic pension plan. If so, it becomes subject to ERISA and other employee benefit rules and laws. Ongoing programs are, for example, difficult to withdraw without appropriate notification, and they must be fully funded. In contrast, a time-limited program is designed to end and therefore is not considered to be a benefit subject to ERISA and other employee benefit rules and regulations.

Some institutions attempt to respond to short-term faculty retirement issues by introducing a temporary incentive plan to induce an immediate, one-time reduction in staff. Other institutions introduce ongoing plans in an effort to permanently raise age-specific retirement rates. Sixty of the seventy-seven plans in the survey were ongoing and seventeen were temporary plans. Most of the temporary plans were offered at public institutions.

The objective of most of these plans was to entice individuals to retire before age 65, well below the former mandatory retirement age of 70. Most important, Keefe found that virtually all of the institutions did not mention mandatory retirement as a reason for the introduction of retirement incentive plans. In fact, only one institution specifically indicated that it had adopted an incentive plan in response to the elimination of mandatory retirement.

Window plans offer special retirement options that are available only for a short period of time and/or to people between certain ages. Used in conjunction with a defined benefit pension plan, window plans typically treat participants as if they were older or had more years of service in the calculation of pension benefits. Of course, and especially in conjunction with a defined contribution pension plan, window plans can also simply offer cash payments for faculty members who retire within the designated time frame. For the most part, the primary objective of window plans is to achieve a short-term increase in retirements consistent with an institution's attempt to reduce the size of its faculty or to redress a significant problem in the composition of its faculty. These plans are less likely to be adopted to solve long-term problems associated with later retirements.

In addition to observing national patterns in the use of retirement incentive programs, it is important to know how knowledgeable administrators on individual campuses are matching incentives to the faculty employment and retirement challenges they face. In a series of chapters, researchers and administrators who participated in the design of retirement incentive programs at Cornell University, the University of California, the University of Wisconsin, and the University of Virginia examine the experience in depth.

In Chapter 5, Ronald Ehrenberg, Michael Matier, and David Fontanella analyze Cornell University's response to the end of mandatory retirement. Cornell is a unique institution with six of its colleges privately funded and four colleges operated by Cornell under contract with the State of New York. All faculty in the six privately funded colleges are enrolled in a defined contribution retirement program, while faculty in other colleges have a choice of participating in a state defined benefit retirement plan or an optional retirement program.[7]

In the fall of 1996, a joint faculty-administrative committee was appointed to make recommendations on how Cornell should respond to the elimination of mandatory retirement. The committee began by examining employment records, which indicated that the average age of retirement fluctuated without trend until 1993–94, but since rose by two years. In addition, some faculty who reached age 70 during this period remained on the job.[8] Fewer retirements reduced hiring opportunities and resulted in an aging of the faculty. The proportion of all faculty under the age of 35 declined from 15 percent in 1982–83 to 5 percent in 1996–97. The percent of the faculty over the age of 60 increased from 13 to 21 percent during the same period. The number of newly hired, tenure-track faculty declined from 108 in 1987–88 to 48 in 1995–96. The committee determined that the decline in hiring had three adverse effects: (1) Cornell was hiring fewer faculty with new ideas and new perspectives; (2) fewer new hires meant the university was less able to diversify its faculty along gender, racial, and ethnic lines; and (3) fewer new hires had the potential to limit Cornell's ability to remain at the frontier in rapidly changing fields and to shift faculty resources into new areas of inquiry.

As it began its deliberations, the committee was instructed by the provost to avoid a buyout plan because of the belief that these plans would not be cost effective. Since a majority of Cornell faculty members retire before age 70, the worry was that any plan that paid people to retire prior to age 70 would be paying many people to do what they would have done anyway.

Moreover, the legal status of defined contribution-based buyout plans that limited participation to faculty prior to a certain age was thought to be ambiguous.

Instead, the committee made a series of other recommendations to increase retirement rates: (1) faculty should be provided financial planning assistance over their life cycles to assure that they make informed investment decisions with their retirement accounts; (2) more information should be available about the importance of investing in tax-deferred supplementary retirement accounts; (3) faculty should be encouraged to discuss their retirement plans beforehand with department chairs or college officials to enable academic units to improve their planning; (4) salary increases should be linked to individual productivity; (5) the status of emeriti professors should be enhanced; (6) university retirement contributions to the defined contribution plans should be capped; and (7) the existing phased retirement program should be expanded.

The Cornell faculty objected to several of the key points in these recommendations. Specific arguments were that the recommendation to match salary increases to productivity was offensive and should be deleted; the phased retirement program was not generous enough and it should be amended; and capping retirement contributions was merely an attempt to cut compensation and should be eliminated. The committee report was been amended to reflect these criticisms at the time of publication the plan was under consideration in the office of the provost.

In Chapter 6, Ellen Switkes looks at one of the largest retirement incentive plans in higher education, the three Voluntary Early Retirement Programs (VERIPs) adopted by the University of California (UC) in the early 1990s. Faced with a disproportionate share of the UC faculty over the age of 55, a state budget crunch, and the immanent elimination of mandatory retirement at what some consider the nation's premier public research university system, administrators designed a retirement incentive plan that used the university's overfunded defined benefit pension plan to bear most of the cost of the incentive plan.

Each of the three VERIPs involved increasing the annual retirement income to which the faculty member was entitled. It did so by adding years of service to the pension formula used to calculate retirement income, thus increasing the faculty member's proportion of final income. In order to target certain age groups, more or fewer years were added, depending on the faculty member's age.

Each VERIP was more generous than the last. But the response did not entirely parallel the program's generosity (for another perspective, see Pencavel 1997). In response to the first plan, which was introduced in 1990, 31 percent of eligible faculty accepted early retirement. The second early retirement plan, which followed in 1992, provided more generous benefits and extended the boundaries of eligibility to older faculty. Only 18 percent of eligible faculty accepted the early retirement offer. The final plan was even more generous, and 33 percent of eligible employees took early retirement in response to this last offer.

The response to these early retirement offers by UC provides an especially useful view of how employee expectations influence acceptance rates. The first offer was almost unprecedented and was billed as a one-time event and not to be repeated. The second offer was also publicized as a last chance, but employees apparently felt they could hold out for another round. In the third instance, word passed among the faculty that there truly would be no future offer this time, likely contributing to the highest acceptance rate of all.

In Chapter 7 Robert O'Neil provides a unique perspective on the effects of ending mandatory retirement. He is former president of the University of Wisconsin and the University of Virginia. He was also a member of the 1989–91 National Research Council Committee on Ending Mandatory Retirement in Higher Education. O'Neil presided over the Wisconsin and Virginia campuses when mandatory retirement was eliminated. He outlines the transition that each institution made to ending of mandatory retirement and other forces that affected both faculty behavior and policy choices available to each institutions. He strongly supports the need for joint planning between administrators and faculty.

In light of the intended and potential unintended incentives associated with retirement incentive programs, in Chapter 8, John Keefe analyzes these programs from the point of view of a faculty member who must decide on the benefits and opportunity costs of continuing to work or accepting the offer. He concludes that the intangible elements of retirement incentive programs, including the nonmonetary aspects, can be critical in the ultimate success of these programs. College and university administrators and faculty would be wise to consider issues such as access to campus facilities, professional status, and similar postretirement issues when formulating retirement incentive programs.

Assessment of Research Findings

A major contribution of this volume is the critical assessment of current and past research on faculty retirement and the identification of unsettled research questions. Some of the foremost authorities on faculty retirement decisions, the ending of mandatory retirement, and the state of the academic labor contributed summary assessments concerning faculty retirement in the twenty-first century.

An important question about faculty retirement behavior in response to the ending of mandatory retirement is whether current ex post patterns are surprising compared to anticipated or ex ante effects. In Chapter 9, Sharon Smith examines the research that predicted changes in retirement behavior before the end of mandatory retirement and compares it to the results of the Ashenfelter and Card study and the Clark et al. study of retirement rates and age structure. She concludes that recent patterns are not surprising and that college and university retirement policies should be based on hard analysis of the circumstances facing each institution rather than on beliefs or attitudes. In particular, spending on retirement incentive programs should be undertaken only in response to a clear analysis of faculty demographics and retirement behavior so that such expenditures will be targeted on a clear need.

In addition to the question of changing retirement behavior and the implementation of retirement incentive programs, colleges and universities face other critical issues associated with faculty retirement. Karen Holden and Lee Hansen analyze several of these issues in Chapter 10. They review the findings of their study of faculty retirement completed prior to the increase in mandatory retirement age that took effect in 1982. They compare these findings to the results reported in this volume.

From these chapters the following conclusions emerge:

Consensus. Views vary among institutions and between faculty and administrators on the impact of ending mandatory retirement. This variation suggests that individual campuses are differentially affected and therefore should examine their own circumstances carefully before choosing future retirement-related policies.

Incentive programs. Most representatives of higher education faculty and administrators believe that ending mandatory retirement has benefited faculty who can now exercise choices available to all other working Americans. However, they both recognize that for planning and budgeting purposes, individual campuses and multicampus systems may need to decrease the uncertainty associated with future retirement patterns by offering individuals the opportunity to retire earlier than they might otherwise choose to do so. Therefore, both faculty and administrators support well-designed, noncoercive retirement incentive programs that increase certainty choice while preserving individual rights.

National demographic trends. At the national level, projecting or predicting future faculty supply and demand is next to impossible because forces affecting this market cannot be fully specified. These include, but are not limited to, future government support, industrial growth patterns, and immigration policies and patterns. Conclusions about the effects of ending mandatory retirement for faculty must be placed in this uncertain context.

Awareness. Few colleges and universities are fully aware of what they can and cannot do to provide retirement incentives to their employees. Education and information programs are needed in this regard, especially now that the law affecting retirement incentives in higher education has changed.

The final word is far from in on this subject. The consequences of eliminating mandatory retirement have not yet been fully felt or understood. Additional studies and discussion of this issue and its effect on higher education are needed.

Guidance for Administrators and Faculty

Taken as a whole, this volume identifies a series of important retirement-related concerns and policies for dealing with those concerns:

Retirement Rates and Patterns

College and university faculties are aging. The surge of faculty hiring in the 1960s and early 1970s continues to dominate the academic labor market. The aging of faculty hired to teach the baby boomers combined with smaller cohorts of subsequently hired faculty are the primary cause of the aging of the academic labor market. These trends show up in aggregate academic labor market data as well as data on the faculties of particular colleges and universities. There has been an increase in the average age of faculty members, a decrease in the proportion of the faculty members under age 40, and an increase in the proportion of the faculty members over age 55.

The elimination of mandatory retirement has led to lower retirement rates for those faculty members who continue to work until age 70. Although older professors remaining at their university posts can be found at nearly all types of institutions, they are concentrated at research universities. In the past, these professors would have been forced to retire. Now many of them are choosing to remain as full-time, tenured faculty members for several additional years. To date, the increase in retirement ages has played only a small role in the aging of faculties. However, the declining probability of retirement among older professors, particularly at research universities, will become more important in coming years as the relatively large number of faculty members hired in the 1960s and early 1970s begins to reach traditional retirement ages.

Future cohorts of retirees will look much different from today's. In the twenty-first century, faculties will include more minorities, more foreign-born scholars, and more women. Future retirement decisions by these faculty are uncertain. Will they be similar to those of today's older professors, who are predominately white men, or will they work longer? Academic administrators should plan for the changing composition of their faculty and its impact on retirement patterns. And institutions that have experienced, as many have, a shift from defined benefit to defined contribution pensions should be prepared for changes in how these programs affect retirement decisions. Even where pension plans haven't changed, colleges and universities should also prepare for the possibility that future cohorts will respond differently to the incentives to retire or to delay retirement that are built in—intentionally as well as inadvertently—to pension plans and retirement incentive programs.

We also need a better understanding of the impact of the increase in stock market values during the 1990s on the retirement decisions of participants in defined contribution pension plans. One study showed that observed retirement rates were higher for those with relatively large defined contribution accumulations, but future retirement rates may be lower if, as is likely, the next generation of older professors in defined contribution plans do not continue to benefit from above-average equity returns.

Effects on Colleges and Universities

Later retirements can significantly affect colleges or universities. At institutions where faculty size is not growing, retirements provide the major opportunity for new hiring. Academic institutions use these hiring opportunities to revitalize teaching and research, reallocate faculty resources, reduce labor costs, and stay on the cutting edge of rapidly changing educational opportunities. Decreases in retirement rates will inhibit new hiring and retard the ability of institutions to achieve these goals. Institutions where the retirement age is increasing will experience a temporary sharp decline in hiring and a less severe, long-term reduction in hiring due to the lengthening of the average faculty career.

Disagreements among administrators and faculty and in the academic literature regarding the impact of a larger number of older faculty members on colleges and universities have more than one source. Some of these disagreements are a result of a lack of empirical information. We simply do not know whether or how faculty retirement ages are changing on many individual campuses. Following the lead of some of the researchers who presented their findings at this conference, individual schools should track retirement patterns at their own campuses.

Much remaining disagreement regarding the impact of faculty aging is normative. Even if retirement ages have, are, or will change at some universities, the question of whether these changes will harm their institutions remains. This answer may be a matter of perspective. Robert O'Neil, perhaps the only former university president to experience retirement uncapping at two institutions prior to 1994, points out that administrators are more likely to focus on the financial burdens associated with an older faculty and fewer hiring opportunities due to the lengthening of faculty careers. Faculty groups are more likely to focus on the many positive contributions older faculty can make to university life.

The most important conclusion here is that the empirical issues should be separated from the normative issues. Empirical questions can be resolved as much as possible through further research and discussion. The normative issues should be clearly identified and confronted through continuing discussions among faculty and administrators on campuses, in state capitols, and in Washington.

Retirement Incentive Programs

Retirement incentive programs have been adopted by a large number of academic institutions and they come in many forms. They can be early retirement buyouts, phased retirement programs, or increased generosity of retirement plans. Limited evidence suggests that these plans can alter faculty retirement behavior; however, it is unclear how cost effective these plans are. Much clearer is the observation that few colleges and universities have targeted their use of these programs to counteract the effects of ending mandatory retirement.

The recent legislation enacting a safe harbor for design of certain types of retirement incentive programs has lifted a legal burden on many colleges and universities. Current legislation now allows colleges and universities *and their faculty members* access to the same sorts of retirement incentives that were available in businesses and in public colleges and universities.

The new safe harbor legislation should be accompanied by efforts to increase awareness of retirement incentive programs. College and university associations have a responsibility to help educate administrators and faculty about the options and appropriate uses of retirement benefit programs and retirement incentive programs in particular. Financial planning programs can help faculty to better prepare for retirement, while education and communication between faculty and administrators concerning incentive plans improves the success rate of most early retirement programs.

Action and Assessment

Action and further needed analysis for the twenty-first century will require cooperative, candid effort on the part of researchers, administrators, and faculty. If we are to understand the full impact of the end of mandatory retirement and faculty aging on colleges and universities, better data is needed both for the academic labor market as a whole and for individual institutions. Analyses must be conducted to document changes in faculty age structure and shifts in retirement patterns, determine the magnitude of potentially adverse effects of higher ages of retirement, and estimate the cost-effectiveness of retirement incentives programs adopted to deal with the consequences of mandatory retirement.

But better research is not enough. All of the major constituents in higher education must be willing to come together to develop and examine the evidence, formulate shared principles and conclusions based on the evidence, and then promulgate policies and programs that address the challenges of an aging faculty in the twenty-first century.

Notes

1. The Age Discrimination in Employment Act was passed in 1967 forbidding discrimination against workers aged 40 to 65. This act explicitly permitted employers to force workers to retire at age 65 without cause. This act was amended in 1978 raising the upper age of protected workers to 70. This prohibited mandatory retirement prior to the age of 70. Academic institutions were given an exemption from this amendment until July 1, 1982. The ADEA was amended again in 1986, outlawing the use of mandatory retirement at any age in most jobs. Once again, educational institutions were given a temporary exemption until January 1, 1994, when the law was extended to cover tenured faculty members.

2. Many of the following issues and ideas were first summarized in Clark and Hammond (1998). Some of the material in this book was presented in preliminary form at a 1998 conference in Washington, D.C. on the effects of ending mandatory retirement, sponsored by TIAA-CREF and the College of Management, North Carolina State University.

3. Tenure does not mean that professors cannot be terminated; however, the university must show that a professor is not performing at an acceptable level. Essentially, termination of a senior professor would require the university to show that the person is incompetent or is not performing required job assignments. Across the country, concern about these issues has produced an increasing trend toward academic accountability and posttenure review. Even with the closer monitoring of faculty performance, the termination of a senior faculty member will be a painful task especially when the person has been a long-term, productive professor.

4. This study received support from the Andrew W. Mellon Foundation, with additional support and cooperation from TIAA-CREF. Throughout the study, Ashenfelter and Card and TIAA-CREF took a number of steps to ensure confidentiality and anonymity. The researchers obtained permission from TIAA-CREF and from the human resources and/or benefits office of each institution involved. They were provided a limited amount of data by the institutions and by TIAA-CREF, all of which was carefully masked to preserve anonymity. As a result, the researchers and the sponsoring and participating organizations cannot identify any individual or institution involved in the study.

5. However, there is no indication of the value of retirement benefits for persons not enrolled in TIAA-CREF. Faculty not enrolled in TIAA-CREF may be participants in other defined contribution plans or in defined benefit plans that are prevalent among public institutions.

6. In a defined contribution pension, retirement benefits are not fixed by any formula, but they do tend to increase with age. For example, many colleges and universities offer employer contribution rates that increase with an employee's age. Moreover, an individual's retirement income typically increases with the length of time contributions remain invested as well as with the actuarial effect of any increase in a person's retirement age. Thus, other things being equal, the person who delays starting a lifetime annuity will receive higher annual retirement income than someone who starts an annuity earlier.

7. Most new faculty have enrolled in a defined contribution plan. Currently there are fewer than twenty faculty in the state retirement plan.

8. Prior to 1994, Cornell rigorously enforced mandatory retirement; however, retired faculty were eligible to be hired back for specified terms on a part-time basis at a renegotiated salary.

References

Ashenfelter, Orley and David Card. 1998. "Faculty Retirement Behavior in the Post-Mandatory Retirement Era: New Evidence from the Princeton Retirement Survey." Paper presented at TIAA-CREF and NC State University conference, "Examining Life After the End of Mandatory Retirement," Washington, D.C., May.

Atkinson, Richard C. 1990. "Supply and Demand for Scientists and Engineers: A National Crisis in the Making." *Science* 248 (April 27): 425–32.

Bowen, William G. and Julie Ann Sosa. 1989. *Prospects for Faculty in the Arts and Sciences: A Study of Factors Affecting Demand and Supply 1987 to 2012*. Princeton, N.J.: Princeton University Press.

Brewer, Dominic J., Susan M. Gates, and Charles Goldman. 1998. *In Pursuit of Prestige: Strategy and Competition in U.S. Higher Education*. Santa Monica, CA: The RAND Corporation.

Clark, Robert L. and P. Brett Hammond. 1998. "To Retire or Not? Examining Life After the End of Mandatory Retirement in Higher Education." *Research Dialogues* 58 (December).

Finkelstein, Martin J., Robert K. Seal, and Jack H. Schuster. 1998. *The New Academic Generation: A Profession in Transformation*. Baltimore: Johns Hopkins University Press.

National Research Council, Committee on Ending Mandatory Retirement in Higher Education. 1991. *Ending Mandatory Retirement for Tenured Faculty: The Consequences for Higher Education*, ed. P. Brett Hammond and Harriet P. Morgan. Washington, D.C.: National Academy Press.

National Research Council, Committee on Science, Engineering, and Public Policy. *Reshaping the Graduate Education of Scientists and Engineers.*. Washington, D.C.: National Academy Press.

National Research Council, Committee on Dimensions, Causes, and Implications in the Recent Career Trends of Life Scientists. 1998. *Trends in the Early Careers of Life Scientists*. Washington, D.C.: National Academy Press.

Pencavel, John. 1997. "The Response of Employees to the Severance Pay Incentives: Faculty of the University of California." Working paper, Stanford University, July.

Rees, Albert and Sharon Smith. 1991. *Faculty Retirement in the Arts and Sciences*. Princeton, N.J.: Princeton University Press.

Chapter 2
Faculty Retirement at Three North Carolina Universities

Robert L. Clark, Linda S. Ghent,
and Juanita Kreps

The educational community has been concerned about the changing state of the academic labor market for some time. One concern is the projection that the demand for faculty will level off and then begin to decline. This projected decline in the total demand for professors is the result of a reduction in the growth of the college-age population and technological innovation in instructional methods such as the shift from the traditional classroom lecture to computer-assisted learning. More recently, questions regarding changes in the age composition of university faculties have emerged as a serious issue facing many colleges and universities. Improvements in health and longevity combined with amendments to the Age Discrimination in Employment Act (ADEA) may further reduce already low retirement rates among older faculty and limit the employment prospects of new Ph.Ds.

When ADEA was first passed in 1967, it prohibited the use of mandatory retirement prior to the age of 65. Amendments enacted in 1978 raised the permissible age for mandatory retirement to 70; however, an exemption for higher education postponed the effective date of this change to July 1, 1982. In 1986, further amendments to ADEA eliminated the use of mandatory retirement at any age; however, once again the effective date for higher education was delayed until January 1, 1994.[1] Thus, since 1994, U.S. colleges and universities have not been permitted to require faculty members to retire at any specified age. The elimination of mandatory retirement, along with other changes in the academic labor market, could result in an increase in the proportion of scholars in their late sixties and seventies remaining on the job.

Later retirement ages for faculty members have important implications for the financial status of the institutions and the long run quality of faculty research and teaching. Since older, more experienced faculty are typically paid substantially more than newly hired assistant professors, later retirement which postpones the transition from older to younger faculty will generally be associated with increases in costs to universities. Moreover, older faculty nearing the end of their careers are not perfect substitutes for younger faculty in relation to research, teaching, university service, and interaction with students. To fulfill its educational mission, a vibrant university needs a mix of faculty at various ages. Delayed retirement may adversely alter the desired age composition of faculty. The impact on the hiring of young scholars could be particularly important at a time when total demand for university faculty is declining. Meanwhile, the number of new doctorates earned continues to rise, reaching over 42,000 per year in the 1990s.

Many factors influence a professor's retirement decision, including workload requirements of the academic position, pension benefits, health status, financial obligations, alternative opportunities for research, and the appeal of travel and other leisure-time activities. Continuing in the classroom or the laboratory past the customary age of 65 or 70, however, is a option newly available to the current cohort of older faculty. Relatively little evidence is currently available to indicate how retirement behavior has changed in response to the elimination of mandatory retirement. Analysis of retirement ages at three North Carolina universities (Duke University, North Carolina State University, and University of North Carolina) since 1988 indicates an aging of the faculties and a reduction in the probability of retiring at ages 69 and 70.

During the past decade, the faculties of Duke University, North Carolina State University (NCSU), and the University of North Carolina (UNC) have been aging rapidly. Between 1988 and 1997, the mean age of the combined faculties increased from 46.5 to 49.0 years of age, an increase of more than two years in age over a nine-year period. Figure 1 shows the increase in the average age of the faculty each of the three universities. During this same period, the proportion of the combined faculties at the three universities less than 40 years of age decreased from 27.4 to 17.9 percent, while the proportion of the faculties 55 years and older rose from 23.7 to 29.2 percent. Each of these aging measures indicates that there have been increases in the relative number of older professors and a decline in the proportion of younger entry level faculty members.

The aging of the faculties is the result of lower rates of hiring of new faculty, relatively low quit rates, and much lower retirement rates. Each of these factors have contributed to an increase in the proportion of the faculties composed of older persons. This dramatic aging of the professorate at the triangle universities is consistent with national trends in the academy, and have raised many questions among academic administrators. Specific concerns include further delays in retirement due to the ending of mandatory retirement, the higher cost associated with more senior professors, the re-

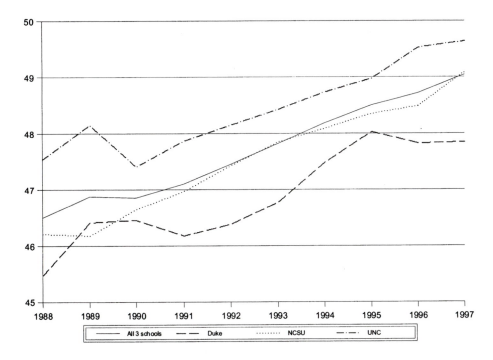

Figure 1. Mean age of faculty, 1988–97. Source: Authors' calculations based on employment records provided by Duke University, North Carolina State University, and the University of North Carolina.

duced ability to hire new Ph.D.s into entry level positions, and the potential for some older professors to remain past their most productive years. This analysis seeks to document the aging of the faculties of the three universities, to examine the prospects for further aging, and to determine the impact of the ending of mandatory retirement on retirement rates and hence the age structure of the faculty.

Faculty Age Structure

The age structure of a university faculty at a point in time depends on an initial age structure in an earlier year, age-specific hiring rates, and age-specific exit rates including quits, retirements, and deaths. In large measure, the current age structure and the recent aging of faculties reflect hiring patterns in the 1960s and 1970s, along with the rather low quit and retirement rates associated with the current state of the academic labor market. The elimination of mandatory retirement at age 70 has exacerbated this aging process by increasing the expected age of retirement.

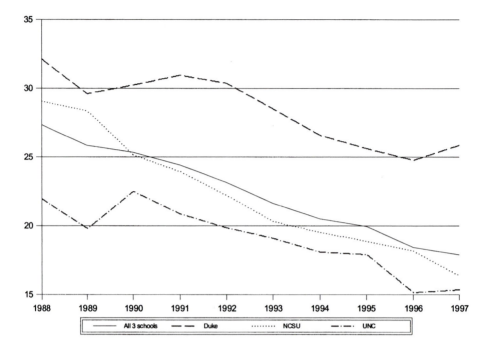

Figure 2. Percent of faculty under age 40, 1988–97. Source: Authors' calculations based on employment records provided by Duke University, North Carolina State University, and the University of North Carolina.

To examine the age structure of the faculties, employment records for the three universities were obtained for the years 1988 to 1997, the data are for tenure-track faculty members not in medical schools. The employment records include information on the date of birth and the date of first employment. This information enables us to calculate age and length of service for each person at each university. Figures 2 and 3 show the dramatic aging of these faculties as reflected in the proportion of the total faculty less than age 40 and the proportion age 55 and older. In each of the universities, the proportion of faculty less than age 40 decline by over 6 percentage points in seven years while the proportion age 55 and over increases between 3.8 and 8.0 percentage points. NCSU has the largest decline in young faculty and the smallest increase in older faculty among the three universities. The age structure for the combined faculties between 1988 and 1997 is shown in Table 1 while the faculty age structure for the three universities separately is presented in Appendix Tables A1–A3.

Duke University. There were 610 faculty employed at Duke University in 1988. The faculty increased to 656 in 1991 and remained relatively stable in

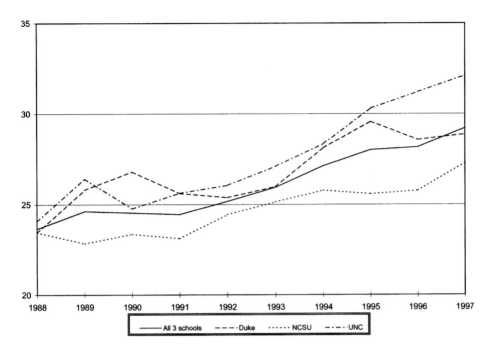

Figure 3. Percent of faculty age 55 or older, 1988–97. Source: Authors' calculations based on employment records provided by Duke University, North Carolina State University, and the University of North Carolina.

size during the following years, before declining in 1996. Until 1994, Duke maintained a strict mandatory retirement policy at age 70; as a result, there was only one faculty member age 70 or older at the beginning of any academic year prior to 1994. After the elimination of mandatory retirement, people begin to delay retirement past age 70. The proportion of the faculty less than 40 years of age declined from 32.1 percent in 1988 to 25.9 percent in 1997 while the proportion of the faculty age 55 and older increased from 23.4 percent in 1988 to 28.5 percent in 1997.

North Carolina State University. There were 1,420 individuals on the faculty at NCSU in 1988. Faculty size remained relatively constant during the sample period reaching a high of 1,506 in 1996. Although NCSU had a policy of mandatory retirement at age 70, there were four or five persons on the faculty over age 70 in each year prior to 1993. In 1988, 29.1 percent of the faculty were less than age 40. The proportion of young faculty declined sharply to only 16.4 percent in 1997. In contrast, the proportion of the faculty age 55 and older rose more modestly from 23.5 percent to 27.3 percent. Reflecting past hiring patterns, a large increase occurred in the proportion

Table 1. Age Structure of Faculty, All Three Schools, 1988–97

Age group	1988	1989	1990	1991	1992	1993	1994	1995	1996	1997
< 30	1.84	1.90	2.04	1.43	1.17	0.94	0.72	0.93	0.77	0.56
30–34	9.25	8.74	8.59	8.20	7.76	7.16	6.70	5.89	5.72	5.95
35–39	16.70	16.04	15.21	14.75	14.21	13.53	13.06	13.12	11.94	11.40
40–44	18.14	18.23	18.39	18.28	18.23	17.88	17.07	16.11	17.05	15.88
45–49	17.36	17.72	17.94	18.38	18.11	17.75	18.48	18.73	18.72	19.12
50–54	13.29	13.29	13.97	14.50	15.35	16.81	16.85	17.20	17.64	17.88
55–59	12.66	12.42	12.57	12.15	11.84	11.97	12.46	12.93	13.30	14.01
60–64	7.09	7.84	7.89	8.74	9.78	10.25	10.08	10.16	9.65	9.44
65–69	3.51	3.68	3.25	3.37	3.32	3.31	4.01	4.18	4.30	4.95
70 +	0.16	0.13	0.16	0.19	0.22	0.41	0.56	0.75	0.90	0.81
N	3048	3099	3143	3145	3159	3200	3193	3209	3232	3211

Source: Authors' calculations using faculty personnel data records from Duke University, University of North Carolina, and North Carolina State University.

of the faculty ages 45 to 54. This group increased from 28.2 percent of the faculty in 1988 to 39.6 percent in 1997.

University of North Carolina. There were 993 faculty employed at UNC in 1988 and the faculty increased in size throughout the period reaching 1,099 in 1995 before declining somewhat in 1996 and 1997. In 1988, 22.0 percent of the UNC faculty were less than age 40. This age group declined to only 15.4 percent by 1997. The aging of this faculty is shown by the large increase in the proportion of faculty age 55 and older from 24.1 percent in 1988 to 32.1 percent in 1997.

Trends in Faculty Retirement

It is important for academic administrators to understand the effect of eliminating mandatory retirement on the retirement rates of university faculty. The following analysis represents an initial assessment of the impact of this important change on retirement patterns at the triangle universities. These findings illustrate the impact of amendments to ADEA on the age structure of the faculties in the 1990s and enable the projection of future retirement patterns in the presence of the larger cohorts of faculty approaching retirement in the next two decades. It is highly likely that the implications of the elimination of mandatory retirement on faculty age structure in the first decade of the twenty-first century will far outstrip those shown in the last decade of the twentieth century.

Using the employment records, age-specific retirement rates were calculated for the three universities separately and for the combined faculties for each year between 1988 and 1997.[2] The employment records are for the academic year, beginning in the year shown. The 1988 data pertain to the 1988–89 academic year while the 1997 data indicate employment at the beginning of the 1997–98 academic year. Faculty retirement is determined by comparing the employment records of successive years. The retirement rates discussed in this analysis indicate the proportion of the faculty of a specific age that were on the payroll in September of one year who were not still employed the next September. For example, the 1988 retirement rate for persons 65 years of age indicates the proportion of persons age 65 employed in September 1988 who were not employed in September 1989. At the older ages, the number of faculty at each individual age is very small. In order to provide more meaningful information on the age-specific probability of retiring, the years before the elimination of mandatory retirement (1988 to 1993) were combined as were the years after the ending of compulsory retirement (1993 to 1997).[3] These retirement patterns are shown in Table 2.

One method of determining the direct impact of eliminating mandatory retirement is to observe the change in the retirement rates for persons reaching ages 69 and 70 before and after January 1, 1994.[4] Retirement rates for people reaching the age of mandatory retirement at the three universities dropped sharply after 1994. Retirement rates for persons aged 70 at the beginning of the academic year declined from 77 percent when mandatory retirement was still being used to 13 percent after it was eliminated while retirement rates for those 69 years of age at the beginning of the academic year dropped from 61 percent with mandatory retirement, to 38 percent without this policy. Although the number of faculty reaching the ages of 69 and 70 during this period is relatively small (81 prior to 1994 and 80 after), the substantial decline in the retirement rate certainly suggests that the ending of mandatory retirement has had a pronounced effect on the retirement rates of faculty at these ages.

Mandatory retirement might also have an indirect effect on the retirement rates of somewhat younger faculty. Persons in their early and mid 60s consider the number of possible remaining years of work when they are deciding whether to continue in their faculty position or retire. Thus, the elimination of mandatory retirement at age 70 could alter the retirement rates of faculty in their 60s. The data for the triangle universities indicate no clear pattern of change in retirement rates at these younger ages. Retirement rates increased slightly after the elimination of mandatory retirement at four ages and declined at three ages. In general, the retirement rates for Duke are lower than those for NCSU and UNC.

Another method of illustrating the changing retirement patterns is to follow only those faculty who were already employed in the first year for which we have data, 1988, and to observe their retirement patterns. Limiting the sample to those employed in 1988 eliminates older faculty who have been newly employed by one of the universities. These newly hired faculty could be expected to have different retirement probabilities than existing faculty.

Table 2. Retirement Patterns by Age

	1988–92			1993–96		
	Employed	Retired	Retirement rate	Employed	Retired	Retirement rate
Age 62						
All	250	14	5.6	272	16	5.9
Duke	51	1	2.0	61	3	4.9
NCSU	109	8	7.3	123	6	4.9
UNC	90	5	5.6	88	7	8.0
Age 63						
All	230	27	11.7	240	32	13.3
Duke	52	6	11.5	56	8	14.3
NCSU	94	13	13.8	105	12	11.4
UNC	84	8	9.5	79	12	15.2
Age 64						
All	180	31	17.2	220	34	15.5
Duke	46	2	4.3	40	3	7.5
NCSU	70	16	22.9	101	22	21.8
UNC	64	13	20.3	79	9	11.4
Age 65						
All	162	41	25.3	171	26	15.2
Duke	43	5	11.6	36	4	11.1
NCSU	63	19	30.2	68	12	17.6
UNC	56	17	30.4	67	10	14.9
Age 66						
All	136	20	14.7	127	29	22.8
Duke	36	3	8.3	28	3	10.7
NCSU	52	11	21.2	52	14	26.9
UNC	48	6	12.5	47	12	25.6
Age 67						
All	119	22	18.5	95	23	24.2
Duke	30	6	20.0	26	1	3.8
NCSU	43	5	11.6	36	9	25.0
UNC	46	11	23.9	33	13	39.4
Age 68						
All	95	30	31.6	64	14	21.8n
Duke	19	12	63.2	25	41	6.0
NCSU	41	9	22.0	24	7	29.2
UNC	35	9	25.7	15	3	20.0
Age 69						
All	59	36	61.0	50	19	38.0
Duke	5	5	100.0	16	7	43.8
NCSU	30	17	56.6	21	7	33.3
UNC	24	14	58.3	13	5	38.5

Table 2. Continued

	1988–92			1993–96		
	Employed	Retired	Retirement rate	Employed	Retired	Retirement rate
Age 70						
All	22	17	77.3	30	4	13.3
Duke	0	0	—	6	0	0.0
NCSU	10	7	70.0	15	3	20.0
UNC	12	10	83.3	9	1	11.1

Source: Authors' calculations using faculty personnel data records from Duke University, University of North Carolina, and North Carolina State University.

Table 3. Retirement Rates, 1988 Faculty Cohort

Age	1988	1989	1990	1991	1992	1993	1994	1995	1996
62	2.2								
63	7.9	8.9							
64	11.1	14.3	26.9						
65	23.7	25.0	33.3	13.3					
66	10.0	13.8	16.7	10.0	19.2				
67	12.0	11.1	32.0	30.0	11.1	14.3			
68	0.0	22.7	58.3	41.2	21.4	31.3	22.2		
69	40.0	41.7	70.6	80.0	70.0	54.6	36.4	53.9	
70	66.7	100.0	71.4	80.0	100.0	0.0	20.0	0.0	33.3

Source: Authors' calculations using faculty personnel data records from Duke University, University of North Carolina, and North Carolina State University.

The first column of Table 3 shows the proportion of persons at each age who retired prior to the start of the 1989 academic year. The second column of the table shows the proportion of those persons who were employed in 1988 and continued on to work during 1989 who retired prior to the 1990 academic year.

These data show that retirement rates at age 70 were over 65 percent for each year between 1988 and 1992. All total, 17 of 20 persons who began an academic year at age 70 retired prior to the next year. In contrast, the retirement rates in the years after 1993 for persons aged 70 at the beginning of the year was much lower, as only 3 of 21 faculty retired. For persons aged 69 at the beginning of the academic year who turned 70 during the year, 34 of 54 faculty retired between 1988 and 1992, while only 17 of 41 retired after mandatory retirement was eliminated.

This analysis of faculty behavior at the three universities reveals that retirement rates are very low for all persons aged 62 and over. In addition, a clear impact of lower retirement rates for persons 69 and 70 is found after the elimination of mandatory retirement. If these patterns continue to hold in the coming years, the faculty at these institutions will become much older.

Duke University. Retirement rates at Duke were extremely low throughout the sample period, except during the year that they became 70 when faculty were required to retire. The number of retirements by persons age 62 to 70 averaged only 8 per year between 1988 and 1997. The retirement rate for persons between ages 62 and 67 was only 9 percent before and after the end of mandatory retirement. In contrast, the retirement rate for persons age 68 and older was 71 percent with mandatory retirement and 23 percent after its elimination. Prior to the elimination of mandatory retirement (1988 to 1993), five individuals reached age 69 and then all five were forced to retire. After the elimination of mandatory retirement (1993 to 1997), six people reached age 70 and none retired. These data clearly show the importance of mandatory retirement as a human resource policy at Duke.

North Carolina State University. Retirement rates prior to age 70 tend to be higher at NCSU than at Duke. When mandatory retirement was in effect, retirement rates for persons age 69 and 70 averaged 60 percent at NCSU; thus, some individuals were allowed to continue employment past the compulsory retirement age. In contrast, the retirement rate for persons of these ages was 28 percent after mandatory retirement was eliminated. Retirement rates for persons aged 66 to 68 were up slightly (from 18 to 27 percent) during the latter period, while the rates for persons 62 to 65 fell slightly (from 17 to 13 percent).

University of North Carolina. Fourteen of 24 people age 69 at the beginning of the academic year retired between 1988 and 1993 and 10 of 12 persons age 70 retired. After the elimination of mandatory retirement only 5 of 13 persons aged 69 and one of nine persons age 70 retired. Retirement rates for persons age 66 to 68 went up between the two periods (from 20 to 29 percent), while retirement rates declined for those age 62 to 65 (from 15 to 12 percent).

Faculty Retirement Decisions

In order to estimate faculty retirement rates, a sample including all faculty age 62 and over at the three universities was constructed. The sample included all faculty meeting this age restriction in each of the years for which we have data, producing a total sample of 2,637 observations.[5] To further investigate the change in retirement rates in response to the ending of mandatory retirement, the sample was also divided into the years before and after academic year 1993–94. This produced a sample of 1,472 observations during the period when mandatory retirement was being used and a sample of 1,165 observations after its elimination. Sample means are presented in Appendix Table A4.

Table 4. Mean Retirement Age of Faculty, 1988–96

	1988	1989	1990	1991	1992	1993	1994	1995	1996
All 3 schools	65.71	66.36	65.92	66.20	66.17	65.98	66.06	65.64	65.86
Duke	—	66.38	66.38	66.58	65.86	66.13	66.00	65.55	—
NCSU	65.45	66.26	66.31	65.82	66.35	66.13	66.36	65.95	66.18
UNC	66.38	66.47	65.42	66.41	66.07	65.64	65.70	64.92	65.61

Source: Authors' calculations using faculty personnel data records from Duke University, University of North Carolina, and North Carolina State University.

The dependent variable (Retirement) in the analysis is a dichotomous variable indicating whether the person retired prior to the start of the subsequent year (Retirement = 1) or remained employed (Retirement = 0). Retirement is estimated using a probit procedure. The probability of retirement is estimated as a function of gender (Male = 1, Female = 0), race (White = 1, Other = 0), salary (in $10,000s), number of years at current university, dichotomous variables indicating rank, participation in the state pension plan, university where employed, and a series of dichotomous variables indicating the age of the faculty member in September of the relevant year.

The sample is comprised almost entirely of whites (95 percent) and males (93 percent). There are very few faculty members in this sample who are not full professors (11 percent) and 56 percent of the sample observations are enrolled in the state retirement plan. The mean age of the sample is 65. Of the 2,637 observations from the entire sample period, only 15 percent retired. For the most part, the sample means do not differ much between the 1988 to 1992 period and the period following the end of mandatory retirement. As expected from the retirement rates presented in Table 2, the percentage of observations indicating retirement between 1988 and 1992 is larger than that for the sample period of 1993 to 1996.

However, the mean retirement age of the sample has not varied much over the nine year sample period. Table 4 presents the mean retirement age for the sample included in this analysis by year. The mean retirement age is also reported for each university separately. Of the faculty members age 62 or older, the average age of retirement fluctuated between 65 and 66 for all of the years of this study.

The data on faculty members ages 62 and older will be used to examine the differences in retirement patterns by personal and professional characteristics. Retirement studies of the general labor force typically find significant differences in the probability of retiring based on these characteristics. A variable indicating whether the observation is from an academic year between 1993 and 1996 is also included in the estimation equation in order to determine the effect of eliminating mandatory retirement. This variable is interacted with a dichotomous variable representing age 70 to allow for the expected effect of the elimination of mandatory retirement on the probability of retiring at age 70.

Economic research has shown that pension coverage, the type of pension, and the monetary incentives associated with each type of pension are important determinants of the timing of retirement (Kotlikoff and Wise 1989; Quinn, Burkhauser, and Myers 1990). For faculty at NCSU and UNC, the records indicate the whether the faculty member is enrolled in the Teachers and State Employees Retirement Plan (the state plan) or an optional retirement plan (ORP). The state plan is a defined benefit plan with considerable early retirement incentives while the ORPs are defined contribution plans.[6] In 1988, over 80 percent of the faculty age 62 and over at NCSU and 84 percent of the faculty age 62 and older at UNC were enrolled in the state retirement plan. All faculty at Duke are enrolled in some type of defined contribution plan. Understanding the effects of pensions on the retirement decisions of older faculty may be central to the future planning of academic administrators.

The results of the estimated retirement equation are shown in Appendix Table A5. The first column reports the results based on the entire sample, while columns 2 and 3 report the results from each sample time period separately. The estimates indicate that (holding other factors constant) gender, race, salary, and length of employment do not have a statistically significant effect on the probability of older faculty at these universities retiring. Faculty holding the rank of assistant professor have a retirement rate that is 18 percentage points higher than the rate for full professors. In addition, the retirement rates are not significantly different among the faculty at the three universities. Given the data presented in Tables 2 and 3, this finding was somewhat surprising; however, differences in pension plan participation examined below explain this seeming contradiction.

An important finding is that participation in the state retirement plan increases the retirement rate by 10 percentage points. Since none of the Duke faculty are eligible to participate in this plan, this finding helps to explain the lower retirement rates observed for the Duke faculty in the data presented in Table 2. The effect of participation in the state retirement plan on retirement rates has important implications for North Carolina State University and the University of North Carolina. In the future, a lower proportion of their faculties in their 60s and 70s will be in the state plan.[7] These results indicate that the decline in enrollment in the state retirement plan will further decrease the retirement rate at NCSU and UNC.

The dichotomous age variables can be used to show the change in the probability of retiring with advancing age. The age effects show that relative to the probability of retiring at age 62, the retirement rate is 11 percentage points higher for someone age 63. With the exception of age 66, the

Table 5. Estimated Retirement Probabilities by Age, 1988–92

Age	State Plan	ORP	State Plan	ORP
62	9.33	2.11	6.75	4.28
63	18.64	5.46	15.62	10.84
64	21.65	6.75	14.07	9.65
65	27.48	9.53	15.73	10.93
66	19.23	5.71	19.81	14.16
67	25.52	8.55	24.15	17.72
68	35.24	13.80	23.25	16.97
69	54.23	27.28	37.64	29.48
70	50.20	24.03	7.89	5.08
71+	36.42	14.51	32.46	24.84

Source: Authors' calculations using faculty personnel data records from University of North Carolina.
Probabilities are estimated using a base case. This base case is a white male full professor at the University of North Carolina, with 25 years of service at UNC and earning $75,000 per year.

probability of retiring increases each year up to age 69. Finally, the analysis indicates that the age 70 retirement rate was 13 percentage points lower in the years after the elimination of mandatory retirement than for the years during which this policy was allowed. The remainder of the retirement age profile was not affected by the elimination of mandatory retirement.

For the most part, the results from both before and after the end of mandatory retirement are quite similar; however, there are three important changes between the two time periods. The first is the sharp decline in the size of the effect of participation in the state plan from an estimated effect of 15 percentage points in the presence of mandatory retirement to only a 4 percentage point effect after its elimination. This finding could indicate that the retirement incentives of a defined benefit plan like the state plan are stronger when the older worker must select a retirement age of 70 or younger. Thus, the ending of mandatory retirement may have weakened the ability of universities to encourage older faculty to retire.

The second major finding in the estimated retirement rates is the difference in the retirement rate at age 70. Prior to the elimination of mandatory retirement, the retirement rate at age 70 was 46 percentage points higher than at age 62. After the elimination of mandatory retirement, the retirement rates for age 62 and age 70 are statistically the same. The third key observation is that, in the post-mandatory retirement period, assistant professors and associate professors are more likely to retire than full professors.

To further illustrate changes in retirement rates, predicted age-specific retirements rates are calculated for faculty members before and after the ending of mandatory retirement based on the estimated effects from the retirement equation (see Appendix Table A5). Table 5 shows the predicted probability of retiring for a white, male full professor at the University of North Carolina earning $75,000. The entries in the table show the predicted age-specific retirement rates for persons in the state plan and those for faculty who are participants in one of the defined contribution plans offered by the universities. In both cases, the age-specific retirement rates are shown before and after the ending of mandatory retirement.

The first column illustrates that the predicted retirement rate for a person age 62 enrolled in the state retirement plan was only 9 percent, prior to the elimination of mandatory retirement. The retirement rate increased to 27 percent for persons age 65, and it was 50 percent for persons aged 69 and 70. At every age, the retirement rates for persons in one of the optional retirement plans were one-half to one-third of those in the state retirement plan.

After the elimination of mandatory retirement, retirement rates declined for persons between the ages of 62 and 65 who are in the state plan. The predicted retirement rate at age 62 in the post-mandatory retirement period is only 7 percent and for persons aged 65 is only 16 percent. Although there is a slight increase in the retirement rate for persons 66, all other retirement rates are lower and the predicted retirement rate for persons aged 70 declines from 50 percent before 1993 to only 8 percent in the more recent years. For persons in a defined contribution plan, the predicted retirement rates are higher for those aged 62 to 69 but are much lower for persons aged 70. Ashenfelter and Card (1998) report a similar increase in retirement rates for TIAA-CREF participants during the 1990s.

Conclusions

The analysis of employment records of three North Carolina universities reveals that the faculties of these institutions have aged considerably in the last decade. The aging of the faculty is the result of past hiring patterns; slow growth in total faculty size, which along with low turnover has lead to relatively few new hires; and a decline in the rate of retirement among older faculty.

Age-specific retirement rates were examined before and after the ending of mandatory retirement at age 70. The results clearly indicate that the age-specific probability of retiring declined following the elimination of mandatory retirement. The decline in retirement rates implies an older faculty and fewer hiring opportunities in the future. Another significant finding is that pension plans influence retirement patterns with participants in defined benefit plans having higher retirement rates than those in defined contribution plans. These results have important implications for developing human resource policies of colleges and universities in the twenty-first century.

Table A1. Age Structure of Faculty, Duke, 1988–97

Age group	1988	1989	1990	1991	1992	1993	1994	1995	1996	1997
< 30	4.43	3.18	3.45	3.05	2.72	2.26	0.77	0.92	1.43	0.79
30–34	11.97	10.19	11.29	13.28	11.78	10.23	10.14	8.09	9.21	10.09
35–39	15.08	15.61	14.26	13.59	15.41	15.79	14.44	15.42	14.13	14.98
40–44	14.43	14.81	16.14	16.34	15.56	15.19	15.67	14.20	15.71	14.51
45–49	17.54	16.56	14.26	14.20	13.60	14.29	16.13	17.71	18.10	17.67
50–54	12.62	12.90	13.48	13.59	14.50	14.89	14.13	13.13	12.86	13.09
55–59	12.13	13.54	13.32	12.06	11.78	11.88	11.67	12.21	12.54	13.41
60–64	8.20	8.44	8.46	8.85	10.12	10.68	11.52	11.76	10.16	9.15
65–69	3.61	4.78	5.33	5.04	4.53	4.81	5.22	5.65	5.08	5.36
70 +	0.00	0.00	0.00	0.00	0.00	0.00	0.31	0.92	0.79	0.95
N	610	628	638	655	662	665	651	655	630	634

Source: Authors' calculations using faculty personnel data records from Duke University.

Table A2. Age Structure of Faculty, NCSU, 1988–97

Age group	1988	1989	1990	1991	1992	1993	1994	1995	1996	1997
< 30	1.74	1.97	1.77	1.07	0.53	0.53	0.73	0.81	0.66	0.47
30–34	9.95	9.44	8.14	7.73	7.21	6.61	5.93	4.86	4.85	4.14
35–39	18.96	18.35	16.60	16.46	15.23	13.67	13.53	13.23	12.68	11.76
40–44	19.36	19.99	20.67	19.72	20.17	19.62	18.60	17.27	17.60	16.78
45–49	15.69	16.32	17.98	19.05	19.10	19.35	20.20	20.99	19.72	20.72
50–54	11.62	11.73	12.07	13.32	13.56	15.59	15.93	17.61	18.73	18.85
55–59	12.75	11.73	11.68	11.26	10.96	10.77	11.07	11.40	12.15	12.57
60–64	6.21	6.95	7.68	8.33	9.62	10.11	9.67	9.24	9.10	9.09
65–69	3.40	3.15	2.95	2.60	3.14	2.97	3.40	3.58	3.52	4.68
70 +	0.33	0.39	0.46	0.47	0.47	0.79	0.93	1.01	1.00	0.94
N	1498	1526	1524	1501	1497	1514	1500	1482	1506	1496

Source: Authors' calculations using faculty personnel data records from North Carolina State University.

Table A3. Age Structure of Faculty, UNC, 1988–97

Age group	1988	1989	1990	1991	1992	1993	1994	1995	1996	1997
< 30	0.50	0.59	1.08	0.85	1.05	0.66	0.64	0.82	0.55	0.56
30–34	7.45	6.09	7.44	6.64	5.63	5.64	5.52	5.55	4.93	6.01
35–39	14.00	13.16	13.99	13.38	13.17	12.79	11.96	11.56	9.67	8.79
40–44	18.83	17.98	17.81	17.55	16.98	16.75	15.92	16.01	17.06	15.45
45–49	18.63	19.45	19.67	19.26	19.18	17.78	18.12	17.02	17.70	17.76
50–54	16.52	16.31	15.26	16.70	17.94	19.29	19.50	18.74	18.89	19.33
55–59	12.29	12.67	12.72	12.52	12.69	13.92	14.17	15.65	15.33	16.37
60–64	7.15	8.55	8.22	9.68	10.21	10.07	9.94	10.01	10.13	10.08
65–69	4.33	4.91	3.82	3.32	2.96	3.01	3.96	4.19	4.93	5.09
70 +	0.30	0.29	0.00	0.09	0.19	0.09	0.28	0.45	0.82	0.56
N	993	1018	1022	1054	1048	1063	1087	1099	1096	1081

Source: Authors' calculations using faculty personnel data records from University of North Carolina.

Table A4. Sample Means

Variable name	1988–96 Sample	1988–92 Sample	1993–96 Sample
Male	0.93	0.92	0.93
White	0.95	0.96	0.94
Salary	$65,503	$61,235	$70,896
Job tenure	27.65	27.10	28.35
Asst. professor	0.02	0.02	0.02
Assoc. professor	0.09	0.08	0.10
Full professor	0.89	0.90	0.88
Duke	0.25	0.23	0.29
NCSU	0.37	0.43	0.30
UNC	0.37	0.34	0.41
Age	64.99	65.02	64.95
State retirement plan	0.56	0.58	0.54
Retirement	0.15	0.17	0.14
N	2637	1472	1165

Source: Authors' calculations using faculty personnel data records from Duke University, University of North Carolina, and North Carolina State University.

Table A5. Estimated Effects from Probit Model

Variable Name	Full Model	1988–92	1993–96
Male	−2.61	−1.21	−2.78
White	3.98	3.19	4.47
Salary / 10,000	−0.10	−0.21	0.05
Job Tenure	−0.10	−0.15	−0.00
Asst. Professor	18.93*	11.18	27.38*
Assoc. Professor	3.50	−0.53	7.16*
Duke	1.45	6.62*	−3.05
NCSU	−1.95	−1.17	−2.45
Age 63	11.12*	11.35*	11.64*
Age 64	12.00*	14.81*	9.83*
Age 65	16.45*	21.11*	12.94*
Age 66	14.19*	12.29*	16.97*
Age 67	20.64*	19.38*	22.12*
Age 68	26.62*	29.80*	21.44*
Age 69	43.89*	48.82*	37.14*
Age 70	25.05*	45.63*	1.72
Age 71 +	31.23*	31.97*	31.95*
State Retirement Plan	10.45*	15.44*	4.47
After 1993	−2.20	—	—
After 1993 *Age 70	−12.72*	—	—
N	2637	1472	1165
Log likelihood	−1055.98	−608.79	−434.34

Source: Authors' calculations using faculty personnel data records from Duke University, University of North Carolina, and North Carolina State University.
* · < 0.10

Notes

1. A useful summary of the changes in the ADEA is provided in National Research Council (1991).

2. The employment records for NCSU and UNC are based on faculty censuses that are compiled in September of each year in accordance with a directive from the Board of Governors of the University of North Carolina. The data for Duke are similar, but the actual employment information is compiled each January. The employment refers to persons on the university payroll at the beginning of an academic year.

3. This division produces five observations for retirement prior to the elimination of mandatory retirement beginning with the retirement rate in the 1988–89 academic year and ending with the rate in the 1992–93 academic year. There are four observations after the end of mandatory retirement for the years starting with the 1993–94 academic year and ending with the 1996–97 academic year.

4. In most cases, faculty were not required to retire on the day of reaching age 70. A more standard rule at most universities was that the faculty could complete the academic year in which they attained the age of 70.

5. This process implies that a person who remains employed during the entire sample period will be in the sample a total of nine times.

6. All faculty hired after 1971 by the University of North Carolina system have had

the option of enrolling in either the state plan or one of several approved optional retirement plans. Over time, more and more faculty have opted for one of the ORPs (Clark, Harper, and Pitts 1997).

7. Clark and Pitts (1999) show that the more recently hired faculty at NCSU have a greater likelihood of being enrolled in one of the ORPs than they do of participating in the state retirement plan.

References

Ahenfelter, Orley and David Card. 1998. "Faculty Retirement Behavior in the Post-Mandatory Era: New Evidence from the Princeton Retirement Survey." Paper presented at TIAA-CREF conference, "Examining Life After the End of Mandatory Retirement," Washington, D.C., May.

Clark, Robert and Melinda Pitts. 1999. "Faculty Choice of a Pension Plan: Defined Benefit vs. Defined Contribution." *Industrial Relations* 38 (1): 18–45.

Clark, Robert, Loretta Harper, and Melinda Pitts. 1997. "Faculty Pension Choices in a Public Institution: Defined Benefit and Defined Contribution Plans." *Research Dialogues* 50 (March).

National Research Council, Committee on Ending Mandatory Retirement in Higher Education. *Ending Mandatory Retirement for Tenured Faculty: The Consequences for Higher Education*, ed. P. Brett Hammond and Harriet P. Morgan. Washington, D.C.: National Research Council, 1991.

Kotlikoff, Laurence J. and David A. Wise. *The Wage Carrot and the Pension Stick.* Kalamazoo, Mich.: Upjohn Institute, 1989.

Quinn, Joseph, Richard Burkhauser, and Daniel Myers. *Passing the Torch: The Influence of Economic Incentives on Work and Retirement.* Kalamazoo, Mich.: Upjohn Institute,1990.

Chapter 3
Age-Based Retirement Incentives for Tenured Faculty Members: Satisfying the Legal Requirements

David L. Raish

Many colleges and universities have begun experiencing fewer retirements among their oldest tenured faculty members. Some of these institutions are exploring, or have instituted, age-based retirement incentive programs under which greater benefits are available on earlier retirement. These programs help institutions to achieve a more orderly turnover of faculty and, in many cases, substantial cost savings. At the same time, the programs offer individual faculty members the opportunity to retire more comfortably at an earlier age, if they choose to do so.

Until recently, the legality of these age-based retirement incentive programs was unclear. In addition, court challenges had become increasingly common under the Age Discrimination in Employment Act of 1967, as amended (ADEA). However, in October 1998, Congress enacted a "safe harbor" exception[1] to the ADEA covering certain age-based retirement incentive benefits offered by institutions of higher education to their tenured faculty members.

A variety of retirement incentives for tenured faculty, age-based or not, are now permitted under the ADEA. However, careful planning is required to satisfy the conditions of the ADEA as well as other federal and state laws.

Assessing the Need for Retirement Incentives

Not surprisingly, expiration at the end of 1993 of the ADEA's special exception permitting mandatory retirement in higher education has led to fewer retirements by tenured faculty members, especially among those nearing, at, or over age 70.[2] Experience will, of course, inevitably vary from one institution to another, depending on a number of factors, including the climate of the institution (meteorological and otherwise), the teaching and other demands placed on senior faculty, the level of retirement income provided by the institution's retirement plans, the availability of postretirement health coverage, and the extent to which retirement or other benefit plans may provide disincentives to retire.[3]

Those institutions that experience fewer retirements among tenured professors of retirement age will generally face increased budget pressures, given the salary differential that typically exists between long-term and entry-level faculty members. This was recognized in the January 1998 report of the National Commission on the Cost of Higher Education. The report recommended legislation to permit age-based retirement incentives for tenured faculty members as one means of checking the skyrocketing costs of a college education (National Commission on the Cost of Higher Education 1998). Institutions also typically need to encourage more retirements in order to respond to changing academic needs, including necessary hires in new and existing fields (National Research Council 1991: 3).[4]

In 1986, Congress commissioned a study from the National Academy of Sciences on the impact on major research institutions of the expiration of the special ADEA exception permitting mandatory retirement of tenured faculty at age 70. The Committee on Mandatory Retirement in Higher Education, formed to conduct the study, concluded in its 1991 report that the mandatory age 70 retirement provision should be allowed to expire (National Research Council 1991: 5). However, it reached this conclusion on the assumption that age-based voluntary retirement incentive plans were available to institutions of higher education, in order to encourage retirements in the normal course (National Research Council 1991: 3). Contrary to this expectation, the Equal Employment Opportunity Commission (EEOC) and others have, in recent years, challenged the legality of some age-based faculty retirement incentives, and some of these challenges have met with success in the courts.[5]

The ADEA in General

With certain exceptions, the ADEA prohibits an employer from discriminating against any individual with respect to "compensation, terms, conditions, or privileges of employment, because of such individual's age." More specifically, the ADEA also prohibits an employer from ceasing or reducing, because of age, contributions under a defined contribution retirement plan or benefit accruals under a defined benefit retirement plan.

The ADEA's definition of "employer" specifically includes "a State or political subdivision of a State and any agency or instrumentality of a State or a political subdivision of a State." Further, the ADEA also incorporates by reference provisions of the Fair Labor Standards Act which allow for private causes of action against federal and state governments. However, the Supreme Court has recently held that the ADEA's purported abrogation of the states' sovereign immunity is unconstitutional, and, therefore, private claims cannot be brought in federal court against state employees, including state colleges and universities.[6] The Court's decision, however, appears to leave open the possibility of enforcement action by EEOC.

Retirement Incentives Available Before the New Safe Harbor

Some retirement incentives were permissible under the ADEA prior to enactment of the safe harbor for tenured faculty in 1998. These incentives remain available. Indeed, Congress expressly provided that the 1998 safe harbor does not affect the application of the ADEA to plans or employers outside the safe harbor.[7]

Plans without benefits that decline with age. If a retirement incentive arrangement does not reduce or eliminate benefits on account of increased age, it does not run afoul of the ADEA prohibition against discrimination on the basis of age. Having a *minimum* age for a given benefit does not violate the ADEA, even if that minimum age is greater than 40. In other words, younger members of the class protected by the ADEA—those age 40 or older—may be denied a benefit that is available to older members of the protected class.[8]

For example, it would be permissible for an institution to offer lifetime medical coverage to faculty members or other employees retiring at or after a stated age, such as age 60. Similarly, it would be permissible for an institution to offer faculty members over a stated age, such as age 62, the ability to make a reduced time commitment for a stated period, give up tenure, and receive disproportionately greater compensation during that period. A phased retirement plan might, for example, permit a faculty member over age 62 to work half-time for up to three years for 75 percent of full-time pay, provided the faculty member gives up tenure at the beginning of the phased retirement period and agrees to retire altogether at the end of that period.

The most common type of retirement incentive arrangement with no reduction or cessation of benefits based on increased age is a "window" plan. Under such a plan, enhanced retirement benefits are offered only if an individual retires during a specified period of months. For example, an institution might establish a "window" plan under which faculty members over a stated age, such as 60 or 65, may elect, between September 1 and December 31 of a given year, to retire on June 30 of the following year and receive certain enhanced benefits. The enhanced benefits might include a lump sum cash payment, a larger pension under a defined benefit plan, postretirement health coverage (or, if that coverage is already available, a greater employer contribution toward that coverage), and perhaps other benefits or perquisites. Those who do not elect retirement during the 4-month window receive no such enhancements on retirement. Because of the incentive provided by the closing of the window on December 31, faculty members are encouraged to retire now rather than later. No upper age limit or age-based reduction is needed to provide such an incentive.

Window plans do, however, have several drawbacks. First, they are often perceived by faculty members as unfair, since they require a decision within a limited period of time during which the faculty member may be unable or unwilling to think seriously about retirement. They also deny the benefit enhancements to those who may choose to retire a year or two later. While well suited for an immediate reduction in force (and, therefore, widely used by other employers for this purpose), window plans are inconsistent with the longer term, orderly turnover of faculty that most institutions and their faculty members prefer. If an institution were to reopen the window and offer enhanced benefits again, the incentive would quickly become diluted, as some faculty members would put off retirement and wait for the next opening of the window.

Incentives in defined benefit pension plans. The ADEA permits certain age-based early retirement subsidies in defined benefit pension plans.[9] First, an employer may offer social security supplements that provide extra benefits only to those retiring before a specified age at which social security benefits are available (so-called "social security bridge benefits"). A defined benefit plan might provide, for example, that individuals retiring between ages 60 and 65 will receive an increase in their monthly retirement benefit equal to the social security benefit they can expect to receive at age 65, if they wait until age 65 to apply for their social security benefit. This eliminates one disincentive to retirement before age 65—that of having no social security income available between ages 60 and 62 and only a reduced Social Security income available for life if the benefit is started between ages 62 and 65.

Other early retirement subsidies are also permitted by the ADEA. For example, a participant who has accrued an annual lifetime benefit under a defined benefit pension plan, starting at age 65, equal to $30,000, might receive only about $15,000 per year if the participant retires and starts the benefit at age 55. This results from the normal actuarial reduction based on the fact that payments will be made for a longer period of time. The plan may enhance that early retirement benefit, so that the participant receives the same annual amount upon retirement at age 55 (or age 60) as he or she would have received if the benefits had started at age 65.

Voluntary early retirement incentive plans consistent with the purposes of the ADEA. The ADEA also permits voluntary early retirement incentive plans (VERIPs) consistent with the relevant purpose or purposes of the ADEA.[10] The relevant purposes of the ADEA are to promote employment of older persons based on their ability rather than age; to prohibit arbitrary age discrimination in employment; and to help employers and workers find ways of meeting problems arising from the impact of age on employment.[11]

The scope of the ADEA exception for VERIPs is unclear. It has no meaning if it does not permit at least some retirement incentive plans under which benefits are reduced or cease as a result of increased age. As discussed above, minimum age requirements are permissible under the ADEA, and a plan that involves no reduction or cessation of benefits based on increased age is already consistent with the ADEA.

The Statement of Managers on the Older Workers Benefit Protection Act of 1990 (OWBPA), which added the VERIP exception to the ADEA, cryptically explains:

Early retirement incentive plans that withhold benefits to older workers above a specific age while continuing to make them available to younger workers *may* conflict with the purpose of prohibiting arbitrary age discrimination in employment.[12] (emphasis added)

This language suggests that *some* age-based retirement incentive arrangements are permitted by the VERIP exception. However, it also suggests that some are not, and it is unclear where the line should be drawn.

In a 1992 request for comments on certain issues to be addressed in future regulations, the EEOC asked:

Does OWBPA allow the reduction or elimination of an early retirement benefit in correlation with increasing age or increasing years of service? If so, under what circumstances?[13]

Not long thereafter, in a different administration, the EEOC answered its own question, taking the position that the VERIP exception permits no voluntary early retirement incentive plan that involves a reduction or cessation of benefits based on increased age.[14] In a 1997 decision of a federal magistrate judge, that position met with success.[15] However, in a 1998 decision of a U.S. Court of Appeals, the VERIP exception was held to apply to a plan that provided special benefits upon retirement only in the first year in which the teacher had both attained age 55 and completed twenty years of service.[16]

The Safe Harbor for Certain Age-Based Faculty Retirement Incentives

The uncertain scope of the VERIP exception, together with the limited usefulness of the retirement incentives otherwise available under the ADEA, prompted the higher education community to seek legislative clarification that voluntary retirement incentive plans, under which benefits end or decline in value based on increased age, could be offered to tenured faculty members. The result was the enactment of a safe harbor for certain age-based plans as part of the Higher Education Amendments of 1998.[17]

Overview of the safe harbor. The safe harbor permits supplemental benefits that are reduced or eliminated based upon age, subject to six conditions:[18]

First, the employer must be an institution of higher education.

Second, the benefits must be offered to employees with unlimited tenure.

Third, the benefits must be payable upon *voluntary* retirement.

Fourth, the institution must not implement any age-based reduction or cessation of benefits other than these supplemental benefits (except as otherwise permitted by the ADEA).

Fifth, the supplemental benefits must be in addition to any retirement or severance benefits that have been available to tenured faculty members generally, independent of any early retirement or exit-incentive plan, within the preceding 365 days.

Sixth, any tenured faculty member who attains the minimum age and satisfies all non-age-based conditions for receiving such a supplemental benefit must have an opportunity for at least 180 days to elect to retire and receive the maximum supplemental benefit that could then be elected by a younger but otherwise similarly situated employee. The faculty member must also have the ability to delay retirement for at least 180 days after making that election.

Institutions of higher education. The safe harbor is limited to plans offered by institutions of higher education as defined in Section 101 of the Higher Education Act of 1965, as amended. That definition generally includes any educational institution that:

- admits as regular students only persons having a certificate of graduation from a school providing secondary education, or the recognized equivalent of such a certificate;
- is legally authorized to provide a program of education beyond secondary education;
- provides an educational program for which the institution awards a bachelor's degree or provides not less than a two-year program that is acceptable for full credit toward such a degree;
- is a public or other nonprofit institution; and
- is accredited by a nationally recognized accrediting agency or association, or if not so accredited, is an institution that has been granted pre-accreditation status by such an agency or association that has been recognized by the secretary for the granting of preaccreditation status, and the secretary has determined that there is satisfactory assurance that the institution will meet the accreditation standards of such an agency or association within a reasonable time.

This definition is essentially the same as the definition of "institution of higher education" in the ADEA provision which, prior to January 1, 1994, permitted mandatory retirement of tenured faculty members at age 70.

Employees with unlimited tenure. The safe harbor is limited to benefits offered to employees serving under a contract of unlimited tenure (or similar arrangement providing for unlimited tenure). This language is identical to the corresponding language of the ADEA provision which, prior to January 1, 1994, permitted mandatory retirement of tenured faculty at age 70. The Conference Committee Report on the Higher Education Amendments of 1998 (the Conference Report)[19] confirms that the language is intended to have the same meaning as it did in that context.[20]

The Conference Report makes clear that a faculty member need not be tenured at the time benefits are actually provided, so long as he or she was tenured at the time the benefits were offered. Take, for example, a phased retirement program under which faculty members give up tenure, reduce their workload to one-half for a specified period, and receive more than one-half of their full-time salary for that period. The institution may also provide additional benefits on full retirement at the end of that period. Neither the benefits paid during the period of phased retirement nor the benefits provided at full retirement will fail to qualify for the safe harbor because of the fact that the faculty member is no longer tenured when those benefits are provided.

Voluntary retirement. The safe harbor is available only for supplemental benefits payable on *voluntary* retirement. The statute does not elaborate on the term "voluntary," nor does the Conference Report. Presumably, the body of law addressing the meaning of "voluntary" for other purposes of the ADEA will apply in this area as well.[21] Thus, for example, a generous retirement incentive plan cannot be challenged as forcing involuntary retirement merely because its attractiveness induces employees to retire. Also, the employee bears the burden of proof that his or her retirement under a retirement incentive plan was involuntary. Among the relevant factors on voluntariness are whether:

- the employee had sufficient time to consider his or her options;
- accurate and complete information was provided about the benefits available under the early retirement incentive plan; and
- there have been threats, intimidation and/or coercion.

Given the protections of the unlimited tenure relationship, it is unlikely that a tenured faculty member could successfully challenge the voluntariness of his or her retirement, absent unusual circumstances.

No age-based reduction or cessation of other benefits. The safe harbor applies to voluntary retirement incentive benefits offered by an institution only if the institution does not, at the same time, implement any age-based reduction or cessation of other, existing benefits (except as otherwise permitted by the ADEA). In other words, a safe harbor plan cannot reward those who choose to retire and punish those who do not choose to retire. For example, a faculty retirement incentive plan could not both provide additional benefits for retirement before age 70 and, for those choosing to remain employed after age 70, take away health coverage, a parking space, or some other benefit or perquisite that is generally available to tenured faculty members.

However, age-based changes in benefits that are permitted by other provisions of the ADEA would not prevent the safe harbor from applying. For example, age-based reductions in benefits are permitted when justified by increased employer cost. In addition, postretirement health coverage can be (and typically is) eliminated or scaled back substantially upon the retiree's eligibility for Medicare. Because these reductions are permissible under the ADEA, they do not defeat the safe harbor. Also, employers frequently change postretirement benefits from time to time, often reducing or eliminating post-retirement health coverage, for example. This, too, would not prevent the safe harbor from applying, where the change applied to all faculty members or to a non-age-based class of faculty members.

Benefits in addition to preexisting retirement or severance benefits. The supplemental benefits described in the safe harbor must be in addition to any retirement or severance benefits that have been offered generally to tenured faculty, independent of any early retirement or exit-incentive plan, within the preceding 365 days. This provision is designed to prevent an institution that currently offers postretirement (or postseverance) lifetime health coverage, or other benefits, to tenured faculty members from instituting a safe harbor retirement incentive plan and offering the lifetime health coverage or other benefits only to faculty members retiring under that safe harbor plan. In other words, the safe harbor does not permit an employer to take existing postretirement (or postseverance) benefits that are available generally to tenured faculty, without any reduction or cessation based on increased age, and transform them into age-based benefits under a retirement incentive plan described in the safe harbor.

However, in recognition of the fact that employers frequently change, replace, or terminate employee benefits, this restriction is limited to preexisting benefits that were in effect during the preceding 365 days. Thus, for example, an employer that ceased providing postretirement health coverage to those retiring on or after January 1, 2000, could, on or after January 1, 2001, institute a safe harbor retirement incentive plan that includes postretirement health coverage as a benefit only for those who choose to retire under the safe harbor plan. For purposes of this 365-day rule, while the language is not entirely clear, it appears that benefits that continue to be provided to those who are already retired are not taken into account. A benefit would presumably cease to "have been offered generally" to tenured faculty when those who retire cease to be eligible for it, and not when the benefit ceases to be available to those already retired. For instance, if the institution in the preceding example stopped offering postretirement health coverage

Table 1. Hypothetical Safe-Harbor Incentive Retirement Program

Retirement at age	Lump sum benefit as percent of final annual salary
65	200
66	160
67	120
68	80
69	40
70 or older	0

Source: Author's calculations.

on January 1, 2000, the fact that those who retired before that date continue to receive postretirement health coverage for many years to come should not prevent the institution from offering retiree health coverage under a safe harbor retirement incentive plan, beginning January 1, 2001.

In addition, a safe harbor plan can provide a benefit previously offered under a prior early retirement or exit-incentive plan, even if offered within the preceding 365 days. This would, for example, permit an institution to replace an existing early retirement incentive plan with a new plan described in the safe harbor, without waiting 365 days. Similarly, an institution that has been negotiating retirement or exit incentives with faculty members on a case-by-case basis could adopt a safe harbor plan within 365 days thereafter and include the same benefits under that plan.

"One bite at the apple" without regard to increased age. The final condition of the safe harbor is often referred to as the one-bite-at-the-apple or the one-bite rule. It is designed to ensure that an otherwise eligible employee is not precluded (by having attained too high an age) from having at least one reasonable opportunity to retire and receive the maximum benefit offered by the safe harbor plan. That opportunity must include at least 180 days to make the election to retire, and at least 180 days after the election to plan for retirement. Since institutions need time to fill positions, change teaching assignments for other faculty members, or change curricula, the second 180-day requirement should generally be in the interest of both the professor and the institution.

The one-bite-at-the-apple condition will generally apply in two circumstances. First, when a safe harbor retirement incentive plan is established, those who are otherwise eligible for the plan, but are too old to receive its maximum benefit, must be given at least 180 days in which they may elect to retire under the plan and receive that maximum benefit. Assume, for example, a safe harbor incentive plan that provides a lump-sum cash benefit determined under Table 1.

A tenured faculty member who was age 71 when the plan was established must be offered a 180-day opportunity to elect to retire and receive a lump sum benefit equal to 200 percent of final annual salary. (A faculty member who does not elect to retire during that time period would not have any future right to any benefit under the plan.) The faculty member must also be given a period of at least 180 days after the election to plan for retirement.

Similarly, a faculty member who was age 67 when the above plan was established would also be entitled to a 180-day period during which he or she could elect to retire and receive the maximum 200 percent benefit (followed by another 180 days to plan for retirement). If the 67-year-old faculty member did not elect during the applicable 180-day period to retire, he or she would be entitled only to those lower benefits available thereafter (for example, a 40 percent benefit if the faculty member ultimately retired at age 69).

The second circumstance in which the one-bite rule will apply is where a faculty member is not yet eligible for the plan, for a reason other than age, at the time the plan is established, and subsequently becomes eligible at an age when the maximum benefit is not normally available. That faculty member, too, must be given the 180-day opportunity to elect to retire and receive the maximum benefit (and another 180 days to plan for retirement, after that election). For example, if a safe harbor retirement incentive plan, providing benefits under the table above, requires fifteen years of continuous service before a faculty member becomes eligible for the plan, a faculty member whose continuous service began at age 56, and who completed the fifteen-year service requirement at age 71, would be entitled to elect at that time to retire and receive 200 percent of pay as a lump sum benefit. The same would be true if the faculty member completed the fifteen years of continuous service at age 66, 67, 68, or 69.

The maximum benefit available under the one-bite rule. The one-bite opportunity must apply to "the maximum benefit that could then be elected by a younger but otherwise similarly situated employee." This means, for example, that if, on completion of the fifteen-year service requirement in the preceding example, the safe harbor plan was no longer in effect (such that no benefit could then be elected by a younger employee), the faculty member completing the fifteen-year service requirement would also be entitled to no benefit. Similarly, if the plan had been modified between the time it was established and the time the faculty member completed fifteen years of continuous service, whether to reduce or increase benefits, the faculty member would be entitled to the maximum benefit available at that time as reduced or increased.

The maximum benefit that must be made available is the benefit that is available to a "younger but otherwise similarly situated employee." This means that, while the older faculty member benefiting from the one-bite condition is assumed to be of the age at which the maximum benefit is available, all other relevant facts are those actually in existence with respect to the faculty member. For example, if the benefit is a percentage of final pay, the final pay is the faculty member's actual final pay, not the final pay that he or she would have had at a younger age, or that some other, younger faculty member may have. If the schedule of benefits differs among the schools or faculties at the university, the maximum benefit would be determined under the schedule that applies to the faculty member's own school or faculty.

According to the statute and the Conference Report, it does not appear relevant that a maximum benefit could grow to a larger amount if the faculty member were permitted to elect to retire after the initial 180-day election period, due to an increase in salary, years of service, or some other factor that may, under a given safe harbor plan, affect the amount of the benefits provided. It appears that the benefits provided under the one-bite condition need not take any such possible increases into account, and that no second bite needs to be made available. For example, if a plan is established offering the benefits described in the table above, and a 71-year-old professor is given six months to elect to retire and receive a benefit equal to 200 percent of final annual salary, it appears that the benefit need only take into account his or her final salary at the time of the election. If the professor declines to retire at that time and earns a higher salary the following year, it does not appear that another election needs to be offered with the increased benefit.

Ascertaining the maximum benefit. In a plan that offers only a lump sum benefit, in the form of a dollar amount or percentage of pay, as in the examples above, it is easy to determine the maximum benefit available to a younger but similarly situated faculty member. However, some retirement incentive plans provide several benefits, and may pay or provide them over a period of years. For example, a bridge benefit might be paid monthly from the time of retirement until age 65 (or until age 70), allowing a faculty member to postpone starting his or her regular retirement benefits until that time, so that they can grow to a higher amount. The safe harbor plan might also offer health coverage from retirement until age 65, or for the faculty member's lifetime. Other benefits might include on-campus parking, office, laboratory or library space, secretarial assistance, and other opportunities to participate in campus life in various ways. The Conference Report provides:

If more than one benefit is offered, or noncash benefits are provided, or benefits are provided over a period of time, the employee will be assumed to retire at the age which, under the applicable formula or formulas, results in benefits with the largest combined present value.

In most cases, the age at which this present value is the greatest will be readily apparent. For example, if a safe harbor retirement plan provides the benefits described above to individuals retiring between ages 65 and 70, the monthly bridge benefit is 50 percent of final monthly pay, that benefit is payable until age 70, and the retiree health coverage is available for the faculty member's lifetime, it is clear that the maximum benefits would be available to someone electing to retire at age 65. Those maximum benefits would be five years of monthly bridge benefits plus lifetime medical coverage and perquisites. A 66-year-old or 68-year-old retiree would receive fewer monthly bridge benefits and other lifetime benefits over a shorter lifetime. Accordingly, a 71-year-old faculty member to whom the one-bite condition applies would be entitled to five years of monthly bridge benefits, at 50 percent of his or her actual final monthly rate of pay, together with lifetime retiree medical coverage and other perquisites. While the Conference Report states that the faculty member will be assumed to retire *at the age* that results in benefits with the largest combined present value, the Conference Report does not suggest that the benefits actually received by the faculty member must have a present value at least equal to that amount. For example, the 71-year-old faculty member exercising his or her right under the one-bite condition will have a shorter life expectancy, so the lifetime medical coverage and other perquisites provided will have a smaller present value. Presumably, no additional benefit must be paid to make up for this difference in present value, although the statute and legislative history are not entirely clear on this point.

The 180-day requirements. Given the two 180-day periods required, as a minimum, to satisfy the one-bite condition, the offer of voluntary retirement incentives would need to be made at least 360 days prior to the intended retirement date. This would allow a tenured faculty member to wait until the last day of the 180-day election period before making his or her election, and still have another 180 days after the election to plan for retirement. For example, if retirements generally occur on June 30, a safe harbor plan could provide for an election to be made between July 1 and December 31 of one year to retire on June 30 of the next year. On the other hand, the Conference Report does make clear that a faculty member may waive the second 180-day period. For example, if a faculty member elected on July 1 to retire on September 1 of the same year, and if the institution were agreeable to that timetable, the safe harbor plan would still satisfy the one-bite condition.

In the case of a phased retirement plan under which a faculty member elects a reduced workload, but does not fully retire for a stated period of years, it does not seem necessary to allow 180 days between the time of the faculty member's election and the time the reduced workload begins, as long as there are at least 180 days between that election and the date of full retirement. However, the Conference Report does not specifically address this point, and the statute is not entirely clear.

Examples of safe harbor plans. The Conference Report offers some examples of faculty retirement incentive benefits that would fall within the safe harbor. The first involves a monthly bridge benefit available to tenured faculty members who voluntarily retire between ages 65 and 70. In the example, the bridge benefit equals 50 percent of the faculty member's final monthly salary, and is paid from retirement until age 70. The Conference Report goes on to explain that the benefit could be made available between other ages, such as 60 and 65, or 62 and 69, could involve a percentage of salary different from 50 percent, and could even include a varying percentage of salary based, for example, on service, rank, the school or department in which the faculty member teaches, or other factors. The Conference Report clarifies that the benefit could also be subject to other conditions, such as a minimum service requirement for eligibility, or limitation of the plan to one or more schools, departments, or other classifications of tenured faculty.

There is, of course, no requirement that the benefit be based on the retiree's actual salary. It could instead be based on an average salary for professors of a given rank, or in a specific discipline, or institutionwide, or at a group of institutions. Alternatively, the benefit could be a fixed dollar amount instead of a percentage of salary, or it could be based on a formula altogether unrelated to salary.

Another example provided by the Conference Report involves a plan that provides lump sum retirement incentive payments that are reduced based on age at retirement, and eliminated at a specified upper age, such as age 65 or 70. As in the case of a monthly bridge benefit, an institution has considerable leeway in structuring its plan. Variables include the age or ages at which the lump sum benefit is available, the amount of the benefit, the extent to which it is reduced based on age, the age at which it ceases to be available, and the eligibility conditions that apply, including a minimum service requirement or limitation of the plan to one or more schools, departments or other classifications of tenured faculty. Institutions that prefer a monthly bridge benefit for a period of years may, in effect, be forced to offer a single lump sum benefit instead, because the monthly bridge benefit may result in up-front taxation on the full present value of the payments to be made, as discussed below.

The Conference Report also discusses a "voluntary phased, planned or similar retirement program" that offers subsidized pay or benefits for part-time work or decreased duties. Even if the amount of the subsidy or the duration of the part-time work or decreased duties, or both, is reduced or eliminated based on age, these programs, when properly structured, also fall within the safe harbor. For example, a phased retirement program might allow a tenured faculty member to teach a one-half course load for a period of one, two, or three years, as elected by the faculty member, with subsidized pay determined on the basis of Table 2, provided the faculty member gives up tenure at the start of the phased retirement period and agrees to retire altogether at the end of the period.

Presumably, the phased retirement opportunity could be eliminated at a stated age, such as age 70 in the above example, despite the fact that the example in the Conference Report does not include that plan feature.

The Conference Report does not give examples specifically addressing

Table 2. Hypothetical Safe-Harbor Phased Retirement Program.

Age when phased retirement commences	Percent of full-time salary paid throughout phased retirement period
62	90
63	85
64	80
65	75
66	70
67	65
68	60
69	55
70 or older	50

Source: Author's calculations.

the provision of various noncash benefits that are common to faculty retire-ment incentive plans, such as health or life insurance coverage, and various perquisites that allow a faculty member to remain part of the campus com-munity, such as a parking space, laboratory or office space, secretarial assis-tance, committee memberships, access to sports, eating or other facilities, and the like. However, the statute is drafted broadly enough to include these and other benefits, and there is no suggestion in the Conference Report of any limitation on the nature of the benefits offered. Of course, any safe har-bor plan, regardless of the amount or nature of the benefits provided, must satisfy all the conditions of the safe harbor that are discussed above.

Application of the safe harbor to plans that predated it. A number of colleges and universities implemented age-based faculty retirement incentive plans prior to the enactment of the Higher Education Amendments of 1998. These in-stitutions have relied principally on the VERIP exception discussed above, which provides that voluntary early retirement incentive plans do not violate the ADEA if those plans are otherwise consistent with the relevant purpose or purposes of the ADEA.

These institutions will now need to examine their existing plans to see if they satisfy all of the conditions of the safe harbor. If an existing plan fails to comply in some respect with the safe harbor, it does not necessarily mean that the plan violates the ADEA. The Higher Education Amendments of 1998 provide that the enactment of the safe harbor does not affect the application of the ADEA with respect to any plan that is not described in the safe harbor.[22] An institution may still have compelling arguments that the VERIP exception applies to such a plan, notwithstanding any age-based reduction or cessation of benefits. However, the institution may be well advised to replace that existing plan with one that satisfies the conditions of the safe harbor, in order to achieve greater protection against ADEA claims.

If a preexisting plan satisfies all of the conditions of the safe harbor, it is not protected by the safe harbor as to any cause of action that may have arisen under the ADEA prior to the date of enactment (October 7, 1998).[23] Enactment of the safe harbor does not affect the application of the ADEA to any plan described in the safe harbor, for any period prior to enactment.[24] However, strong arguments can be made that such a plan falls within the VERIP exemption and, therefore, did not violate the ADEA. Going forward, it appears that the plan may continue unchanged and benefit from the protection of the safe harbor.

It might be possible to construct an argument that the safe harbor requires the "one-bite" condition to be satisfied after enactment of the safe harbor provisions. For that reason, an institution may, out of caution, want to reintroduce its faculty retirement incentive plan and offer a new 180-day period to elect the maximum benefit. While this may result in additional costs, it also has the advantage of providing a new impetus for retirement by those older faculty who earlier declined to retire. In any event, it is unlikely that any plan in existence before the 1998 legislation met *all* of the detailed conditions of the safe harbor.

ERISA Issues to Consider

For many colleges and universities, the Employee Retirement Income Security Act of 1974, as amended (ERISA), may significantly limit the nature of the benefits that can be provided under a faculty retirement incentive plan, or the faculty members who may be made eligible for those benefits, or both.

Exemption for state institutions and church-affiliated colleges or universities. ERISA does not apply to benefit plans of state or local governments or their agencies or instrumentalities.[25] Therefore, state colleges and universities, as well as community colleges, are not subject to ERISA. Religiously affiliated colleges or universities are also generally exempt from ERISA, provided that they are controlled by a church (or by a convention or association of churches) or share common religious bonds and convictions with that church (or convention or association).[26] Accordingly, these colleges and universities need not be concerned with the ERISA constraints discussed below. However, these institutions do need to be mindful of state statutes prohibiting age discrimination, since they cannot rely on the defense that ERISA preempts such a statute with respect to a retirement incentive plan subject to ERISA.[27]

Plans that are subject to ERISA. Unless they fall within ERISA's exemptions for governmental and church-affiliated institutions, discussed above, colleges and universities are subject to ERISA with respect to their pension and welfare benefit plans. Faculty retirement incentive plans will presumably fall within the ERISA definition of a "welfare benefit plan"[28] to the extent they provide such benefits as health coverage, disability benefits, or death

benefits. Since ERISA contains few content requirements for welfare benefit plans, it is unlikely to affect the design of a faculty retirement incentive
plan with respect to welfare benefits.

Of much greater concern are the ERISA rules applicable to "pension
plans." ERISA defines a pension plan to include:

any plan, fund, or program established or maintained by an employer . . . to the extent that by its express terms or as a result of surrounding circumstances such plan,
fund, or program—
(i) provides retirement income to employees, or
(ii) results in a deferral of income by employees for periods extending to the termination of covered employment or beyond,
regardless of the method of calculating the contributions made to the plan, the
method of calculating the benefits under the plan or the method of distributing
benefits from the plan.[29]

Faculty retirement incentive plans that offer cash benefits after termination of employment, such as bridge benefits or lump sum payments on
retirement, as described in examples above, would generally fall within
ERISA's definition of a pension plan. These plans, if age based, would generally fail to satisfy at least five of ERISA's requirements for pension plans.
First, the minimum age for participation is normally 60, 62, or 65, well in excess of ERISA's age 21 or 26 limit.[30] Second, benefits do not accrue and vest
as generally required.[31] Instead, they get smaller the later one retires. Third,
ERISA specifically prohibits the reduction of contributions or benefit accruals based on increased age.[32] Fourth, retirement incentives are not typically
offered in a joint and survivor annuity form providing lifetime income to the
surviving spouse.[33] Fifth, the plans typically are not funded through a trust
or other vehicle that protects the assets from creditors of the employers.[34]
Instead, benefits typically are paid from the institution's general assets.

Exception for top hat plans. ERISA does exempt from these and other pension plan requirements a "top hat" plan—that is, a plan "which is unfunded
and is maintained by an employer primarily for the purpose of providing
deferred compensation for a select group of management or highly compensated employees."[35] There are no regulations providing guidance on the
meaning of "select group," "management," or "highly compensated employees." In a nonbinding advisory opinion, the Department of Labor has stated
that the top hat provisions should be interpreted in light of Congress's intent to limit the provisions to individuals who, by virtue of their position or
compensation level, have the ability to affect or substantially influence the
design and operation of the plan.[36]

It is doubtful that all faculty members at any college or university constitute a select group of management or highly compensated employees. However, if the retirement incentive plan is limited to a narrowly defined eligible
group, such as tenured, full-time professors over age 60 with at least fif-

teen years of service, the salary levels may be high enough at a given institution, and the number of eligible individuals low enough, that the group will qualify for the top hat exemption. The argument that tenured faculty members constitute management, if not highly compensated, employees would be enhanced if the eligible tenured faculty members had some voting power or other influence as a group over the design of the retirement incentive program and other benefits. As a practical matter, however, to satisfy the top hat exception some institutions may need to limit their faculty retirement incentive plans to more select groups of higher paid faculty members, such as faculty members at the business, law or medical school, or those whose annual pay exceeds a stated amount.

Phased retirement programs. If a phased retirement program provides benefits only while the individual continues to work, and not after termination of employment, it is unlikely to be a pension plan under ERISA.[37] Thus, the troublesome ERISA requirements for pension plans would not apply. However, a phased retirement program that falls outside of ERISA's definition of a pension plan would need to be designed with any applicable state age discrimination laws in mind, since the ERISA preemption argument would not be available unless the program constituted a welfare benefit plan under ERISA Section 3(1).[38]

Window plans. Window plans discussed above may also be exempt from ERISA, at least if they provide only for a single lump sum cash payment and no welfare benefits described in ERISA Section 3(1), because such an arrangement may not constitute a plan under ERISA.

In *Fort Halifax Packing Co. v. Coyne*, in the context of severance payments, the Supreme Court held that no ERISA plan existed, stating that "the theoretical possibility of a one-time obligation in the future simply creates no need for an ongoing administrative program for processing claims and paying benefits."[39] Subsequently, lower courts have examined potential ERISA plans to determine if they require an ongoing administrative scheme.[40] Factors considered in the determination of whether an ongoing administrative scheme is implicated include the type of payment (one-time lump sum or continuous, periodic payments), the duration of the employer's obligation, the trigger for payments (a one-time event or termination in general), and the necessity of case-by-case eligibility determinations.[41]

If a window plan does not constitute either a pension or welfare benefit plan under ERISA, the ERISA preemption argument would again be unavailable with respect to any applicable state age discrimination laws. Thus, it is generally inadvisable for a window plan to have an upper age limit or to reduce benefits based on increased age. Fortunately, such age-based features are not necessary to provide the incentive to retire; the incentive comes from the closing of the window at the allotted time.

Federal Income Tax Issues to Consider

Under the Internal Revenue Code, an individual who has a right to deferred compensation from a tax-exempt or governmental employer is taxed on the value of that right at the time the right ceases to be subject to a "substantial risk of forfeiture," even if the individual does not (or could not) receive the deferred compensation at that time.[42] Unlike ERISA, this Code provision applies to deferred compensation payments by both state and private colleges and universities, including most religiously affiliated institutions.[43]

The first question under the Code is whether a faculty retirement incentive plan is providing deferred compensation. In general, it seems likely that the Internal Revenue Service would take the position that benefit payments promised under a faculty retirement incentive plan, whether a lump sum at retirement, periodic bridge payments for a specified period, or lifetime payments would constitute deferred compensation.[44] On the other hand, if retirement before a stated age is required in order to receive the retirement incentive benefits, a strong argument can be made that the faculty member faces a substantial risk of forfeiting those benefits until the day that he or she retires (before reaching the stated age) and becomes entitled to the benefits.[45] Similarly, with respect to subsidized payments made during part-time employment as part of a phased retirement plan, since those payments would normally be conditioned on continued part-time employment, they would be subject to a substantial risk of forfeiture until actually paid.

Once a faculty member is fully retired, any remaining payments to which he or she is thereafter entitled will not normally be subject to a substantial risk of forfeiture, unless the faculty member is obligated to provide some continuing, substantial services in exchange for those payments—e.g., as a consultant.[46] Thus, the faculty member is subject to tax on the full present value of those payments at the time of retirement. For this reason, most colleges and universities have designed their faculty retirement incentive plans to provide benefit payments in a single lump sum. However, this is not compelled by the Code. An institution could make periodic payments over a fixed period, or over the faculty member's lifetime. As a practical matter, the first payment should be large enough to cover the taxes on the present value of all payments, or the institution should be prepared to make a loan to the faculty member to cover those taxes and to obtain repayment of that loan through monthly deductions from the subsequent periodic benefit payments. In either instance, the tax treatment of the actual benefit payments is quite complicated. A portion of each periodic payment is treated as a tax-free recovery of the present value already taxed, while the balance of the payment is subject to ordinary income tax. To avoid these tax (and associated reporting) complexities, institutions have normally opted for lump sum retirement incentive payments.

Legislation was proposed and almost enacted in 1992 exempting certain faculty retirement incentive plans from the adverse tax treatment of deferred compensation. Perhaps the higher education community will again seek such legislation.

In the case of a window plan, under which all employees over a minimum age may elect to retire within a specified period of months and receive additional benefits, those benefits would similarly be subject to a substantial risk of forfeiture in the normal case. The risk of forfeiture arises because the benefits would normally be conditioned on retirement on the date specified in the window election (and on continued employment until that date). If the payments were to be made over a period of time, or over the faculty member's lifetime, an argument can be made that they do not in this context constitute deferred compensation. In its regulations defining deferred compensation under a similarly drafted statute relating to FICA taxes, the Internal Revenue Service takes the position that benefits paid under window plans, or certain similar arrangements, should be treated as severance payments instead of deferred compensation.[47] Arguably, the same approach should be taken for income tax purposes, with the result that periodic payments under a window plan would not be taxed until received.

A U.S. district court in 1999 held that one-time early retirement incentive payments to tenured faculty members in exchange for their release of tenure rights are not "wages" for purposes of FICA taxes.[48] The court concluded that the early retirement payments to tenured faculty members were for the purchase of their tenure rights, which constitute property interests. According to the court, the payments used to purchase the property interests were not "wages" or "remuneration for services" and so were not subject to FICA taxes. Arguably, the court's rationale also extends to early retirement payments made over a period of time in exchange for tenure rights. The same rationale would support the argument that such payments are not "deferred compensation" for federal income tax purposes. However, the court's opinion is flatly contrary to the position taken by the Internal Revenue Service,[49] and it is not clear whether other courts will agree.

State Age Discrimination Laws

The ADEA does not preempt state age discrimination laws, to the extent they offer broader protection than the ADEA.[50] Thus, the safe harbor for certain age-based faculty retirement incentive plans has no effect on the applicability of state age discrimination laws. With respect to faculty retirement incentive plans (including top hat plans) that constitute employee benefit plans as defined in ERISA, ERISA should preempt any state age discrimination law to the extent such state law prohibits conduct which is lawful under the ADEA.[51] However, as discussed above, some faculty retirement incentive plans are not subject to ERISA and, therefore, do not benefit from the ERISA preemption of state law. Plans not covered by ERISA include, as discussed above, plans of state colleges and universities and community colleges, plans of certain religiously affiliated colleges and universities, phased retirement programs of all institutions, where such programs provide no ERISA-covered benefits, and window plans providing only lump sum cash payments. Accordingly, institutions considering such plans will need to take into account any state age discrimination laws that apply to the institutions.

Summary of Available Options

The variety of possible faculty retirement incentive benefits can be divided into three categories: window plans, ongoing retirement incentive plans that provide benefits on full retirement, and phased retirement plans that offer benefits during a phase-down of the work load for a specified period, followed by full retirement.

A faculty retirement incentive plan may, of course, include elements of two or even all three of these categories—for example, an enhanced benefit at the outset, during a window period, followed by the option to take phased retirement or full retirement with differing benefits. Of course, institutions may offer retirement incentives to faculty members on an individually negotiated basis, without any formalized plan at all. Such arrangements, however, are outside the scope of this chapter.

Window plans. As discussed above, a window plan offers faculty members a set period of months in which they can elect to retire with enhanced retirement benefits. For example, a window plan might give faculty the opportunity to elect between September 1 and December 31 of a given year to retire the following June 30 and receive a lump sum payment or periodic payments with or without postretirement health coverage or other enhancements. While the opportunity is typically limited to faculty members over a minimum retirement age, such as 60 or 62, window plans do not normally have a maximum age. An age cap is generally not necessary to provide the incentive to retire, since the end of the window (December 31 in the above example) provides that incentive.

From a legal standpoint, window plans raise the fewest concerns under the statutes discussed above. With no upper age limit and no reduction of benefits based on increased age, and assuming retirement is voluntary, such a plan does not discriminate on the basis of age and, therefore, does not need to fall within the new safe harbor, or any other specific exemption, in order to comply with the ADEA. For these same reasons, state age discrimination laws should not be of concern. For institutions subject to ERISA, the retirement incentive benefits are unlikely to constitute a separate ERISA plan, at least where benefits are paid in a single lump sum payment, because the plan is temporary and requires no ongoing administration. Finally, the adverse tax treatment of deferred compensation is arguably avoided on the grounds that the payments are in the nature of severance pay and not deferred compensation.

On the other hand, window plans are unattractive to many institutions, given the perceived unfairness of offering substantial benefits only to those few faculty members who are eligible—and prepared—to retire during a limited period of time. Window plans also have little effectiveness if offered more than once, or if other circumstances exist that may cause faculty members to believe they can simply wait for the next window to retire.

Other plans providing benefits on full retirement. Plans in this category are normally more ongoing in nature although subject, of course, to the institution's ability to modify or terminate them. These plans typically offer retirement incentive payments, as a single lump sum or periodic payments, with or without postretirement health coverage or other enhancements, on full retirement from the institution. In order to provide some incentive to faculty members to retire, and to limit the additional retirement benefits to earlier retirement when the faculty member most needs them, these ongoing plans have not only a minimum retirement age for eligibility but also a maximum age. They also typically include a reduction in benefit based on increasing age. Thus, institutions need to structure these plans to avoid age discrimination claims by older faculty. Unless institutions are prepared to take the risk of relying on the uncertain scope of the ADEA's VERIP exception, these plans should be designed to satisfy the conditions of the 1998 safe harbor. This means assuring that:

- The institution falls within the definition of "institution of higher education" in the Higher Education Act of 1965, as amended.
- The plan is limited to faculty members (or other employees) who are under a contract of unlimited tenure, or a similar arrangement providing for unlimited tenure.
- The benefits provided are "supplemental" to other benefits existing at the time the plan is implemented.
- With respect to tenured faculty members who do not choose to retire, the institution does not take away other, existing benefits, or reduce existing benefits, as a result of increased age.
- The plan does not make available, solely to those retiring under the plan, benefits that were generally available to tenured faculty members retiring within the preceding 365 days (except for benefits under another early retirement or exit incentive plan).
- When the plan is established, every faculty member who would be eligible for the maximum benefit except for attainment of too high an age is given a 180-day opportunity to elect retirement and receive that maximum benefit, and another 180 days to plan for retirement.
- Any faculty member who, at the time the plan was established, did not meet all eligibility criteria other than age (such as a required number of

years of service) and later satisfies those criteria will have a 180-day opportunity to receive the maximum benefit then available to a younger, but otherwise similarly situated, employee.

Ongoing retirement incentive plans of this nature should be structured with consideration of the employee's tax consequences. Unless they pay the cash incentive benefit (if any) in a single lump sum payment, the institution will probably want to frontload the payments sufficiently to cover the up-front tax liability on the present value of all periodic payments, or loan a similar amount to the employee to pay that tax liability, with repayment to be made through payroll deduction from the remaining payments.

Institutions subject to ERISA — that is, colleges and universities other than state institutions and certain religiously affiliated institutions — must limit this second category of plans to a select group of management or highly compensated employees within the meaning of ERISA's top hat exemption. This top hat exemption presently is unclear in scope, given the absence of guidance from the Department of Labor.

In the case of a state college or university, community college, or religiously affiliated college or university that is exempt from ERISA, the institution will need to consider any applicable state age discrimination laws. This is unlikely to be true of an institution subject to ERISA, assuming the retirement incentive plan constitutes an ERISA pension plan, because of ERISA's preemption of state law affecting such benefit plans. Nevertheless, this does not appear to have been tested yet in the courts in the context of early retirement incentive plans.

Phased retirement plans. This third category of plans provides enhanced salary or benefits, or both, prior to full retirement during a period of years (usually three years or less) during which a faculty member's workload gradually decreases. Typically, the faculty member gives up tenure at the beginning of the phase-down period, and agrees to retire fully at the end of the period, although these elements are not always required. The phase-down may be in stages, such as 75 percent, 50 percent, and 25 percent workloads over a three-year period, or it may involve a simple cutback to a 50 percent (or other percentage) workload throughout the phased retirement period. Phased retirement plans might have an upper age limit, or they might reduce the enhanced salary or benefits based on increased age, or both. However, some institutions offer the phased retirement option with the same enhanced salary or benefits to all tenured faculty over a minimum age, such as 55 or 60.

If the phased retirement plan has an upper age limit on eligibility, or reduces benefits based on age in some respect, an institution is generally well-advised to design the plan to fall within the safe harbor discussed above. This means, as a practical matter, that the following must be true:

- The institution falls within the definition of institution of higher education in the Higher Education Act of 1965, as amended.
- The plan is limited to faculty members (or other employees) who are under a contract of unlimited tenure, or a similar arrangement providing for unlimited tenure.
- The salary subsidy paid (and any other extra benefits provided by the plan) during the phase-down period are in addition to salary amounts (and benefits) generally available to part-time faculty with the same workload.
- The phased retirement plan does not involve any age-based reduction or cessation of benefits other than the salary subsidy (and any other extra benefits provided by the plan), except as otherwise permitted by the ADEA.
- The salary subsidy (and any other extra benefits provided by the plan) generally have not been available to part-time tenured faculty members, with similar workloads, during the preceding 365 days, except under another early retirement or exit-incentive plan.
- Any faculty member who is otherwise eligible at the time the plan is established, but is over the highest age at which the maximum phased retirement plan benefits are available, has at least a 180-day opportunity to elect phased retirement and receive the maximum benefits available to a similarly situated younger faculty member and another 180 days to plan for retirement.
- Any faculty member who, at the time the plan was established, did not meet all eligibility criteria other than age (such as a required number of years of service) and later satisfies those criteria, but is then older than the highest age at which the maximum benefits are generally available, has a 180-day opportunity to elect phased retirement and receive the maximum benefits.

If the benefits under a phased retirement plan are provided solely while the individual continues to work, and not after termination of employment, such a plan will not generally fall within the meaning of a pension plan under ERISA. Therefore, such a plan need not be limited to a select group of management or highly compensated employees in order to avoid ERISA's onerous requirements for pension plans.

On the other hand, the absence of ERISA pension plan status deprives the institution of the argument that state age discrimination laws are preempted by ERISA, unless the plan's age-based benefits are health coverage, disability benefits, death benefits, or other benefits that fall within the ERISA definition of a welfare benefit plan. The institution will, therefore, have to consider the effect of any such law that may apply.

The adverse tax rules for deferred compensation should not be of con-

cern in a phased retirement plan, so long as the enhanced salary or benefits are conditioned upon continued provision of services during the phase-
down period.

Conclusion

Many institutions of higher education—and their faculties—value ongoing
retirement incentive plans. The institutions benefit from more orderly faculty turnover and, in many cases, substantial cost savings. The individual faculty members have the opportunity to retire more comfortably at an earlier
age, if they are inclined to do so.

For an ongoing retirement incentive plan to accomplish these objectives,
it is important that the benefits decrease at higher ages and end at a specified age. Otherwise, there would be no incentive to retire, and older retirees
may reap a windfall given the growth in their retirement accounts, older retirees are less likely to need an extra benefit to produce a comfortable level
of retirement income.

Until enactment of the ADEA safe harbor in 1998, the legality of age-
based retirement incentive plans was uncertain. The safe harbor now affords
them protection. However, the safe harbor includes a number of conditions
that need to be satisfied. In addition, other federal and state laws need to
be taken into account. Thus, careful planning is required in designing and
implementing age-based retirement incentive plans for tenured faculty.

The author gratefully acknowledges the assistance of Ellen V. Benson, an
associate at Ropes & Gray in Boston, Massachusetts, and the helpful comments of Ann H. Franke, Director of Employment Liability Services, United
Educators Insurance Risk Retention Group, Inc., in Chevy Chase, Mary-
land.

Notes

1. Higher Education Amendments of 1998, Pub. L. No. 105-244, §941, 112 Stat.
1581, 1834–35, adding section 4(m) to the ADEA.
2. See Clark, Kreps, and Ghent (this volume) and the discussion of the research by
Ashenfelter and Card (1998) Clark and Hammond (this volume) for an assessment
of the change in retirement ages since the ending of mandatory retirement.
3. See Keefe (this volume) for discussions of retirement incentive programs and
intangible factors in retirement decisions.
4. See Ehrenberg et al. (this volume) for an examination of the implications of
delayed retirement on Cornell University.
5. *Solon v. Gary Community School Corp.*, 180 F. 3d 844 (7th Cir. 1999); *Equal Employment Opportunity Commission v. Crown Point Community School Corp.*, 1997 WL 54747
(N.D. Ind. 1997). Challenges have been rejected by *Auerbach v. Board of Education of
the Harborfields Central School District of Greenlawn, New York*, 136 F. 3d 104 (2nd Cir.

1998), although with dicta suggesting gradual age-based reductions would violate the ADEA, and by *Lyon v. Ohio Education Association*, 53 F. 3d 135 (6th Cir. 1995).

6. *Kimel v. Florida Board of Regents*, M U.S. M, 2000 WL 14165,* 16 (January 11, 2000).

7. Higher Education Amendments of 1998, §941(c)(2)–(3).

8. ADEA §4(*l*)(1)(A), 29 U.S.C. §623(*l*)(1)(A); see *Stone v. Travelers Corp.*, 58 F.3d 434, 437 (9th Cir. 1995) (holding that ADEA section 4(*l*)(1)(A) precludes the ADEA claim of a 52-year-old individual asserting that he was denied pension benefits in violation of the ADEA because he was under age 55).

9. ADEA §4(*l*)(1)(B), 29 U.S.C. §623(*l*)(1)(B).

10. ADEA §4(*f*)(2)(B)(ii), 29 U.S.C. §623(*f*)(2)(B)(ii).

11. ADEA §2(*b*), 29 U.S.C. §621(*b*).

12. 136 Cong. Rec. S13594-01, S13596 (September 24, 1990) (S. 1511 Final Substitute: Statement of Managers) (hereafter "OWBPA Statement of Managers").

13. Equal Employment Opportunity Commission, Request for Comments, Age Discrimination in Employment Act, 57 Fed. Reg. 10626, 10628 (March 27, 1992).

14. See, e.g., Brief for Plaintiff at 21–22, *Equal Employment Opportunity Commission v. Crown Point Community School Corp.*, No. 2893 CV237, 1997 WL 54747 (N.D. Ind. 1997); Brief for Appellants at 12–14, *Lyon v. Ohio Education Association*, 53 F.3d 135 (6th Cir. 1995).

15. *Equal Employment Opportunity Commission v. Crown Point Community School Corp.*

16. *Auerbach v. Board of Education.* In dicta, the court suggested that the VERIP exception would not apply if the benefits were gradually reduced as higher ages were attained. However, it is unclear why this distinction would be warranted.

17. Higher Education Amendments of 1998.

18. ADEA §4(*m*), 29 U.S.C. §623(*m*).

19. H.R. Rep. No. 105-750, pp. 403–7 (1998).

20. See C.F.R. §1625.11(*e*)(1) (1998) (amplifying the meaning of "unlimited tenure" to some extent).

21. See, e.g., OWBPA Statement of Managers, at S13596; *Auerbach v. Board of Education.*

22. Higher Education Amendments of 1998.

23. Ibid.

24. Ibid.

25. Employee Retirement Income Security Act of 1974 (ERISA) §§3(32) and 4(*b*) (1), 29 U.S.C. §§1002(32) and 1003(*b*)(1).

26. ERISA §§3(33) and 4(*b*)(2), 29 U.S.C. §§1002(33) and 1003(*b*)(2).

27. ERISA §514(*a*), 29 U.S.C. §1144(*a*) (providing that ERISA "shall supersede any and all State laws insofar as they may now or hereafter relate to any employee benefit plan described in section 4(*a*) and not exempt under section 4(*b*)").

28. ERISA §3(1), 29 U.S.C. §1002(1).

29. ERISA §3(2)(A), 29 U.S.C. §1002(2)(A).

30. ERISA §202(*a*)(1), 29 U.S.C. §1052(*a*)(1).

31. ERISA §203, 29 U.S.C. §1053.

32. ERISA §204(*b*), 29 U.S.C. §1054(*b*).

33. ERISA §205(*a*), 29 U.S.C. §1055(*a*).

34. ERISA §302, 29 U.S.C. §1082.

35. ERISA §§201(2) and 301(*a*)(3), 29 U.S.C. §§1051(2) and 1081(*a*)(3).

36. Department of Labor Advisory Opinion No. 90-14A.

37. *But see* Department of Labor Advisory Opinion No. 81-27A.

38. ERISA §514(*a*), 29 U.S.C. §1144(*a*).

39. *Fort Halifax Packing Co. v. Coyne*, 482 U.S. 1, 12 (1987).

40. See, e.g., *Shahid v. Ford Motor Co.*, 76 F.3d 1404, 1409 (6th Cir. 1996); *Delaye v. Agripac, Inc.*, 39 F.3d 235, 237 (9th Cir. 1994); *Champagne v. Revco D.S. Inc.*, 997 F.Supp. 220, 221–22 (D.R.I. 1998).

41. *Champagne v. Revco D.S. Inc.*, 997 F. Supp. at 222, quoting *Gilmore v. Silgan Plastics Corp.*, 917 f. Supp. 685, 688 (E.O. No. 1996).

42. Internal Revenue Code of 1986, as amended, §457(*f*).

43. A religiously affiliated institution is exempt from Section 457(*f*) if it is church or a "qualified church-controlled organization" within the meaning of Section 3121 (*w*)(3)(B) of the Code. I.R.C. §457(*e*)(13). However, a religiously affiliated college or university falls within that exemption only if it is not open to the general public or no more than 25 percent of its revenues normally consist of tuition or other payments from the public or of government-source funds. I.R.C. §3121(*w*)(3)(B).

44. See Treas. Reg. §31.3121(*v*)(2)-1(*b*)(3)(i), (defining "deferral of compensation" for purposes of a special timing rule for FICA tax payments in Section 3121(*v*)(2) of the Code, which is worded very similarly to Section 457(*f*)).

45. See Treas. Reg. §1.83–3(*c*).

46. Ibid.

47. Treas. Reg. §31.3121(*v*)(2)-1(*b*)(4)(*v*).

48. *North Dakota State Univ. v. United States*, No. A3-98-50, Slip. op. at 18–20 (D.N.D. Nov. 22, 1999).

49. See IRS Technical Advice Memorandum 9711001.

50. 29 CFR §1625.10(*g*); *Moody v. Pepsi-Cola Metropolitan Bottling Co.*, 915 F.2d 201, 209–10 (6th Cir. 1990), *Bailey v. Container Corp. of America*, 594 F. Supp. 629, 632–33 (S.D. Ohio 1984).

51. See *Shaw v. Delta Airlines, Inc.*, 463 U.S. 85, 103–4 (1983); *Devlin v. Transportation Communications International Union*, 173 F. 3d 9y (2nd Cir. 1999).

References

Ashenfelter, Orley and David Card. 1998. "Faculty Retirement Behavior in the Post-Mandatory Retirement Era: New Evidence from the Princeton Retirement Survey." Paper presented at TIAA-CREF and NC State University conference, "Examining Life After the End of Mandatory Retirement," Washington, D.C., May.

National Research Council, Committee on Ending Mandatory Retirement in Higher Education. 1991. *Ending Mandatory Retirement for Tenured Faculty: The Consequences for Higher Education*, ed. P. Brett Hammond and Harriet P. Morgan. Washington, D.C.: National Academy Press, 1991.

National Commission on the Cost of Higher Education. 1998. *Straight Talk About College Costs and Prices.* Washington, D.C.: III(I)(1)(6).

Chapter 4
Survey of Early Retirement Practices in Higher Education

John Keefe

This chapter presents the findings from a survey on early retirement at colleges and universities in the United States. TIAA-CREF commissioned the survey to assist university administrators and faculty in dealing with the human resources challenges of an aging faculty base. After changes in employment law in 1993 eliminated mandatory retirement, incentives for early retirement have become the only means to encourage faculty to relinquish tenure, and to allow administrators to reallocate the positions and salary dollars of senior faculty.

To observe the types of early retirement measures in place and their effectiveness in meeting the institutions' human resource goals, we contacted 167 large and small colleges and universities, both public and private. We received 66 responses on 77 different plans. Drawing on the responses, we discuss the prevalence of early retirement plans and the structure of the plans we encountered. We also present critiques from the institutions using the several different types of plans, and statistics on plans' "success rates" (acceptances versus offers).

To preview our findings, about 80 percent of both public and private institutions in our sample offered early retirement plans of some type. By comparison, the National Center for Education Statistics surveyed higher education institutions on the topic of faculty retirement arrangements in 1992–93, and concluded that 60 percent of all higher education institutions offered early retirement incentives at that time (U.S. Department of Education 1997b). We also found that the 1994 legislative end to mandatory retirement for professors at 70 had little effect on most institutions' early retirement policies: many of the programs observed had started after the legislative change and encouraged retirement as early as age 55.

Types, Features, and Motivations for Retirement Incentive Plans

An early retirement plan for higher education faculty is the product of staffing challenges typical to educational institutions—a short planning horizon, departments out of balance with enrollment needs, or underperforming faculty—combined with an individual school's context of financial and human resources, state and federal employment regulations and pension plan rules.

Although early retirement arrangements in academe are rarely identical, most have common structures with respect to compensation and other variables. In the course of our survey of seventy-seven early retirement plans at 66 schools and systems, we encountered two primary types of early retirement plans:

- *incentive payment plans*, in which faculty receive severance payments as an incentive to retire
- *phased retirement plans*, in which senior faculty teach reduced course loads and are paid adjusted salaries.

Several plans formally combined incentive payments with phased retirement, and a few plans offered little or no incentives, simply allowing faculty to take retirement earlier than the conventional age.

Although the primary difference among plans is the structure of compensation they provide to faculty, plans also vary according to the length of time they are offered to faculty, and the flexibility they give to school administrators. To illustrate this range of options, we next describe typical, as well as some unusual, applications of each structure.

Basic Plan Types

Retirement incentive plans. Under an incentive payment plan, an institution makes a special payment to a faculty member, in return for which the faculty member relinquishes tenure, leaves the employment of the school, and starts to draw benefits from a retirement account.

The size of incentive payments varies widely among types of schools. For private institutions, the lowest payment observed in our survey was 40 percent of final salary; the highest was 200 percent. Most private institutions with a payment plan in our sample offered between 100 percent and 200 percent of final salary. The payments offered by public schools and systems were generally smaller, ranging from 12 percent of final salary to 100 percent. At many public institutions, early retirement benefits were tied to the length of the employee's service in his state or system pension plan.

Payments for early retirement are meant as a substitute for, or a supplement to, retirement income in the years between the date of early retirement and normal retirement age. A 1994 study by Bruce Palmer indicates that pensions in the United States provide average income replacement from 70 to 80 percent for employees in defined contribution plans (Palmer 1994). Thus an incentive payment of 100 percent of final salary allows a retiring employee a cushion of about 1.5 years of average retirement income, allowing the employee to delay drawing on their retirement assets.

Although most institutions paid incentives in one lump sum or a series of payments over two years, we did encounter some variation of payment methods. One private university paid a lump sum of 30 percent of salary to the employee at retirement and then made five annual contributions, totaling 70 percent of salary, to an annuity for the retiree's benefit. Another private university paid $9,500 to the employee at departure, followed by a series of monthly checks up to the amount of the employee's social security earnings limitation.

We observed two institutions—one public and one private—that built time-based expiration incentives into their plans. In one case, the lump sum payment started at 100 percent of salary at age 55, and dropped 10 percent per year as the employee delayed retirement. In the other, the institution paid 200 percent of salary to retirees ages 60 to 65, and sharply reduced the payments in subsequent years. In the latter case, employees retiring at age 69 received 60 percent of final salary; employees retiring at 70 or older received no payment.

Phased retirement plans. Our definition of phased retirement plans includes part-time teaching arrangements that are formally structured and uniformly applied, as well as less formal part-time or consulting plans that are negotiated case by case. In our sample of 66 schools, we noted formal phased plans at nine institutions and informal plans at 16 others.

Clouding the distinction between formal and informal phased plans further are those institutions which offer a formal payment type plan, but separately offer part-time posts to faculty after they retire. In our sample, we found 17 schools with this arrangement. Only 11 institutions in the sample, or about 17 percent, said they did not offer any part-time employment to retired faculty.

The types of part-time employment offered to retired faculty varied from institution to institution. One institution limited the term of reduced teaching assignments to one year, but most arrangements provided for three to five years of part-time teaching. Some allowed an instructor to teach all of his or her courses in one semester, thus granting a synthetic full retirement during the rest of the year. Several public institutions noted that regulations governing state employment and retirement benefits imposed limits on the amount retirees could work.

Of the 25 institutions with phased plans, seven responded that retirees teaching part-time received salaries in direct proportion to their reduced course load. There were five institutions paying more than a pro rata share, ranging from continuation of full-time salary, to 70 percent of salary for teaching a 50 percent course load, to a pro rata salary plus 10 percent.

Combination plans. We found three institutions—all fairly small, privately controlled, and located in the Northeast—that offered early retirement plans that integrated incentive payment and phased retirement arrangements. Only one of these three formally articulated the package. At that institution, employees received a lump sum of 25 percent of final salary at retirement, and agreed to teach, for up to five years, a course load ranging from 33 percent to 50 percent of full time for which they received 50 percent to 65 percent of full-time pay. Arrangements at the other two schools followed a similar pattern, but individual compensation packages were negotiated with retirees.

Other plan types. For two small liberal arts colleges on the east coast, early retirement appears to mean simply that—the opportunity to leave employment early (beginning at ages 55 and 58) and start to draw on a pension account and receive retiree health benefits. At one of these institutions, retired faculty are offered part-time teaching posts on a case-by-case basis. At the other there are no part-time teaching or consulting relationships between the school and the retired faculty.

Plan Features

Ongoing plans versus window offers. A second key element in the early retirement plans we observed is whether the plan has an indefinite life, and thus is an ongoing plan that potentially applies to all future employees, or is a "window plan," and thus offered only to a group of employees who meet age and service requirements on a specified date or during a specified time interval.

The distinction between ongoing plans and window offers is significant to the legal and tax status of a given plan, and thus beyond the scope of our research. However, employees' expectations can be very different under the two types of plan, which we consider in Chapter 8 of this volume.

Sixty of the 77 plans observed in our survey were ongoing and had no explicit closing date. In most of those cases, an employee who met the age or service requirements of the plan could elect early retirement at any time, often up to age 65. Seventeen of the plans in our survey, or 22 percent of the total, were window offers with an explicit end and no guarantee of an opportunity in the future. Nearly all window offer plans included incentive payments, and the majority were offered at public schools or systems.

Eligibility. Responses to our survey indicated that the focus of the plans at most institutions truly is encouraging faculty to retire early—that is, before the conventional retirement age of 65—rather than displacing faculty who have stayed until 68 or 70. Twenty-seven of the 77 plans observed offered early retirement before age 60, and most of these were effective at age 55.

The requirement for years of service varied widely, although most institutions allowed participation in early retirement after 10 or 15 years of employment.

Formal versus informal plans. We also inquired in our survey whether the plan was formal—that is, a written, publicized policy offering similar terms to all employees meeting age or service requirements—or informal, individually negotiated and offered to selected employees. Twenty-one of the 77 responses indicated that plans were informal (by their nature, window plans are formal plans, while ongoing plans can be either formal or informal).

Motivations for Early Retirement of Faculty

To close our discussion of plan characteristics, our survey asked several questions about institutional objectives in adopting particular plans and whether those objectives had been met. Most institutions declined to answer, but we managed to gather 16 observations. Five institutions said they adopted early retirement in order to reduce costs; another five noted that the plan was adopted as a tool for managing faculty performance; and five more claimed their goal was greater flexibility in faculty hiring and department balancing.

The objective stated by the sixteenth responding institution, a well-known private research university in the northeast, was "to continue rates of retirement after the end of mandatory retirement." *This institution was the only one to cite the end of mandatory retirement as a motivation for adopting early retirement incentives.* Moreover, only three institutions indicated that the end of mandatory retirement at age 70 in 1993 was a significant factor in developing their early retirement policies. Very few institutions mentioned mandatory retirement at all in their responses. Consider, however, the response of an administrator at a small institution in the Northeast, who claimed to speak for all of higher education: "They are doing this to get rid of bad teachers, and if anyone tells you any different, they are lying."

Institutions' Application of Plan Types

Survey Design and Coverage

The population of interest for this project included public four-year institutions or university systems in all fifty states, as well as large and small private four-year schools.

We contacted benefits administrators and other executives at 167 separate institutions or systems and sent a four-page questionnaire to those who

Table 1. Institutions Contacted for Early Retirement Study

	Private	Public	Total	Percent
Northeast	27	14	41	24.6
Southeast	24	15	39	23.3
Midwest	21	19	40	24.0
Southwest and west	20	10	30	18.0
	5	12	17	10.2
Total	*97*	*70*	*167*	*100.0*
Percent	*58.1*	*41.9*	*100.0*	

Source: Author's calculations.

Table 2. Institutions Responding to Survey

	Private	Public	Total	Percent
Northeast	15	8	23	29.9
Southeast	5	8	13	16.9
Midwest	9	12	21	27.3
Southwest and west	3	9	12	15.6
	4	4	8	10.4
Total	*36*	*41*	*77*	*100.0*
Percent	*46.8*	*53.2*	*100.0*	

Source: Author's calculations.

agreed to participate. The questionnaire asked for details on the participating institutions' current early retirement plans, as well as any past plans. In view of the sensitive nature of early retirement measures, we promised at the outset to avoid naming individual institutions in papers or presentations. Most replies came back via mail or fax. As a quality control measure, we conducted many interviews by phone and contacted participants to offer assistance with answering the questions. We received replies to the survey from 66 institutions. We were able to observe 77 different plans, including ten instances where institutions had multiple plans in operation or prior plans that had ceased. Thirty-six of the responses (46.8 percent) pertained to plans at private institutions, and 41 (53.2 percent) to public schools or systems.

Table 1 details, the number of institutions contacted to participate in the survey by region and institution control. Table 2 indicates the sources of responses received. The western region, which includes the Pacific Coast states as well as Alaska and Hawaii, may seem underrepresented both as to contacts and responses. However, this shortfall is compensated for by the extensive data and analysis on the region provided by Ellen Switkes (this volume) who examines early retirement in the University of California system (see also Pencavel 1997).

A second apparent discrepancy in our survey data is the apparent overrepresentation of private institutions. Our survey reports on private and public institutions in nearly equal numbers, while for the United States as a whole, about 70 percent of higher education faculty works at public institutions, and about 30 percent is at private schools (U.S. Department of Education 1997a). However, many of the survey responses for public institutions cover statewide systems or universities with multiple campuses, and thus represent a larger faculty base than the responses of private schools. In any case, a disproportionate number of responses in one category or the other does not change the aim of this project, which is to identify and interpret different policies and practices of early retirement rather than make a precise statistical estimate. As a final comment on how our sample relates to the population of higher education faculty, we note that the responses to our survey include, directly or indirectly, 23 of the 50 largest institutions in the U.S. (*1998 Higher Education Directory*).

Although we were satisfied with the picture that emerged from the surveys we received, it is important to consider the significance of those institutions who did not respond. A small number of institutions—five or so—declined because they do not participate in surveys as a matter of policy. A dozen others also declined, saying they could not afford the time. In the remaining cases, our calls went unreturned. What other systematic reasons might have kept the remainder from responding? One reason might be that their institutions had no plan. We indicated in the questionnaire that the absence of a plan was one response we were looking for; indeed, about 19 percent of responses indicated no plan. Nevertheless, it is logical to assume that some administrators at schools without early retirement chose to disregard the survey. Another possible explanation is the desire for privacy. Early retirement measures can be controversial, and, unlike public institutions where plans are public information, private institutions may have chosen to remain silent. Only 37 percent of the private schools we contacted submitted a survey response, versus 59 percent for public institutions.

Patterns in Retirement Incentive Plans

Patterns in early retirement plans were evaluated according to the key variables of institutional control, Carnegie classification, geography, and size. Due to several limitations on the information we gathered—a small sample size, many missing observations, and data that is qualitative rather than quantitative—the statistical analysis is fairly simple. For example, we compare the proportions of the types of plans offered at private institutions to the sample as a whole, and then perform the same comparison for public schools.

Public versus Private. Are the plans offered by private institutions different from those offered by public schools? Table 3 below suggests that public and private institutions' early retirement plans differ in just one respect:

Table 3. Plan Types for Public and Private Institutions Responding

Type	Private	Percent	Public	Percent	Total	Percent
Payment	12	33.3	18	43.9	30	38.9
Phased	12	33.3	13	31.7	25	32.5
Payment and phased	3	8.3	1	2.4	4	5.2
Other	2	5.6	1	2.4	3	3.9
None	7	19.4	8	19.5	15	19.5
Total	*36*	*100.0*	*41*	*100.0*	*77*	*100.0*

Source: Author's calculations.

Table 4A. Early Retirement Programs at Surveyed Institutions, Numbers of
Programs According to Carnegie Classification

Carnegie classification	Payment	Phased	Payment phased	Other	None	Total
Baccalaureate 1	4	3	1	2	2	12
Baccalaureate 2	1	1	—	—	1	3
Doctoral 1	—	1	—	—	1	2
Doctoral 2	3	2	—	—	3	8
Fine arts	—	1	—	—	1
Master's 1	5	4	2	—	1	12
Master's 2	—	1	—	—	—	1
Research 1	7	6	—	—	4	17
Research 2	2	2	—	—	1	5
System	8	5	—	1	2	16
Grand total	*30*	*25*	*4*	*3*	*15*	*77*
Percent of total	*38.9*	*32.5*	*5.2*	*3.9*	*19.5*	*100.0*

Source: Author's calculations.

public institutions have a somewhat greater proportion of plans involving payments to the retiree than private schools (44 percent versus 33 percent). Public and private institutions in our sample show the same proportion for "no plan"–about 19 percent.

Carnegie classification. Do early retirement programs differ according to the nature of the school offering them? Table 4 switches the axis orientation of Table 3 and shows the details of plan types according to the institutions' Carnegie classifications (developed by the Carnegie Foundation for the Advancement of Teaching). At this level of detail, the small size of our sample limits inferences on the proportions of plan types within a particular class of school. That said, the distribution of program types within Carnegie classifications is very close to the overall proportions in the sample. Fewer payment plans were offered by Baccalaureate I and Doctoral II schools than by the responding institutions overall, while public systems offered payment plans

Table 4b. Percentages of Program Types for Carnegie Classifications

Carnegie classification	Number of plans	Payment	Phased	Payment and phased	Other	None	Total
Baccalaureate 1	12	33.3	25.0	8.3	16.7	16.7	100.0
Baccalaureate 2	3	33.3	33.3	—	—	33.3	100.0
Doctoral 1	2	—	50.0	—	—	50.0	100.0
Doctoral 2	8	37.5	25.0	—	—	37.5	100.0
Fine arts	1	—	—	100.0	—	—	100.0
Master's 1	12	41.7	33.3	16.7	—	8.3	100.0
Master's 2	1	—	100.0	—	—	—	100.0
Research 1	17	41.2	35.3	—	—	23.5	100.0
Research 2	5	40.0	40.0	—	—	20.0	100.0
System	16	50.0	31.3	—	6.3	12.5	100.0
Total	77	Nm	Nm	Nm	Nm	Nm	Nm

Source: Author's calculations.
Percentages refer to the number of plans for a given school classification, not plan type; thus columns total across to 100 percent. Percentages within columns are not comparable, and do not add to 100 percent. Nm = not meaningful

Table 5. Early Retirement Plans by Geographic Region

Region	Payment	Phased	Payment and phased	Other	None	Grand total
Northeast	7	5	3	1	1	17
Southeast	5	8	—	1	5	19
Midwest	11	7	—	1	2	21
Southwest and mountain	3	3	—	—	6	12
West	4	2	1	—	1	8
Total	30	25	4	3	15	77

Source: Author's calculations.

slightly more frequently. The proportions of Doctoral II and state systems' plan offering payments did not deviate much from the sample overall.

Geography. Does the school's region make a difference to its early retirement offering? Table 5 shows the survey data grouped for geographical analysis. Only the west had a distribution of plans that was in line with the proportions of the overall survey. In the northeast region there was a concentration of combined payment and phased early retirement plans, and fewer than the proportional number of institutions offering no plan at all. In the southeast, more institutions offered payments and fewer offered phased plans. In the midwest, sample proportions led us to expect 11 payment type plans, but only 8 were observed. We also expected to find 4 institutions without plans but saw only 2. The southwest region had a higher than expected proportion of plans offering payments, as well as a surplus of institutions with no plan.

School size. Is there a relationship between the size of responding schools and early retirement offerings? Two different measures of correlation to school size and plan types indicated no strong measure of association with early retirement arrangements.

Indirect observations: effective control and plan funding. Although we did not measure these factors in our survey, we were able to discern two other important influences in early retirement plans through the responses we received. The first was the degree of control the institution exercised over the design of the plan. Public institutions generally are exempt from the requirements of ERISA legislation, meaning that these schools can avoid contention with rules that prohibit discrimination in favor of high earners. On the other hand, as public institutions are funded with public monies, they are subject to greater taxpayer scrutiny than private institutions, and thus likely would feel constraints in the amounts of incentives they can grant. In fact, we found that early retirement offers were disallowed or limited in a number states, due to specific employment laws at the state level.

A second observation was that plans take different shapes according to the source of their funds. We observed several plans that were part of a larger state employment initiative, and thus did not require the university to build early retirement into operating budgets. In other cases, state authorities granted permission to allow early retirement, but left it to the public institution to allocate the funds. For the most part, private institutions must fund their early retirement plans entirely on their own, so that the generosity of any plan is a function of the institution's wealth (we did encounter one private university, however, which had received a foundation grant to encourage early retirement of faculty).

Last, we noted that the type of basic pension plan can have a bearing on plan design. The University of California system was able to afford several waves of early retirement in the early 1990s, thanks to its overfunded defined benefit pension plan. In a few other cases, an institution compensated early retiring employees through additions to the defined benefit pension accounts, or allowed them to purchase additional service credits in state plans. None of the institutions in our survey with defined contribution basic pension plans had devised ways to reallocate funds within their plans.

Schools without early retirement. How do schools that offer no early retirement programs differ from those that do? About 19 percent of our sample reported no early retirement plan. Doctoral II and Research I institutions averaged fewer plans than expected by the sample proportions, while Master's I schools and state systems offered more. As noted, the southwest had a higher proportion of schools without early retirement, the southeast was in line with the total, and the other regions were below the average.

When compared to research from the National Center for Education

Table 6. Institutions Without Early Retirement: Comparison of Studies

Carnegie class and control	Percentage of institutions with no early retirement plan	
	NCES, 1993	This survey, 1998
Private liberal arts	67.2	20.0
Private comprehensive	44.8	12.5
Public comprehensive	45.6	0.0
Private coctoral	55.2	20.0
Public coctoral	34.2	60.0
Private research	29.6	28.6
Public research	23.0	20.0
Public systems	not measured	12.5
Overall	40.3	19.5

Source: Author's calculations.

Statistics (U.S. Department of Education 1977b) the "19 percent without" proportion from our stury suggests that the use of early retirement plans has increased significantly during the 1980s. Table 6 reorganizes our findings to match a summary presentation of the NCES estimates. The NCES study estimated that for U.S. higher education as a whole, about 40 percent of institutions offered no early retirement plans. The proportion of four-year institutions having no plans in 1993 varied widely across Carnegie classifications, ranging from 67 percent for private liberal arts colleges to 23 percent for public research institutions.

Our findings suggest that early retirement plans are now present at a much larger proportion of schools. With the exception of the Public Doctoral group, early retirement plans were present at over 70 percent of institutions observed (we point out that our sample was much smaller than that of the NCES). Our results also offered their own explanation for the increase: twenty-four out of seventy-seven responses, or close to one third of our observations, indicated that institutions had adopted early retirement after 1993, when the NCES sample was drawn.

Success of Early Retirement Programs

Few of the institutions responding to our survey included evaluations on how well their early retirement plans have met their goals, or were able to provide statistics on the acceptance of early retirement offers. Hence we were unable to draw general conclusions about which plan designs are most effective. We can nonetheless glean some insights from the responses of a few individual programs.

One important factor in the retirement decision may be that the generations facing retirement today and in the future are simply not prepared for any retirement, much less an early one. A large state system that offered a cash incentive program to both faculty and staff commented that the administration had been unpleasantly surprised by the older employees' lack of financial preparedness for retirement.

Incentive payment plans. All of the institutions that commented on incentive payment plans had negative remarks. Both small and large private institutions remarked that their payment plans turned out to be more expensive than they had anticipated. A mid-sized public university wrote that faculty accepted the plan in greater numbers than expected. A very large state system responded that administrators had a "mixed picture" of the cost savings from their plan, which involved options for both incentive payments and phased retirement. One public system stated that its incentive payment plan had been effective when initiated in the 1980s. Over time, however, it had grown too expensive and evolved into a "golden handcuff" that faculty had come to expect as a part of their retirement.

Phased plans. We received few comments from institutions on their phased retirement plans. The comments we did receive also cited phased plans as being too expensive, and noted that they resulted in the loss of many good instructors.

Payment and phased plans together. In two cases—a small liberal arts college and a large three-campus state system—we obtained offer and acceptance statistics for institutions that offer prospective early retirees a choice of payment incentives or phased retirement. These cases are especially valuable as they show how groups of people working in a common management and compensation environment interpret and choose from options that place different values on retiring versus continuing to work.

The smaller institution (student enrollment of 2,000) typically offers either incentive payments of about one year's salary, or a 50 percent teaching load lasting three years for which the early retiree is paid 70 percent of final salary. Major benefits are continued under both arrangements (early retirement is not offered to all employees, and every offer is negotiated separately). Over the two-year life of the plan, 21 employees in total had been offered early retirement; seven had selected phased retirement, and three had taken the lump sum package. Administrators indicated that since creating the phased plan in 1996, they favored phased retirements to avoid speculation among employees on amounts granted in buyouts.

The second case pertains to the university system of a state in the Great Plains; one of its campuses is among the 50 largest universities in the United States. This system has offered a phased retirement plan since 1982 and an early retirement incentive since 1986. Employees, both faculty and staff, aged 57 or older are eligible. This early retirement incentive does not make a payment in lieu of salary. Instead, it pays for medical insurance coverage until the employee is eligible for Medicare, provides a small paid-up life insurance policy, and makes contributions to the employee's pension account for several years. The phased plan offers a five-year transition to retirement with pay in direct proportion to the years of service. In the past three fiscal years an average of 31 people per year have chosen phased retirement, while an average of 129 people per year have opted for the early retirement incentive.

The logic behind the choices made by the retirees at the two institutions seems to conflict: although the payment offer was more lucrative at the small school than the large one, a majority of the small school's employees chose phased retirement. The opposite applied at the state system, where more faculty chose what appears to be a less lucrative payment over the option of phased retirement.

The two offers are hardly equal and opposite; both of the options at the small school are quite generous, while the payment offer at the large school yielded no cash upon retirement. Moreover, many factors could be responsible for leading the employees to these decisions: the environment of a small school versus a large one, health considerations, differing options for spending their retirement years, or "guidance" by the administration. Even so, we present these contrasting examples to show that monetary considerations are only one factor driving the early retirement choice (Chapter 8 in this volume evaluates the importance of the nonmonetary factors in a retirement decision).

Offer and acceptance statistics. Only 11 schools reported fully on how many people had become eligible and then accepted offers of early retirement. Table 7 below summarizes these plans and their acceptance rates. The number of observations is small, but the information contained is very useful, as it illustrates the wide range of acceptance for plans of different designs. Acceptance rates ranged from zero to 100 percent; most rates came in between 12 and 33 percent. In general our contacts knew how many faculty had accepted early retirement, but few had kept track of the numbers of faculty who became eligible. This lack of information is not surprising, but it is unfortunate. Institutions invest considerable time and energy in designing early retirement plans and then spend large sums to carry them out. Establishing targets for costs and success rates of early retirement arrangements, and the analyzing actual results—including measuring retirees' expectations of and satisfaction with retirement—will give administrators insights into how highly professors value their work and service, thus providing important feedback for fine-tuning early retirement plans and development of other retirement measures.

Case histories. Because the number of observations is small and their range wide, we believe that calculating an average acceptance rate would not generate a meaningful measure. Instead we have provided some of the context of the cases in Table 7.

In one unusual but instructive case, a small liberal arts institution in the

Table 7. Summary of Experience, Early Retirement Plan Offers Accepted

Carnegie classification	Enroll-ment	Plan type	Eligible	Accepted	Rate (%)	Comment
Research 2	22,000	Payment/window	1,000	220	22	—
Master's 1	5,000	Phased/ongoing	42	36	86	—
Baccalaureate 1	2,000	Payment/window	21	7	33	—
—	—	Phased/window	—	3	14	—
Baccalaureate 1	2,000	Payment/ongoing	2	2	100	Designed case by case
Master's 1	7,000	Payment/window	50	12	24	Final year of plan
Master's 1	2,000	Payment and phased/ongoing	15	5	33	Plan ended
Baccalaureate 1	2,000	Payment and phased/ongoing	37	0	—	Plan "not rich enough"
Doctoral 2	7,000	Phased/ongoing	5	5	100	Plan used to retain faculty
State system	—	Payment/window	3,500	472	13	—
Research 1	27,000	Phased/ongoing	250	30	12	—

Source: Author's calculations.

northeast devised a phased retirement plan offering 50 percent of salary and full benefits in compensation for a reduced course load for a term of two years. To the surprise of the administration, none of the 37 eligible faculty accepted the offer. In the 1980s the school had offered an unusually generous phased plan, and the new generation of prospective retirees thought the revised plan was "not rich enough" in comparison (our contact also volunteered the opinion that if the school were to offer a plan consisting only of payment to cover health insurance coverage, many faculty would likely opt for early retirement).

At the other extreme, a well-known liberal arts college offered a payment incentive of 40 percent of a faculty member's last annual salary, paid monthly, starting at age 60, for up to five years. Thus, a retiring faculty member could receive up to two years' salary, plus commensurate contributions to his or her retirement account, in exchange for retiring and relinquishing tenure. The early retirement incentive is reduced, however, if the faculty member waits to retire, and the offer expires at the end of five years. The plan was adopted in October 1997; since then seven faculty members became eligible for the incentive, and all elected to receive it.

Another small liberal arts college said that it offered early retirement payment incentives to just one or two faculty members per year, usually as a means to retire faculty who were no longer meeting the school's teaching standards. All these offers were accepted as well, but incentives were formulated case by case, so that the school's management was able to meet the needs of each prospective retiree.

The University of California (UC) system undertook three waves of payment incentives for early retirement between 1991 and 1994. The UC system had a greatly overfunded defined benefit pension plan, and chose to use the excess to fund early retirements. The offers and resulting retirement were studied in detail by Ellen Switkes (this volume; see also Pencavel 1997). In the first offer, which was publicized as a one-time event and not to be repeated, 31 percent of eligible faculty accepted early retirement. The second offer was more generous than the first and extended the boundaries of eligibility, but only 18 percent of offers were accepted. In the final offer, which was more liberal and generous still, 33 percent of eligible employees took early retirement.

A look at the University of California case is especially useful in view of the different states of employee expectations in each round. The first offer was unprecedented, and billed as a one-time event. The second offer was also publicized as a last chance, but employees apparently felt they could hold out for another round. In the third instance, word passed among the faculty that there truly would be no future offer, likely contributing to the highest acceptance of all.

Comparison to NCES study results. As with the availability of early retirement plans, the acceptance rates revealed by our survey may be compared to a 1992 survey conducted by the National Center for Education Statistics (U.S. Department of Education 1997b). In that study, 11,000 faculty were surveyed on their views of retirement, and the sample results were extrapolated to the entire higher education faculty of 528,000 (note that the NCES survey asked about intentions and preferences, but did not measure actual retirements).

Of the faculty sampled, 26 percent were aged 55 or older. About one third of the respondents aged 55 to 64 said they would accept the offer of an early retirement incentive, and about another third were undecided. As only one third answered a definite "no" to the prospect, about two thirds of the retirement-minded population were at least candidates for early retirement. The sample also contained about 24,000 faculty over the age of 65; of this group, over 50 percent said they would decline an offer of early retirement. The NCES survey also asked faculty about their job satisfaction levels. Only 20 percent of those who were willing to take early retirement indicated that they were generally dissatisfied with their jobs. In sum, early retirement is a complex decision that takes into consideration the relative values—both monetary and nonmonetary—of working life and retired life, and the risks of moving from one to the other.

References

Palmer, Bruce A. 1994. "Planning for Retirement Using Income Replacement Ratios." *Research Dialogues* 37. New York: TIAA-CREF, July.

Pencavel, John. 1997. "The Response of Employees to Severance Pay Incentives: Faculty of the University of California." Working paper, Stanford University, July.

Switkes, Ellen. This volume. "The University of California Voluntary Early Retirement Incentive Programs."

U.S. Department of Education, National Center for Education Statistics. 1997a. *Digest of Education Statistics 1997*. NCES 98–015. Washington, D.C.: NCES.

———. 1997b. *Retirement Plans and Other Departure Plans of Instructional Faculty and Staff in Higher Education Institutions*. NCES 98–254. Washington, D.C.: NCES.

1998 Higher Education Directory. Falls Church Va.: Higher Education Publishers.

Chapter 5
Cornell Confronts the End of Mandatory Retirement

Ronald G. Ehrenberg, Michael W. Matier, and David Fontanella

As a major research university, Cornell University was cognizant of predictions that the ending of mandatory retirement in 1994 might affect its faculty since this type of university has faculty members often so tied to their work that they cannot conceive of leaving their positions unless compelled to do so (National Research Council 1991; Rees and Smith 1991). Consequently, Cornell's faculty and administrators worried about what the change in the law would might for the institution.

Cornell is unique among major American research institutions, in that it is a hybrid of private and publicly assisted colleges. Six of the colleges located on its Ithaca, New York, campus (the Colleges of Art and Sciences, Engineering, Law, Management, Hotel, and Art, Architecture, and Planning) are private colleges that charge tuitions comparable to those of other selective private institutions. Faculty in these six colleges, referred to as the endowed colleges, participate in a defined contribution retirement program. The other four colleges on the Ithaca campus (Agriculture and Life Sciences, Human Ecology, Veterinary Medicine, and Industrial and Labor Relations) are operated by Cornell under contract with the State of New York and, in exchange for state assistance, charge tuitions considerably lower than those charged in the endowed colleges. These statutory colleges are integral parts of Cornell, but many of their benefit programs are part of the benefit programs provided to the State University of New York (SUNY) campuses by the State of New York. As such, faculty members in the statutory colleges have a choice of participating in a state-defined benefit retirement program or an optional defined contribution program. Over time, most new faculty have elected to participate in the defined contribution program and there are currently less than twenty faculty in the statutory colleges who belong to the defined benefit system.[1]

Table 1. New Tenure-Track Appointments, Total University, 1982–83
Through 1997–98

Year	Full professor	Associate professor	Assistant professor	Instructor	Total
1982–83	15	15	50	2	82
1983–84	5	3	54	0	62
1984–85	11	9	51	0	71
1985–86	7	13	53	0	73
1986–87	15	9	75	0	99
1987–88	20	8	79	1	108
1988–89	10	23	69	0	102
1989–90	6	15	43	0	64
1990–91	11	12	48	2	73
1991–92	12	8	33	0	53
1992–93	10	11	38	2	61
1993–94	4	6	29	1	40
1994–95	9	7	44	0	60
1995–96	6	6	36	0	48
1996–97	8	9	33	1	51
1997–98 *	10	8	46	1	65

Source: Authors' calculations from Cornell University Academic Personnel Database.
Faculty (including acting) and instructors are eligible for tenure-track appointment. Health
Services, ROTC, and Medical College excluded from this table.
*As of March 24, 1998.

In July 1995, the first author of this paper was appointed vice president of academic programs, planning and budgeting at Cornell and, at his initiative, a joint faculty-administrative committee was subsequently established, with him as chair, to look into how the university should respond to the elimination of mandatory retirement. In this chapter, we discuss the environment in which the university found itself when the committee was established, the recommendations of the committee, faculty reactions to the recommendations, and the actions that the university ultimately decided to pursue.

The Environment at Cornell

In the fall of 1996 when this committee was first established, changes in the age distribution of the Cornell faculty and changes in the economic environment in which both the statutory and endowed colleges operate, had come together to drastically restrict the flow of new faculty into the university. As Table 1 indicates, the total number of new tenure-track faculty appointments in the university peaked at 108 in 1987–88 and had fallen to only 48 in 1995–96. The comparable numbers for the endowed and statutory colleges during the same period, respectively, were 56 to 29 and 52 to 19. Put

Table 2. New Tenure-Track Appointments, Total University, 1982–83
          Through 1997–98

Year	Assistant professors	Total	Percent assistant
1982–83	50	82	61.0
1983–84	54	62	87.1
1984–85	51	71	71.8
1985–86	53	73	72.6
1986–87	75	99	75.8
1987–88	79	108	73.1
1988–89	69	102	67.6
1989–90	43	64	67.2
1990–91	48	73	65.8
1991–92	33	53	62.3
1992–93	38	61	62.3
1993–94	29	40	72.5
1994–95	44	60	73.3
1995–96	36	48	75.0
1996–97	33	51	64.7
1997–98*	46	65	70.8

Source: Authors' calculations from Cornell University Academic Personnel Database.
Faculty (including acting) and instructors are eligible for tenure-track appointment. Health
Services, ROTC, and Medical College excluded from this table.
*As of March 24, 1998.

another way, in the aggregate, new faculty hires at Cornell fell by almost 60
percent during the period.[2]

Fewer new hires meant that fewer faculty with new ideas and new perspectives were coming to the university. Fewer new hires also meant a reduced
ability for Cornell to diversify its faculty along gender, racial, and ethnic
lines. Finally, fewer new hires had the potential to limit Cornell's ability to remain at the frontier in rapidly changing fields and to shift faculty resources
into new and exciting areas of inquiry.

Historically, Cornell has concentrated its faculty hiring at the assistant
professor level, provided good opportunities for these new assistant professors to flourish and to receive tenure, and thus grown its own "stars." This
strategy is designed to build a faculty who are committed to the institution,
as well as to their own disciplines, and who are willing to devote time to doing
things that benefit the institution as well as themselves personally. As Table 2
indicates, the strategy of hiring primarily at the assistant professor level has
continued in recent years. Over the last fifteen years, approximately 70 percent of all new faculty hires university-wide came at the assistant professor
level.

In spite of this emphasis on new young faculty, the decline in the overall number of new hires led to a decline in the number of younger faculty

Table 3. Distribution of Faculty by Age Group, Total University, 1982–83
        To 1997–98

Year	Less than 35	35–49	50–59	60 and older
1982–83	15.2	45.0	25.3	14.5
1983–84	14.5	45.8	25.8	13.9
1984–85	13.1	47.1	25.6	14.1
1985–86	12.8	48.2	24.3	14.6
1986–87	12.2	49.0	24.3	14.5
1987–88	11.8	49.8	23.6	14.8
1988–89	10.3	51.3	23.3	15.0
1989–90	9.5	51.7	23.5	15.3
1990–91	8.8	51.3	24.3	15.6
1991–92	7.6	50.9	24.4	17.1
1992–93	6.3	50.7	25.7	17.3
1993–94	5.4	50.0	26.2	18.5
1994–95	5.1	48.3	27.8	18.7
1995–96	5.0	47.8	30.2	17.0
1996–97	5.3	44.9	32.5	17.3
1997–98	5.9	42.3	33.9	17.9

Source: Authors' calculations from the Cornell University Academic Personnel Database (February 1 each year).
Faculty include part-time and acting appointments but exclude courtesy, visiting, adjunct, emeritus, Health Services, and ROTC appointments. Age is computed as of June 30 of the academic year.

at Cornell. While over 15 percent of all faculty were under age 35 in 1982–83, by 1996–97, this had fallen to around 5 percent (Table 3). The decline in the endowed colleges was only to 7 to 8 percent, but the decline in the statutory colleges was to 2 percent.

Interestingly, the percentage of faculty over age 60 had risen from roughly 13 to 21 percent in the endowed colleges during the period. In contrast, the percentage of faculty over age 60 in the statutory colleges was lower at the end of the period than it was at the start of the period, primarily because of a number of early retirement incentive programs that the State of New York provided at zero cost to Cornell University during these years. As noted, statutory faculty have the option of choosing to belong to a defined benefit retirement program or to a defined contribution (TIAA-CREF) program.[3] Because the latter option was first permitted in the late 1960s, many of the recently retired statutory faculty were enrolled in the former program. Defined benefit programs can be structured in ways to provide incentives for participants to retire and retirement incentive programs can be developed that enhance these incentives. The retirement incentives provided under the state defined benefit program did appear to be effective in inducing statutory faculty to retire.[4] In contrast, defined contribution programs provide only limited incentives for participants to retire and the effectiveness of

Table 4. Age of Faculty at Retirement, All Faculty, 1982–83 to 1996–97

Year	Endowed			Statutory		
	Number	Mean age	Median age	Number	Mean age	Median age
1982–83	7	66.4	65.0	46	63.4	64.0
1983–84	13	66.2	66.0	7	62.6	64.0
1984–85	8	68.5	70.0	19	63.5	64.0
1985–86	11	66.9	67.0	19	64.8	66.0
1986–87	12	67.2	69.0	14	63.4	64.0
1987–88	16	65.3	66.5	25	64.1	65.0
1988–89	15	67.2	69.0	19	64.6	66.0
1989–90	15	66.3	68.0	16	65.6	65.5
1990–91	11	65.4	66.0	14	63.0	64.0
1991–92	12	68.4	70.0	23	64.4	65.0
1992–93	17	64.5	64.0	12	67.4	68.0
1993–94	11	65.7	66.0	8	65.9	65.0
1994–95	10	64.8	66.0	9	63.3	63.0
1995–96	11	66.1	67.0	42	64.9	65.0
1996–97	8	68.4	69.0	19	64.1	65.0

Source: Authors' computations from the Cornell University Academic Personnel Database. Age computed as of retirement date.

retirement incentive programs in inducing retirement under them, is limited by tax law. As of early 1997, only 16 of the 665 statutory faculty were enrolled in the defined benefit retirement system.

How did the elimination of mandatory retirement at age 70 in 1994 influence the ages at which Cornell faculty retire? Table 4 summarizes the mean and median age at retirement for faculty in the endowed and statutory sectors who retired since 1982–83. There is only little evidence in these data of increases in retirement ages after the elimination of mandatory retirement. The endowed mean and median ages at retirement fluctuated without any discernible trend until 1993–94, but since then have increased by about three years. The comparable statutory numbers show virtually no change. On average, the data suggest Cornell faculty members retire well in advance of their seventieth birthdays so that at first glance the elimination of mandatory retirement seems, not to have had a large impact on their retirement behavior.[5]

Means or medians can be deceiving, however. Figure 1 shows the age distribution of endowed faculty at retirement during the 1982–83 to 1996–97 period. Many faculty retired well in advance of their 70th birthdays, but approximately one third retired at age 70 or older (older could occur only after January 1, 1994, when the law changed). Indeed, in February 1998, there were 27 endowed faculty age 70 and above whom were still actively employed. These represent the faculty who turned 70 after January 1, 1994,

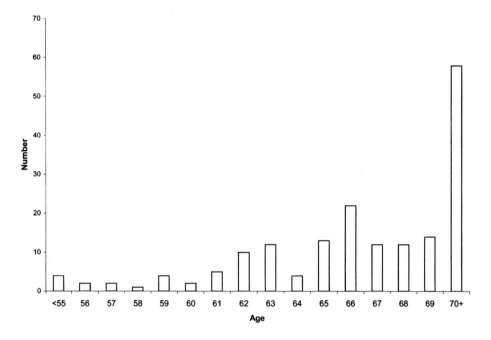

Figure 1. Age of faculty at retirement endowed, 1982–83 through 1996–97. As of February 1, 1998, there were 27 active endowed faculty age 70+. Source: Authors' calculations from Cornell University Academic Personnel Database.

and who still had not retired as of February 1998. Similarly, Figure 2 show that approximately 11 percent of the statutory faculty who retired over the period did so at age 70 or older and seven faculty age 70 or older were still active in February 1998.

Inspection of data on the annual percentage of faculty retirees who were age 70 showed no upward trend over time. However, this masks what statisticians and economists call the truncated sample problem. Here the data on retirees ignore the people continuing in active faculty status. For example, while the mean retirement age of the 11 endowed faculty who retired in 1995–96 was 66.1, there were also 10 endowed faculty who turned age 70 that year and remained active. Moreover, of the 21 endowed faculty who were 70 to 73 years old in 1995–96, all 21 were still active faculty at the start of the 1996–97 academic year. In contrast, the mean retirement age of the 42 statutory faculty who retired in 1995–96 was 64.9 and only 5 statutory faculty turned age 70 that year and remained active.[6,7]

A number of the faculty who are age 70 and above remain employed under part-time phased retirement agreements. Nonetheless, the inescapable conclusion is that the abolition of mandatory retirement for faculty is

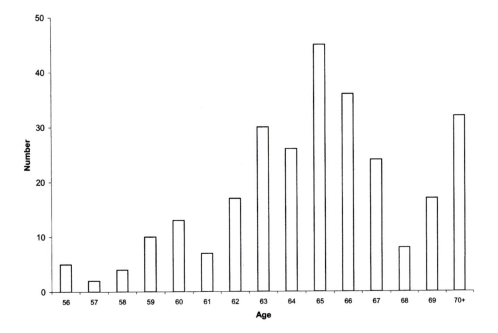

Figure 2. Age of faculty at statutory retirement, 1982–83 through 1996–97. As of February 1, 1998, there were 7 active faculty age 70+. Source: Authors' calculations from Cornell University Academic Personnel Database.

leading to an increase in retirement ages for endowed Cornell faculty. To the extent that faculty retire at later ages, this reduces the flow of new faculty into the university. To take a simple numerical example, suppose a university employs 1,750 faculty, each is initially employed at the university at age 30 and each retires at age 65. In this case, an average of 50 faculty a year will be hired. If, however, faculty retire at age 70 instead of age 65, annual hiring of new faculty will fall by one-seventh to about 43.

Thirty-five percent of the Cornell faculty in 1996–97 had been hired prior to 1978, when the mandatory retirement age for faculty was raised from 65 to 70, and these faculty all began their careers at Cornell with the expectation that they would retire no later than age 65. The Cornell retirement and benefits packages as well as the tenure system had been designed with this retirement age in mind. Twenty-seven percent of all faculty as of 1996–97 were hired between 1978 and 1987, when the law eliminating mandatory retirement for faculty was enacted (although it did not become effective until 1994). All of these faculty began employment at Cornell with the expectation that they would retire from Cornell no later than age 70. Thus, the majority of faculty at Cornell at the time our committee began its deliberations had received the opportunity to remain employed for longer than they or the university expected at their time of hire.

Most faculty nearing retirement ages at Cornell are highly productive. Their contributions to the university are numerous, and the fact that some now choose to retire after age 70 means that the university is benefiting from their skills for a longer number of years. These extra benefits must be balanced, however, against the costs to the institution of the limitation on new faculty hires that later faculty retirement ages induce, as well as the impact of delayed retirements on faculty salaries.[8]

The Preliminary Report of the Committee

The preliminary report of the joint faculty-administration committee on the transition of faculty to emeritus status (henceforth the "transition committee") was circulated to the Cornell community in April of 1997.[9] The committee had been instructed to rule out the option of expensive buy-out plans because evidence from a number of campuses suggested that such plans are often not cost effective.[10] Indeed, Table 4 and Figures 1 and 2 indicated that the majority of Cornell faculty are currently retiring before their 70th birthdays and hence any plan that paid people to retire before age 70 would be paying the vast majority of faculty for doing what they would have done without extra compensation anyway.

The committee's first set of recommendations dealt with financial planning over the life cycle. The committee wanted financial resources not to be a constraint for those faculty members who wished to contemplate retirement at age 70 or younger. In the absence of additional resources to increase the university's contribution into faculty retirement plans, a cost-efficient strategy is to provide financial planning assistance to faculty over their life cycles to ensure that they make informed investment decisions with respect to the assets in their retirement accounts. The committee was also concerned that only about half of Cornell's faculty participated in tax-deferred supplementary retirement accounts (SRAs) and only 20 percent contributed the maximum amount into such accounts that they were legally permitted. Hence, the transition committee also recommended that information should be provided to faculty on the importance of taking advantage of tax-deferred savings opportunities and that faculty be fully informed that, due to the power of compound interest, saving early in the career would have a greater impact on wealth at retirement than savings later in the career.

A second set of recommendations viewed retirement planning from the perspective of the academic unit, and urged faculty to discuss with chairs or college officials what their plans were as they approached what typically were seen as the latter years of the faculty life cycle. The ability of an academic unit to plan for its future depends on its having a sense of when its faculty members plan to retire, and the recruitment of replacement faculty is often a multiyear process. These discussions should take place, of course, in full recognition that retirement is a decision protected under federal and state law.

Still viewing things from the perspective of academic units, the committee felt that the abolition of mandatory retirement increased the importance of making sure that tenure does not imply a lack of accountability. Hence it recommended that steps be taken to ensure that faculty workloads be equitably distributed across all departmental faculty and that annual salary increases be awarded judiciously throughout a faculty member's life cycle to match the individual's productivity.

A third set of recommendations dealt with allowing faculty to "phase" into retirement. The university had a long established phased retirement program that allowed faculty in the endowed part of the university to move to half-time appointments, typically for five years, during which time they would receive half salary but full health benefits and full retirement system contributions. On signing an agreement to enter into such a program, the faculty member voluntarily agrees to give up tenure and retire at of the end of the period. This plan dated back to a time when age 65 was the mandatory retirement age and it had be revised to conform to the new federal law. It also needed to be extended to faculty in the statutory part of the university.[11]

The transition committee recommended extension of the program with a five-year maximum term specified to the half-time appointments. In addition, it specified that after an initial period during which all faculty would be eligible to participate in such agreements if they were at least age 55 and had 10 years of service at the institution, eligibility for the plan should be restricted to faculty who were below the age of 70. The motivation for such a restriction, which it believed to be legal under the law, is that this would provide an incentive for faculty to begin the retirement process prior to age 70.

A final, and probably the most important, set of committee recommendations was to greatly enhance the status of emeritus professors so that becoming an emeritus professor would be seen as a natural and desirable stage of one's career rather than as being "put out to pasture." Recommendations here included providing small research stipends ($2,000/year) for five years, guaranteeing emeritus professors at least shared office space, allowing them to maintain virtually all of the privileges of active faculty members, increasing their use in part-time postretirement teaching, enhancing the status of the emeritus professors' association, and encouraging emeritus faculty to get involved in volunteer activities on the campus and in the local community.

Inasmuch as the university was facing tight financial circumstances, there was the issue of where the funds for the emeritus professor research stipends would be found. The committee suggested capping university contributions into the defined contribution retirement plan after some point in a faculty

Table 5. Age of New Assistant Professor to Tenure Track, 1982–83 to 1997–98

Year	Endowed			Statutory		
	Number	Mean age	Median age	Number	Mean age	Median age
1982–83	23	31.1	30.0	27	32.3	33.0
1982–84	29	31.3	29.0	25	31.0	30.0
1984–85	26	31.1	30.0	24	31.1	31.0
1985–86	28	32.7	32.0	25	33.3	33.0
1986–87	39	30.8	30.0	36	33.9	33.5
1987–88	38	31.4	31.5	41	34.0	34.0
1988–89	43	32.1	31.0	26	34.5	34.0
1989–90	34	33.7	32.5	9	34.6	31.0
1990–91	22	33.4	33.5	26	34.9	33.5
1991–92	22	33.4	33.0	11	36.5	37.0
1992–93	24	33.9	31.5	14	37.8	36.5
1993–94	17	33.8	33.0	12	37.7	36.5
1994–95	29	32.9	31.0	15	35.6	33.0
1995–96	21	33.1	31.0	15	37.2	36.0
1996–97	18	30.7	30.0	15	38.0	38.0
1997–98*	38	34.0	34.0	8	36.1	36.5

Source: Authors' calculations from Cornell University Academic Personnel Database.
*As of March 24, 1998.

member's career as a way of helping to free up the funds. One proposal was to cap university contributions after 37 years. This mimics the maximum years of service credit that faculty members can accrue under the statutory college defined benefit plan. As Table 5 indicates, the typical assistant professor began his or her career between the ages of 30 and 35 and the mean age of retirement in the university for faculty has been in the range of 65 to 68. Hence, the only faculty who would see the university's contributions stopped would be those who started careers early at the university and/or postponed retirement until later ages.

An alternative way of accomplishing the same objective is to effectively convert the defined contribution retirement system into a form of defined benefit system, as both Yale and Chicago have done. Each caps the university's contributions into a faculty member's retirement account, when the cumulative university's contributions during the faculty member's career (assumed to have been invested in a conservative manner) are deemed sufficient to provide the individual with an annuity equal to a specified percentage of the individual's final salary. If the stock market falls, and hence the value of the individual's hypothetical account, university contributions are again resumed until the required annuity is again attainable. In practice, only a small number of faculty at either Chicago or Yale have been affected by such provisions and they tend to be in their late 60s or 70s.

Cornell's endowed retirement plan was established in July 1976; it provides for the university to contribute 10 percent of the faculty member's salary each year into the faculty member's retirement account. At the time the plan was adopted, faculty members were compelled to retire at age 65, which was also the age at which full social security benefits could be received. The presence of mandatory retirement meant that there was a de facto cap on the total number of years of contributions that the university would make.

The increase in the mandatory retirement age to 70 in 1978, and then its subsequent abolition (effective January 1, 1994) meant that Cornell now contributes to its faculty retirement plan for more years than framers of the retirement plan originally intended. To the extent that faculty members retire at later ages, retirement benefits will be higher as a percentage of final salary than was anticipated. Of course, the age at which full social security benefits can be received is gradually being increased and will reach age 67 within 20 years. Hence, some increase in the number of years of Cornell contribution would be required to maintain the same level of expected retirement income for faculty who retire prior to the age at which full social security benefits can be received. However, to achieve this does not require contributions to be made indefinitely by the university.

Faculty Responses and Cornell's Change of Policies

The faculty response to the transition committee report was one of indignation. The report's mention of matching productivity and salary increases over the life cycle was assumed to be a statement disparaging senior faculty and to be "ageist." The committee quickly dropped this recommendation from its final report.

The faculty also felt that the "carrots" that had been proposed were too small; Congress had made tenure truly indefinite and, from their perspective, the university had to "buy out" their property rights if it wanted them to retire. While they were correct that Congress had given them a new property right, the notion that the university in its role as an employer could take actions to try to offset the effects of the change in the law was foreign to many of them. Economists who evaluate the effects of changes in federal policies such as the minimum wage often argue about what the magnitudes of employer responses actually are; however, no economist questions the right of employers to respond (see, for example, the recent debate on the effects of changes in the minimum wage in Card and Krueger 1995; Neumark and Wascher 1995). In general, all faculty do not think like economists and some faculty even asserted that if the university tried to pursue policies to encourage voluntary retirement it would be violating the intent of the federal law.

Indeed, faculty response to the one remaining "stick" in the interim report, limitations on retirement contributions, is instructive. Many saw it as an attempt to cut total faculty compensation, even though it was explicit that any money saved would be used to provide benefits for emeritus faculty. Most did not comprehend that the contribution rates chosen by universities to make to their faculty members' retirement accounts were based on a number of assumptions including the expected age of retirement. To the extent that faculty are retiring later, a smaller contribution rate would be required to fund any desired level of annuity because the annuity would be paid out over a smaller number of years, and because savings in the account would experience compound earnings tax-free over a longer number of years. Rather, faculty saw the contribution rate, rather than the implied annual pension benefit, as something that was "due" to them. Ultimately, given faculty perceptions that their salaries were too low, which the Cornell administration actually agreed with, the committee backed off this proposal in its final report.[12]

The administration had agreed that the faculty senate would also get a chance to comment on the committee's final report, and comment it did. It argued that rather than a phased retirement program, in which one had to agree to voluntarily relinquish tenure at the end of the period, it preferred the option of going to part-time tenured appointments indefinitely. The committee patiently explained to them that such appointments, while possible at any time if deans agreed, were not retirement programs. It stressed that it believed such an option would prolong active faculty careers rather than shortening them, and it would not aid departments in planning for replacements. The provost also made it clear that he did not support such an option.

The faculty senate then urged the provost to eliminate the upper age limit for eligibility for the phased retirement program arguing that it was discriminatory and would discourage rather than encourage the use of phased retirement. The committee did not believe that voluntary retirement incentive programs that have age restrictions of the type proposed above are in violation of the law—many institutions already have, for example, retirement incentive programs in which the magnitude of the "retirement bonus" that a faculty member receives varies inversely with the age at retirement and falls to zero at a specified upper age.

In fact, there was some ambiguity as to whether age-based incentives to encourage retirement are legal. Because of this, since 1994 the college and university community has sought legislation that would explicitly recognize the legality of such incentive plans. A provision to accomplish this was part of the 1998 bill to extend the Higher Education Act. In late April 1998, the American Association of Retired Persons (AARP) and House staff members reached a compromise under which the AARP agreed to drop its opposition to the provision (see Lederman 1998). Given that the AARP has dropped its opposition to the provision, it was expected that it would be approved by Congress and enacted into law as part of the Higher Education Act extension. In October 1998, Congress did approve the bill and the president signed it into law.

The compromise language makes clear that the legality of age-based incentives to encourage retirement would apply only to tenured college professors. Typically age 70 is specified as the maximum age of eligibility under such incentive programs, and the bill also requires that all professors over age 70 at the time of the bill's enactment will have six months to decide if they wanted to take advantage of such an incentive. Finally, it requires that any professor who turns age 70 and who was ineligible to take advantage of such an incentive before that age because of the failure to have met a minimum service requirement, will become eligible for a six month period as soon as he or she reaches the minimum service requirement, regardless of his or her age at that time.

Cornell's provost issued his "Provost's Policy Statement on the Transition of Faculty to Emeritus Status" on May 8, 1998. The university policy that was spelled out in this statement closely followed the recommendations of the committee. In particular, it included the phased retirement policy recommended by the committee because this policy already met all of the conditions required in the congressional bill. However, because the bill had yet to be passed, and nothing in life is certain, all faculty were made eligible for phased retirement for the first two years after the policy begins (July 1, 1998, in the endowed colleges at Cornell). The initial two-year open window was chosen by the university to facilitate the transition to the new policy and to give the legislation time to be enacted by Congress.

Postscript 2000 (Ronald Ehrenberg)

It is still too early to tell how successful Cornell's policy will to be in helping the university maintain an adequate flow of new faculty and a sufficient pool of funds for salary increases for continuing faculty. The median age of endowed faculty at retirement remained 66 during the 1997–98 and 1998–99 period. During that period, 26 percent of the faculty retirements took place at age 70 or greater, and most of the latter took place at ages over 70. Indeed by July 1999, the number of active endowed faculty ages 70 and above had increased to 30. Of the latter total 4 were 73, 1 was 74, and 3 were 75.

Lest one be discouraged by these numbers, there are indications that the program is providing real benefits to Cornell's present and retired faculty members. For example, one of my responsibilities as an administrator was space planning. So I negotiated for, and obtained, an office for the Cornell Association of Professors Emeritus (CAPE). This office was needed to symbolize the importance of emeritus professors to the university and to provide a work space for CAPE. The office is to be adjacent to the dean of faculty, who is an elected faculty leader, to stress the connection of the emeritus faculty to the faculty as a whole.

It has been a joy for me to watch the speed with which CAPE has begun working to help both emeritus and nonemeritus faculty. The association has compiled a list of volunteer opportunities on and off campus and developed information on finances and other matters that faculty need to know as they contemplate retirement. Indeed, the emeritus professors have begun to assume the role of peer retirement counselors. An emeritus professor lecture series has even been started on campus and in a local retirement community.

In a program initiated by my wife, who is an assistant superintendent of the Ithaca City School System, several groups of Cornell retirees (staff as well as faculty) now serve as volunteers in our local schools. The impact of their efforts on Ithaca's elementary school students, and the influence of the students on them is extraordinary. Few families have three generations living in Ithaca, so benefits besides academic progress accrue from having volunteers in local schools. The students serve as surrogate grandchildren for the retirees, and the retirees as surrogate grandparents for the students.

Not every element of the new program evokes enthusiasm. For example, although compensation for part-time teaching by emeritus faculty is negotiated individually, it is usually lower than the professors would have received on a per-course basis if they had not retired. Some faculty have threatened to postpone retiring because they view the compensation as inadequate.

I have tried to persuade colleagues who have raised this issue with me that they should consider their cut in salary as analogous to the gifts that alumni make to Cornell each year. Certainly, those of us who have been fortunate enough to spend most of our academic lives at institutions like Cornell should feel extremely lucky to have had such wonderful careers. While many of us lack the financial wealth that the university's alumni often have, we do have extraordinary amounts of human capital. Our time as emeritus professors gives us an opportunity to donate that capital to the university, whether it be in the form of advising graduate students, teaching, serving on committees, or continuing our research. The reduced payments that emeritus professors get for teaching do not seem "out of line" when viewed in this way.

Perhaps Cornell's situation is somewhat unique. Its faculty members, like their peers at other research universities, are motivated mainly by the love of what they do, not by money. In addition, Cornell represents the type of institution to which faculty members can easily become attached. Its location in a small community in which faculty can easily walk or drive to campus made it possible and important for us to design a mutually beneficial program that enables emeritus professors to remain vigorous parts of the community.

A successful program must offer retiring professors an opportunity to continue to do what they love. Thus the effectiveness of Cornell's response to the end of mandatory retirement will depend on whether the institution shows that it truly values emeritus professors and creates an environment in which they can remain professionally active. Whether Cornell's policies can be applied to other institutions is unclear. An institution that differs from Cornell in having many faculty members who are not as eager to continue their research, as satisfied with their relationship with the institution, or as interested in continuing to reside near it may need to stress different things than we did.

Appendix A. Defined Benefit and Defined Contribution Retirement Plans

A *defined benefit* retirement plan provides a retiree with an annual retirement benefit that is specified to be a function of the individual's salary and years of service. A simple form of defined benefit plan is

$$(1) \qquad\qquad\qquad B = kts,$$

where B is the individual's annual retirement benefit, k is a measure of the generosity of the plan, t is the individual's years of service, and s is the individual's average salary over some specified period of time. Under the defined benefit retirement plan in effect for statutory college faculty at Cornell, k is 0.02 and s is the average of the individual's three highest annual salaries. Hence, a statutory faculty member who retired after 30 years of service would receive an annual pension equal to 60 percent of the average of his or her three highest years of salary.

Defined benefit plans provide incentives for retirement because the later one retires, the smaller the number of years that the retirement benefit payments will be made. Ignoring issues relating to salary increases, after some age, the increase in the annual benefit level the faculty member would get from working one more year is more than offset by the loss of one year's retirement benefits from delaying retirement. Thus, after some age, failing to retire reduces the individual's lifetime value of retirement benefits. In addition, maximum percentage benefit levels can be specified that, after some point, eliminate the increase in annual retirement benefits that comes from working one more year. For example, the maximum benefit percentage under the statutory defined benefit plan is 75 percent of salary, which means that once the faculty member reaches 37.5 years of service, working additional years does not increase his or her annual retirement benefit level.

Retirement incentive programs can be straightforwardly developed within defined benefit systems. For example, several retirement incentive programs in Cornell's statutory colleges provided a faculty member with an additional month's service credit for each year worked, if the individual retired within a prescribed period of time. Hence, faculty members who had been employed for 24 years received an additional two years of credit. For an individual with an "average salary" of $80,000, this would lead to an increase in annual retirement benefits of $3,200 a year ((.02)(2)$80,000). If the faculty member turned down the retirement incentive, in the absence of salary increases, the faculty member would have to work two more years before he or she could receive the same annual retirement benefit, which he or she would then collect for two fewer years. Thus, the programs provided a strong incentive to retiree.

Under *defined contribution* retirement systems, the employer contributes a specified percentage of the employee's salary each year to a fund, which is then invested to provide benefits at retirement for the employee. The fund "belongs" to the employee so that as long as the market return on the assets in the fund are positive, the value of the fund is larger the later the age at which an employee retires. Pure defined contribution plans thus do not provide strong economic incentives to retire for faculty members, because delaying retirement leaves the faculty member with a larger retirement fund.

Retirement incentive programs under defined contribution systems typically provide for additional employer payments to the employee if the employee retires within a prescribed interval of time. These additional payments are subject to federal and state income taxes, however, in the year they are made. The retirement incentive programs for statutory college faculty provided for an additional payment of 0.15 of one month's salary for each year of service.[13] Continuing with the example above, a faculty member with 24 years of service and an $80,000 annual salary, would get a payment of $24,000 ((.15)(24)(80,000/12)). After federal and state income taxes were deducted, which we assume would average 23 percent, the faculty member would have about $16,000 to invest in an annuity.[14] However, if he or she worked one more year, the university's retirement contribution for the year, plus the earnings that would occur on all the assets already in the employee account, would far exceed the value of the lump sum payment.[15] In addition, working one more year delays the withdrawal of any of the assets for a year. Not surprisingly, very few eligible statutory faculty enrolled in the defined contribution program participated in the statutory college retirement incentive program.

Appendix B. Tenure Probabilities, Retirement Ages, Hiring, and Faculty Salaries at Cornell

This appendix presents some simple steady state models to illustrate how Cornell's faculty retirement age influences average faculty salaries, the number of faculty that we can hire each year, and the annual salary increase available for continuing faculty. We begin with a baseline model that is meant to represent endowed Ithaca prior to the abolition of mandatory retirement. We then show how changes in faculty retirement ages influence faculty members' salaries and the new hire rate.

The initial model assumes that the university is in a steady state in which it hires the same number of faculty each year, and faculty size remains constant over time. Salaries in each rank are assumed not to vary with age and each faculty member in the model receives the current average endowed salary for his or her rank. Finally, only assistant professors are hired and there is no turnover other than when people are turned down for tenure or retire.[16] The model is then generalized in to allow for salary growth in the full professor rank and we illustrate how changes in retirement ages affect Cornell's ability to increase continuing faculty salaries. This model is a steady state model and assumes a uniform distribution of faculty by age, which is not the situation Cornell actually faces. Consequently, Appendix C presents analyses from a more complex tenure flow simulation approach that permit us to analyze how endowed Cornell's actual faculty flows and faculty salaries over the next twenty years will likely depend on changes in retirement behavior.

A Simple Baseline Model

Suppose the university hires 6 new assistant professors each year who are 30 years old. After 6 years 2/3 (4 of the 6) are promoted to associate professor.[17] These 4 individuals stay as associate professors for 6 years and then in turn are all promoted to professor. Professors each work for another 24 years until they all retire at age 66. There is no other turnover or hiring in this model.

Under these assumptions, at any point in time the university will employ 6×6 or 36 assistant professors, 4×6 or 24 associate professors and 4×24 or 96 full professors. There will be 156 faculty employed and the tenure rate will be 120/156 or 0.77. Each year the number of new faculty hired, 6, will represent 3.8 percent of the faculty (6/156). The faculty salary bill is constructed by assuming that all faculty in each rank earn the 1996–97 endowed Ithaca salaries. Thus, the salary bill will be $36 \times \$50,800$, or $1,828,800$, $24 \times \$62,100$, or $1,490,400$, and $96 \times \$85,600$, or $8,217,600$, for a total of $11,536,800$.

In actuality, we note that the current endowed Ithaca faculty size is roughly 900. Thus one could multiply all of the numbers presented above by roughly 6 if one wanted to scale up to current endowed totals. For simplicity, we do not do this until the final section.

Changing the Retirement Age

Suppose now that the career of a full professor lasted 29 years rather than 24. Put another way, each faculty member retires at age 71 rather than age 66. Under these assumptions, if we hired 6 new assistant professors each year, our total faculty would consist of 6×6 or 36 assistant professors, 4×6

or 24 associate professors, and 4 × 29 or 116 full professors. This would yield a total of 176 faculty and a tenure rate of 140/176 or 0.80. This faculty level is too high, however, since we are assuming that we need 156 faculty to run the university. Hence, the number of newly hired faculty each year, as well as the number present at each age, would have to be reduced by 156/176 or 0.886. Put another way, the number of newly hired faculty members each year would fall to 5.318, a decline of roughly 11 percent from the base scenario. Under this new scenario, we would therefore have 5.318 × 6 or 30.828 assistant professors, 3.546 × 6 or 21.276 associate professors, and 3.546 × 29 or 102.834 full professors, for a total faculty size of 155.938 (which differs from 156 only because of rounding error).

Our total faculty salary bill in this case would be 30.828 × $50,800 (or $1,566,062), 21.276 × $62,100 (or $1,321,240), and 102.834 × 85,600 (or $8,802,590), for a total of $11,689,892. This is $153,092 higher than the total salary bill in the base scenario. One could get back to that total salary bill by cutting each faculty member's salary by $982, or by 1.3 percent. Alternatively, one could cut only full professors' salaries by an average of $1,489, or 1.7 percent of the average full professor salary level.

Salary Growth for Full Professors

The models presented so far assume that there is no salary growth within a rank. To illustrate the impact of changes in the retirement age on salary growth, in this section we relax this assumption for full professors.

The current endowed tenured faculty average salary for individuals in the age range 40–44 is $71,600. Allowing this to be the starting salary for a 42-year-old professor and assuming that each full professor receives an annual "seniority-related" salary increase of $1,165, and that each retires at each 66 when his or her salary is $99,600, yields an average full professor salary of $85,600, which is the current average endowed full professor salary.

Note that in this stylized world, the average percentage salary increase that each full professor receives each year simply because he or she ages one year is (1165/85600) × 100 or 1.36 percent. Put another way, even if there were no general salary pool increase, the average salary increase for full professors each year would be 1.36 percent. This occurs because each year faculty who retire do so at salaries that are $28,000 more than the young full professors that replace them and this difference is available to distribute to all other full professors in the form of seniority-related salary increases.[18]

Now suppose that we increase the retirement age by 5 years to 71. If we continue to assume that all full professors receive the same seniority-related increase each year and keep the average full professor salary at $85,600, the annual increment in salary will fall to 24/29 of $1,165 or $965.50 a year. As a percentage of the average professor salary, the raise will be 1.12 percent. Hence, the increase in the retirement age has led to a decline in the seniority-related increment that professors can receive each year.

Alternatively, suppose that the increment remains at $1,165 a year. In this case, professors will retire at age 71 at an annual salary of $105,425 and the average full professor salary will be $88,012.50. Thus, the average costs of full professors will have risen by 2.8 percent. Unless compensating action is taken (e.g., fewer faculty or lower salaries for associate or assistant professors), total faculty costs will have increased above and beyond the baseline increase.

Extensions

We have shown that, if faculty salaries are assumed to be constant within rank, an increase in the retirement age of 5 years will lead to about an 11 percent decrease in annual faculty hiring, as well as a 1.3 percent decrease in the average faculty member's salary. The model can be generalized to allow full professors' salaries to increase with age. Here we found that an increase in the retirement age of 5 years would reduce the average seniority-related increase that full professors can receive annually from 1.36 to 1.12 percent. Are these effects of changes in the mandatory retirement age large enough to warrant the university's concern? They assume a constant overall faculty size and, to the extent that there will be further shrinkage of its faculty size, hiring will be less in each case. The issue then, is what number of new hires is needed by the university each year to maintain the intellectual vigor of the university and to diversify the faculty?

Perhaps one way to address this question is to scale these numbers up to what the endowed portion of Cornell really looks like. With 900 endowed faculty rather than 156 in steady state, endowed Cornell would be hiring roughly 36 new faculty a year in the first scenario. An 11 percent decrease (the second scenario) would decrease this number to below 32. Whether 32 is sufficiently smaller than 36 is the crux of the concern over whether the elimination of mandatory retirement should concern the university.

Finally, this model assumed all hiring is at the new assistant professor level and that there is no turnover of faculty save at retirement. To the extent that tenured faculty members do leave the university prior to retirement, this leaves open the possibility of hiring some new senior faculty to replace them.[19] If our tenured faculty turnover rate prior to retirement was 2 percent (0.02) a year, we would have roughly 2.4 (120 × .02) senior faculty vacancies a year in the first scenario. Scaled up to the size of the current endowed faculty, this would equal roughly fourteen senior vacancies a year. If our tenured faculty turnover rate prior to retirement were closer to 0.015, the number of senior vacancies we could fill each year would be closer to 10.8.[20] Indeed, staying with the first scenario, our fraction of senior hires would be 10.8/43 or 0.16. Historically, Cornell has filled over 30 percent of its endowed faculty positions at the senior level. The model suggests this is too high a percentage for a steady state.

Appendix C. Simulations Using the Faculty Flow Model

Appendix B reported steady state simulations assuming a uniform distribution of tenured faculty across age groups. It also implicitly assumed that any tenured faculty member that leaves prior to retirement is replaced by another tenured faculty member of the same age and salary, and that no other external tenured appointments are made. Since none of these assumptions is accurate, it is useful to use a faculty flow model developed by Cornell's Office of Institutional Planning and Research (IPR) ago to simulate what is likely to occur over the next 20 years.[21]

This faculty flow model divides the faculty into first through seventh year assistant professors and thirteen age categories of tenured faculty. For each category, the proportions of people who leave the university, who stay in the same category, or who move to each other category each year are calculated using actual data for the endowed colleges for the October 1994–October 1997 period.[22] These "transition probabilities" are initially assumed to remain stable in the future.

The average salaries of faculty in each of the 20 categories are calculated and also are assumed to remain unchanged over time. Put another way, we ignore general increases in the salary pool that may occur each year. Finally, when vacancies occur due to departures or retirements, replacements are assigned to each of the 20 categories by using the proportion of external hires that occurred in each of the categories during the last 4 years. This assumption also means that the size of the endowed faculty is assumed to remain constant at 870 during the period and thus that no further contractions in faculty size will occur.[23]

Baseline Scenario

Using the actual numbers of endowed faculty in each of the 20 categories in 1997–98, the various transition probabilities and the distribution of external hires across categories, the simulation model is "run" for 20 periods to take us out to the year 2018. The oldest endowed faculty member is currently 74 years old and some assumptions must be made about the "continuation rate" for faculty this age and older. It is assumed in these analyses that the probability of continuing as an active faculty member in the next year is 0.75 for 74-year-olds and that this probability drops to 0.5, 0.25, and 0 during the next three years. This implies that all faculty will be fully retired from the university at age 77.

Panel I of Appendix Table C1 summarizes the results from this simulation. New faculty hires rise from a predicted 35 in the current year to 47 in 2018 as the "bulge" of professors currently in the 40 to 60 age range begin to retire. The number of faculty age 60 and higher increases for 10 years but then begins to fall. The percent of endowed Cornell faculty that is tenured falls gradually from its current level of 83.7 percent to 76.6 percent because of the relative large number of retirements that eventually occur. After 5 years, the faculty salary bill begins to decline as the fraction of full professors declines due to retirements. Indeed, 20 years from now, the faculty salary bill is predicted to be about 1.8 percent lower in constant dollars than it is this year. The saved funds would be available to redistribute back to faculty in the form of one-time larger salary increases. If all of the savings were given to full professors, their salaries would be 2.7 percent higher.

Changing Retirement Rate Parameters of the Model

Panel II of Appendix Table C1 reports the result of simulations in which a key parameter of the model is changed. The simulations that underlie panel II assume going forward that all faculty retire no later than age 70. This is achieved by having all faculty currently older than age 70 retire next year and changing the retirement probability for faculty age 70 to 1.0 for future years. Otherwise, all of the other assumptions of the model are assumed to continue to hold. The results show that, if all faculty were to retire no later than age 70, there would be a big effect on the number of new hires that could be made initially (as those currently above age 70 retire and are replaced) but only a smaller long-run effect. Contrasting rows B of panels I and II, over the 20-year period we could hire a total of 959 new faculty rather than the 881 faculty that would be hired if current retirement practices continue. This represents an increase in faculty hiring of roughly 9 percent over the period. This is somewhat less that than the 11 percent change predicted by the steady state model presented in Appendix B for a 5-year change in the average retirement age because the change in the average retirement age being simulated in this appendix is actually smaller than 5 years.

The reduction in retirement ages would have a significant effect on the faculty salary bill. Five years out, the faculty salary bill would be 1.8 percent lower under this scenario than under the base scenario (67,267/68,496). These funds could be redistributed to all continuing faculty in the form of one-time salary increases. In the longer run (20 years), the differential is somewhat smaller, but still in the 1.3 percent range.

Appendix Table C2 provides a more detailed summary of the differences in annual faculty hiring, cumulative faculty hiring, number of faculty age 60+, percent tenured and total faculty salary bill between the two scenarios. Reducing the retirement age will further reduce the overall tenure rate, but the additional reductions that they would lead to are never larger than 2 percentage points. The drop due to the changing age structure of the faculty that Cornell can expect over the next twenty years is considerably larger.

Finally, Appendix Table C3 presents estimates of the average annual salary increase that faculty members can expect each year as they age, even if there is no general increase in the salary pool. This is computed by taking all of the continuing faculty each year, computing the increase for those people who move between any two categories of faculty each year as the difference between the average salaries in the two categories, summing these increases across all faculty, and then dividing by the current average endowed faculty salary.

These average increases range between roughly 1.0 and 1.2 percent across years. These numbers are less than the 1.36 percent predicted using the steady state model Appendix B because that model assumed that fraction of external faculty hires that occur at the tenure level would be less than actually has been the case, and that such newly hired tenured faculty would receive salaries equal to those of the people that they replaced. Often these newly hired tenured faculty are paid more.

Table C1. Simulations from the Faculty Flow Model for Endowed Ithaca Faculty

	1997–98	2002–3	2007–8	2012–13	2017–18
I. Baseline scenario					
Number faculty hires	35	40	45	47	47
Cumulative faculty hires	35	190	410	643	881
Number faculty age 60+	191	236	247	240	225
Percent tenured	83.7	81.3	78.7	77.1	76.6
Faculty salary bill (000s)	$68,304	$68,496	$68,022	$67,489	$67,096
II. Induce all faculty to retire by age 70					
Number faculty hires	57	44	48	49	49
Cumulative faculty hires	57	233	469	714	959
Number faculty age 60+	191	199	207	199	189
Percent tenured	83.7	78.3	77.0	75.9	75.8
Faculty salary bill (000s)	$68,304	$67,267	$66,881	$66,462	$66,231

Source: Authors' calculations using Cornell faculty flow model described in Appendix C.
I: Actual transition probabilities during the last 4 years with assumed continuation rates of .75 for 50- and .25 for 74-, 75-, and 76-year-olds.
II: Same as case I, except all individuals who have not retired by age 70 are assumed to retire at age 70.

Table C2. Percentage Differences from the Baseline Scenario

	1997–98	2002–3	2007–8	2012–13	2017–18
Number of faculty hires					
RRA	62.9	10.0	6.7	4.3	4.3
Cumulative faculty hires					
RRA	62.9	22.6	14.4	11.0	8.9
Number faculty age 60+					
RRA	0.0	−15.7	−16.2	−18.1	−16.0
Percent tenured (% point difference)					
RRA	0.0	−2.0	−1.7	−1.2	−0.8
Faculty salary bill					
RRA	0.0	−1.8	−1.7	−1.5	−1.3

Source: Authors' calculations.
Where: RRA = Reduced Retirement Age.

Table C3. Average Annual Percentage Faculty Salary Increase Due to Normal
        Progression Through the System

	1997–98	2002–3	2007–8	2012–13	2017–18
Percentage increase	1.08	0.96	1.11	1.14	1.17

Source: Authors' calculations.
Baseline model save that all faculty are assumed to retire by age 74.

Notes

1. The Cornell University Medical College, located in New York City, has a separate retirement program, not discussed here.

2. Interestingly, new faculty hiring rebounded back up to 65 in 1997–98, with new endowed faculty appointments increasing to 54, the third highest annual level during the 1982–83 to 1997–98 period. This spurt of hiring in the endowed colleges partially reflected an inflow of endowment funds to the university that resulted from an endowment campaign concluded several years earlier and partially "prefills" in anticipation of future faculty retirements. The reader should view this increase as a temporary "blip," rather than a steady state increase in endowed faculty hiring. Faculty hiring in the statutory colleges continued to decline through 1997–98 because of state funding cutbacks described below.

3. Appendix A explains the difference between defined benefit and defined contribution pension plans and elaborates on the points made in this paragraph.

4. Due to funding cutbacks from the State of New York, the number of statutory tenure-track and tenured faculty fell from 717 in 1988–89 to 631 in 1997–98. It is believed that many statutory faculty retired during the period to avoid seeing younger colleagues laid off. Hence, it is difficult to estimate what the impacts of the early retirement programs, per se, were on statutory faculty retirement behavior.

5. Prior to the elimination of mandatory retirement, Cornell rigorously enforced its mandatory retirement policies. Retired faculty were nevertheless eligible to be hired back for specified terms on a part-time basis, at a renegotiated (usually lower) salary.

6. A reasonable conjecture is that because the vast majority of statutory faculty is now enrolled in the TIAA-CREF system, retirement ages will move closer to the endowed faculty retirement ages over time.

7. More generally, during the 1994–95 to 1996–97 period, universitywide, 80 percent of all faculty who had not retired by age 70 continued on active status the next academic year. The comparable percentages for faculty turning ages 71 and 72 were 70 percent and 100 percent, respectively.

8. Appendices B and C analyze these two issues using a steady state and a Markov process faculty flow model, respectively.

9. A copy of this report is available at <www.ipr.cornell.edu/emeritus/transrpt. html>.

10. The recent retirement incentive plan at the University of California (UC), analyzed by Switkes (this volume), did induce substantial faculty retirements. However, the UC faculty were covered by a defined benefit plan and the cost of "sweetening" their benefits was borne by the state retirement system, not the university. For a discussion of why it is more difficult to "encourage" retirement when faculty are covered by a defined contribution retirement system rather than a defined benefit system, see Appendix A.

11. The plan is actually more complicated and allows for less than half-time employment.

12. The November 1997 final report is available at <www.ipr.cornell.edu/Faculty_to_Emeritus/FinalReport.html>.

13. This is a slight simplification of the actual formula. Annual benefits are reduced if the faculty member retires before age 65 and also if similar benefits are guaranteed to the faculty member's spouse.

14. This was payable in three installments and capped at 45 percent of salary.

15. To see this, note that if the individual's salary had averaged $60,000 and that if 10 percent had been contributed by the state to his or her retirement account each year, after twenty-four years, the value of the account (ignoring investment returns) would be $144,000. If the investment return in this tax-sheltered account were 10 percent in the next year, the earnings of $14,400 would almost equal the value of the incentive. After one factors in tax-sheltered investment earnings on contributions to the account over the previous 24 years, as well as the next year's payment by the state into the individual's account of $8,000, one realizes how ineffective this defined contribution retirement incentive was.

16. We drop these two assumptions in the final section.

17. The actual proportion of newly hired assistant professors during the 1982–83 to 1990–91 period who ultimately were awarded tenure was 63.7 percent.

18. In this model, all new faculty hires still occur at the new assistant professor level. The "young full professors" who replace retirees are newly promoted associate professors.

19. If all tenured faculty who leave prior to retirement are replaced by externally-hired tenured faculty of the same age and salary, none of the other results are altered.

20. The actual number of nonretirement related departures of tenured faculty at Cornell is quite low. In the endowed colleges, they averaged 11.2 a year over the 1992–93 to 1996–97 period on a base averaging 722 tenured faculty, or 0.016

21. See IPR (1994) for an earlier use of the faculty flow model.

22. Endowed college data are used throughout because, as explained in the text, funding cutbacks in the statutory colleges coupled with various retirement incentive programs make it difficult for us to compute stable transition probabilities for statutory faculty.

23. The endowed Cornell actual faculty size exceeds 870 because these analyses

refer only to tenured and tenure-track faculty who are not on leave in a given year and are not administrators. The actual number of endowed faculty in 1997–98 was over 900.

References

Card, David E. and Alan B. Krueger. 1995. *Myth and Measurement: The New Economics of the Minimum Wage.* Princeton, N.J.: Princeton University Press.

Lederman, Douglas. 1998. "Senior-Citizens Group and Colleges Compromise on Early-Retirement Measure." *Chronicle of Higher Education,* April 29 (Internet version).

National Research Council, Committee on Ending Mandatory Retirement in Higher Education. 1991. *Ending Mandatory Retirement for Tenured Faculty: The Consequences for Higher Education,* ed. P. Brett Hammond and Harriet P. Morgan. Washington, D.C.: National Academy Press.

Neumark, David and William L. Wascher. 1995. "Reconciling the Evidence on Employment Effects of Minimum Wages: A Review of Our Research Findings." Board of Governors of the Federal Reserve System, Finance and Economics Discussion Paper 95/53, December.

Office of Institutional Planning and Research. 1994. "Uncapping Faculty Retirement Age." Occasional Report 1, March.

Rees, Albert and Sharon P. Smith. 1991. *Faculty Retirement in the Arts and Sciences.* Princeton, N.J.: Princeton University Press.

Switkes, Ellen. This volume. "The University of California Voluntary Early Retirement Incentive Programs."

Chapter 6
The University of California Voluntary Early Retirement Incentive Programs

Ellen Switkes

Public colleges and universities face considerable challenges in preserving and maintaining their missions and their operations while coping with serious budget problems. The economy of the state, state budget appropriations, and federal research funding are of enormous importance to the very core of the institution and its faculty and students, although the institution can impact these only peripherally if at all. Salaries of faculty and staff make up the majority of university spending, and in a budget crisis there are only limited ways to tighten the collective belt without reducing the payroll. Delayed hiring may have some effect, and hiring freezes are a common method of dealing with temporary or short-term crises. Reduction in the workforce through layoff or retirement incentives may be needed if the budget crisis is severe and prolonged. Such actions may address budget problems, but they engender grave concerns over program quality and continuity.

The University of California (UC) faced a serious budget crisis in the early 1990s and responded to it by instituting a series of Voluntary Early Retirement Incentive Programs (VERIPs). These programs were designed to encourage retirement of staff and faculty in order to reduce the payroll sufficiently to deal with the looming budget crisis. The institutional planners could only guess at the outcome and impact of these programs, because they had little experience with retirement incentive programs and could not know how attractive the incentives would be to faculty and staff. Nor did they know, as the budget crisis developed, how long it would continue and how deep it would eventually cut. Balancing incentives to encourage sufficient reduction in workforce without decimating academic programs was the challenge, and there was little guidance available to the planners. The premise behind VERIPs was fairly simple: encourage retirement of faculty and staff to reduce the payroll through voluntary employee actions, replace as few employees as possible until the budget crisis eased, and later replace them with junior personnel at lower salaries. At the same time, the university needed to maintain the quality of instruction for students; maintain the university's ongoing research programs; maintain the University of California as a destination of choice for excellent undergraduate and graduate students and for new faculty recruits; and also maintain the prestige of academic programs with high quality scholarships. How could these seemingly conflicting objectives be accomplished?

The University of California experienced reductions in state appropriations of over 20 percent from 1990 to 1996. In response to these dramatic budget cuts, in 1991 the university offered the first in what was to become a series of three VERIPs. More than 10,000 staff and 2,000 tenured faculty retired in these programs. Those 2,000 tenured faculty members constituted over 20 percent of all regular faculty. This chapter describes the incentives offered, a profile of faculty who were eligible and of those who elected these programs, and information on the impact on the university's academic programs.

The Retirement System

The University of California is a system with nine campuses and over 150,000 students. The University of California retirement plan (UCRP) is a defined benefit pension plan with over 115,000 active members, 30,000 annuitants, and 21,000 inactive members eligible to receive a benefit. The defined benefit pension formula is determined by years of service, the average of the highest consecutive three years' salary highest average plan compensation (HAPC), and a factor based on age. Because of outstanding performance of investments of the university's retirement plan, neither the employees nor the university made retirement contributions to the plan since 1990. The incentives as well as all of the costs associated with administering the VERIP programs were borne by the retirement system and were not paid from the university's operating budget.

Figure 1 shows the age factors in place during the VERIPs. The minimum retirement age is 50. The age factors increase in a nonlinear fashion and reach a maximum at age 60. After age 60, the age factor remains constant but years of service and HAPC continue to increase until retirement. For example, if Professor Jones retired at age 57 with 16 years of university service and a three highest years average salary of $75,000, the standard pension (P) upon retirement of $20,400 would be calculated based on the age factor for age 57 (0.0170) as $P = (0.0170)(16 \text{ years})(\$75,000) = \$20,400$.

In addition to the university pension, many faculty and staff who retired also received social security benefits, 403(b) distributions, and almost all were eligible for annuitant health insurance on a basis comparable to active employees. (This latter affords a substantial incentive to retire.)

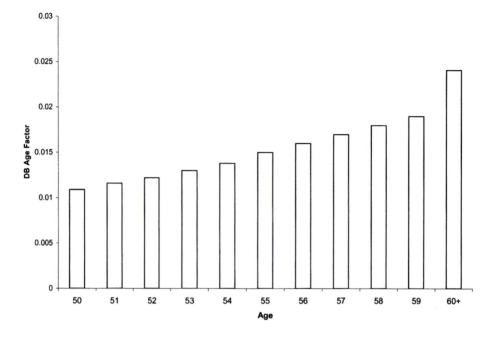

Figure 1. Defined benefit plan age factors in effect during the VERIP programs. Source: Author's calculations.

The Budget Crisis

Figure 2 shows the change over time in the university's budget, enrollment, and faculty numbers during the period preceding and following the deep budget cuts. From 1990 to 1994, the university experienced a budget cut of almost 20 percent, while at the same time the student enrollment decreased only slightly. Also marked in this figure are the three VERIP programs. Budget appropriations for the University of California grew steadily from 1985–86 to 1990–91; substantial enrollment growth spurred aggressive faculty hiring, capital projects, and campus expansion around the system. When the budget crisis hit, a reduction in workforce was the most feasible way to deal with such substantial budget cuts in such a timely and effective way. While layoffs of other staff could have been effected, it was impossible to lay off sufficiently large numbers of tenured faculty within a short time to meet substantial salary saving targets. When the first VERIP program was announced in October 1990, the budget crisis was still young and the total reduction in workforce that would ultimately be needed wasn't yet known.

The university had little experience with large-scale workforce reductions. The VERIP program was designed based on what turned out to be

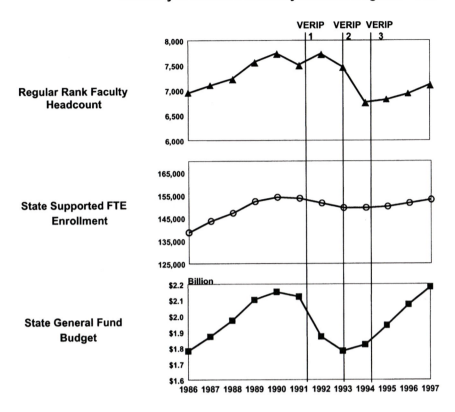

Figure 2. University of California faculty count, student enrollment, and California state budget, 1986–97. Source: Author's calculations.

rather good guesses about the kinds of incentives that would encourage retirement without decimating the workforce. In fact, the university's faculty senate provided substantial support for the incentive plan, in large part because of the anticipated opportunity for a large-scale faculty renewal. In fact, substantial hiring of new faculty was delayed for several years as the budget crisis continued to deepen.

The Incentive Programs

Figure 3 is a time line for the VERIP programs. VERIP 1 was announced in October 1990. Faculty were required to make a binding decision by March 31, 1991 and to retire on July 1, 1991. VERIPs 2 and 3 were announced in July 1992 and June 1993 respectively, with retirement dates for faculty of January 1, 1993 and July 1, 1994. Each VERIP was anticipated to be the final

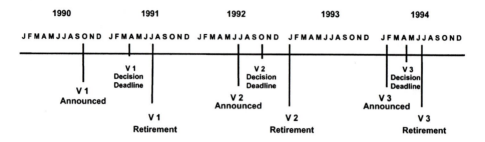

Figure 3. VERIP timeline faculty programs. Source: Author's calculations.

program. Eligible employees were presented with the choice to take the program offered in a window period or to continue in active employment. Each successive program provided broadened eligibility requirements to encourage retirements in response to a worsening state budget forecast. Some employees who selected the earlier programs were unhappy to learn later that if they had chosen not to retire when they did, they could have elected the last program with more valuable incentives. However, by the time VERIP 3 was offered, the incentives were sufficiently generous that a large number of employees elected the program rather than wait for the possibility that an even richer program would be offered later.

Figure 4 describes the three VERIP programs for faculty. Faculty who were subject to mandatory retirement were permitted to retire with the incentives provided in VERIPs 1 and 2, even though they would have had to retire anyway. Mandatory retirement was no longer in place at the time of VERIP 3.

In the first VERIP, faculty with a sum of age plus service of 80 or above were eligible. In the example above, Professor Jones at age 57 with 16 years of service had age plus service of 73 and was not eligible, while faculty colleagues age 60 with 20 or more years of service were eligible. For VERIP 2, faculty needed a combination of age and years of service of 78 to be eligible; for VERIP 3, faculty needed a combination of age and years of service of 73 to be eligible. Three years later Professor Jones was eligible for VERIP 3. At that point she was 60 years old with 19 years of service, so her age plus service equaled 79. Program eligibility for staff employees was more generous. A special set of incentives was established for VERIP 3 for the Berkeley campus because the faculty at this campus had higher average age and service than the rest of the system. The administration was concerned that a very high take rate at Berkeley could create a crisis by jeopardizing important academic programs.

Incentive. Figure 4 shows the incentives offered to faculty under each VERIP program. All three programs provided a lump sum cash payment

	Eligibility Requirements (Age + Service Years)	Retirement Incentives	Retirement Date	Takers
VERIP 1	80 and above	1) 5 years of service credit 2) lump-sum cash payment: 3 months' salary	7/1/91	675
VERIP 2	78 and above	1) 5 years of service credit 2) lump-sum cash payment: 3 months' salary	1/1/93	371
VERIP 3	73 and above [75 and more for Berkeley]	1) 5 years of service credit and 3 years of age, or up to 8 years of service credit* 2) lump-sum cash payment: 3 months' salary	7/1/94	938

* For Berkeley campus: 5 years of service credit plus 2 years of age

Figure 4. Faculty eligibility requirements, retirement incentives, and retirement dates. Source: Author's calculations.

equivalent to three months salary immediately upon retirement as a transition allowance, subject to Internal Revenue Code Section 415 limitations. In addition, faculty who elected VERIP 1 or 2 received five years of service credit. For a professor with 15 years of University of California service, adding 5 years of service credit would result in a pension formula crediting 20 years of service rather than 15 years, resulting in a 33 percent increase in pension. For VERIP 3, the incentives were more complicated as they were based on both an increase in age and service totaling eight. Faculty could add up to three years of age plus five years of service credit. For Berkeley, the numbers were two years and six years respectively.

Examples of the impact of VERIP 3 on retirement benefits for three fictious faculty are shown in Figure 5. These illustrate how the incentives might influence an individual's decision to accept the incentive and to retire.

- Professor Holst was age 68 at the time she elected VERIP 3. She had been eligible for VERIP 1 and 2 but had not retired. Because the age factor reaches a maximum at age 60, Professor Holst had already reached the maximum age factor; additional age credit would not increase her pension. Thus Holst received an incentive of eight additional years of service, which resulted in a 27 percent increase in her pension from an

	Professor Holst		Professor Ramos		Professor King	
Employee status when VERIP is offered	68		55		57	
Actual age	30		20		16	
Years of service credit earned and accrued	$91,000		$80,000		$75,000	
Average salary rate (HAPC)						
VERIP incentives (based on age of employee)						
Additional years of age	0		3		3	
Additional years of service	8		5		5	

Benefits	Standard Benefit	Benefit with VERIP	Standard Benefit	Benefit with VERIP	Standard Benefit	Benefit with VERIP
Benefit percentage (Represents the retirement benefit as a percentage of average salary)	72%	92%	30%	45%	27%	51%
Approximate annual retirement benefit	$65,793	$83,338	$24,000	$36,000	$20,400	$37,957

Figure 5. Examples of impact of VERIP 3 on retirement benefits. Source: Author's calculations.

annual benefit of $65,793 to a benefit under VERIP 3 of $83,338. Had she not retired under VERIP 3, she figured that with a merit increase of about 9 percent every three years and no cost of living increases due to the bad budget, she would have to work to age 73 or more to receive a pension similar to the one offered to her now at age 68. She had been thinking about retiring soon anyway, and so she took the offered incentive.

• Professor Ramos was age 55 with 20 years service when VERIP 3 was offered. He hadn't been eligible for VERIP 1 or 2. VERIP 3 changed his pension calculation by adding three years of age and five years of service to provide a pension 50 percent greater than he would receive if he retired without VERIP at age 55. A significant factor in his decision to retire was the possibility that he might later be recalled to partial active service and could retain his office, graduate students and research grants. Although no guarantees of recall could be made due to retirement plan restrictions, he was reasonably confident that his expertise would be needed, so the prospect of "retiring" without totally giving up his work was quite attractive.

• Professor King was age 57 when he considered electing VERIP 3. He also had not been eligible for VERIP 1 or 2. King's incentive of three additional years of age credit to age 60 (the maximum age factor) and five years of service credit increased his total years of service from 16 to 21. Under VERIP 3 his pension would increase to $37,957; it would have been at $20,400 if he had retired without the added incentives. This was an overall increase of 86 percent in his pension at retirement.

However, King figured that the increase in the age factor from age 57 to 60 combined with a substantial merit increase he was expecting would give him the equivalent of the VERIP 3 benefit with a few more years of work. He was not ready to retire at age 57 and anticipated working many more years, so the VERIP 3 incentive was not sufficiently attractive to Professor King.

The campaign. The university undertook an extensive information campaign with each VERIP program. All eligible employees received a package of information about the VERIP program including individualized statements of what their pension would be if they elected the program. In addition, there were information sessions to which spouses were invited, videos describing the program, and individual retirement counseling for all professors and spouses.

Faculty had many factors to consider in addition to the financial arrangements of their university pension, such as additional income available from other sources, their health and the health of family members, postretirement plans, recall possibilities, and opportunities for other employment. Many faculty were relieved to find the time in retirement to complete a book manuscript, to become more active in their professional societies, or to assume leadership roles in faculty governance. Many were happy about opportunities to teach without having to attend department meetings or serve on committees. Although the university was unable to make any guarantees about future part-time appointments, many faculty considered this a likely option.

Outcome

There were several variables across the three VERIP programs. The demographics of eligible faculty for each VERIP program was different. The eligibility criteria varied as each succeeding VERIP made more faculty eligible; in addition, many formerly eligible faculty had already retired with each successive VERIP offering. In addition, each successive VERIP left a group of eligible faculty less inclined to retire (Pencavel 1997).

Figure 6 shows the take rate for faculty for each VERIP program. This varied from 18 percent for VERIP 2 to 34 percent for VERIP 3. VERIP 2 had a lower take rate because although more people were eligible for VERIP 2 than for VERIP 1, those newly eligible had less seniority and many did not want to retire because their pension, even enhanced by the incentive, was too small. Many faculty were eligible for more than one of the VERIP programs. Overall, of those faculty eligible for any of the programs, 40 percent (which amounted to 2,000 tenured faculty) took advantage of one of the VERIP programs and retired.

The average age of faculty who retired for VERIP 1 was 66 (about the nor-

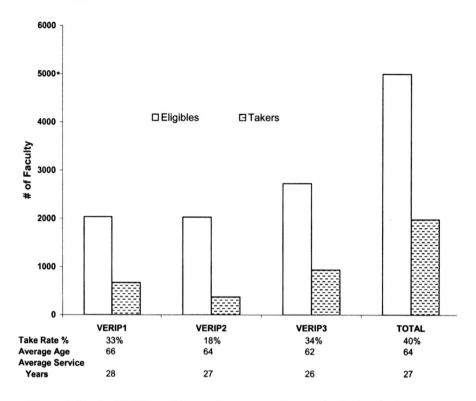

Figure 6. Faculty VERIP participants by program. Source: Author's calculations.

mal retirement age for University faculty). For VERIP 3 the average retirement age was 62, so a younger group of faculty retired with the changes in
eligibility and with the added incentive of this third program.

Figure 7 shows the take rate for various age ranges. Not surprisingly, older
eligible faculty tended to retire at a higher rate than younger eligible faculty.
Of special interest is the group who were 70 or older and eligible for one
or more VERIP programs. This group had the highest take rate of all; 110
of the 145 who were eligible chose to retire. However, the remaining 35 (24
percent) who did not retire might have to work for up to eight more years
before their pension would equal that offered under VERIP 3.

The average age of those eligible for a VERIP program who did not retire
was 60, and the average age of those who retired under these programs was
63.5. Those with more years of service also had a higher take rate, but this
effect was surprisingly modest. The average years of service of those eligible
who did not retire was 25.5 and of those who did retire was 26.6 years.

Campus variation. Overall, 1,984 ladder-rank faculty retired under all three

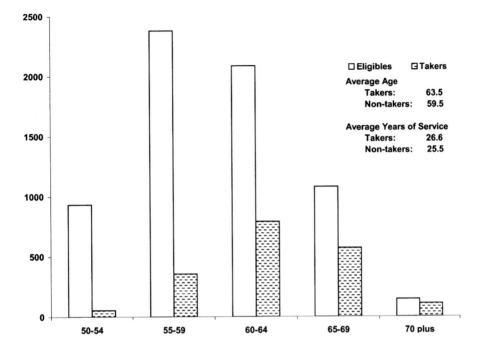

Figure 7. Acceptance rates of VERIP eligible faculty by age. Source: University of California, Office of the President, Academic Affairs.

VERIP programs. In April 1991 when the first election took place, the University's regular faculty numbered 9,802. By July 1994, more than 20 percent of those had retired under a VERIP program. In general, campuses with older faculties had higher take rates. These varied from 13 percent at the San Francisco health science campus to 27 percent at the Berkeley campus, in spite of the decreased eligibility criteria under VERIP 3 at Berkeley.

Disciplinary variation. Early retirement incentive programs were available to everyone who met the eligibility criteria. Growing or newer programs such as molecular biology and ethnic studies tended to have younger faculty than did stable, long-established programs such as engineering and physics. Reports after VERIP 1 were that engineering and physics programs were seriously impacted. However, after all three VERIP programs were completed, there were only small variations in take rate by discipline, as shown in Figure 8. It should not be assumed that the take rates were uniform within disciplines across all nine campuses. In fact, within disciplines, the pre-VERIP ages and years of service among faculty did vary across the campuses. Figure 8 shows only the systemwide averages. It is interesting to

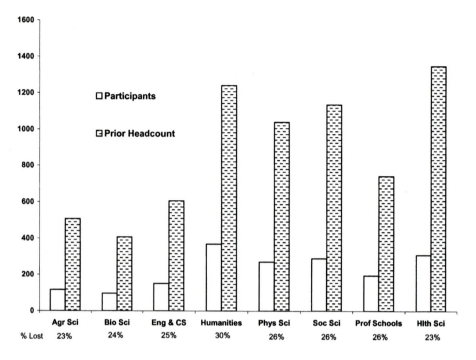

Figure 8. Faculty count prior to first VERIP, VERIP participants, and percent lost. Source: University of California, Office of the President, Academic Affairs.

note that disciplines where faculty might be expected to have other employment opportunities (such as engineering and computer science, biological sciences, and health science) had lower take rates than other disciplines, and humanities had the highest take rate of all.

Profiles of the "Takers"

It is difficult to characterize those who took the retirement incentives. A study of all UCLA faculty eligible for VERIP 3 examined publication output, and it found that the faculty with the most recent publications tended to retire at a slightly lower rate than faculty with fewer recent publications (Kim 1995). In addition, Figure 9 shows the variation of take rate with salary step. At the University of California, faculty are assigned a rank and step to chart their academic progress. Figure 9 shows the steps for the professor rank. Faculty who make normal progress are advanced to a higher step at a higher salary every three years. Thus, the salary step is a rough indicator of academic progress. In addition, those who do not advance beyond step 5 to higher levels are likely to have lower scholarly output. Faculty with higher

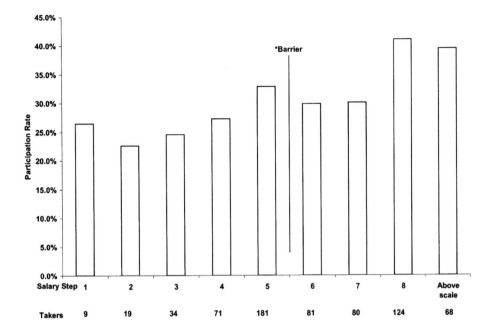

Figure 9. Number and acceptance rates of VERIP 3 participants, full professors by salary step. Promotions from step 5 to step 6 involved a more extensive and intensive review process than for promotions to steps 2–5. Source: University of California, Office of the President, Academic Affairs.

salaries tended to be older and in general did have a higher take rate, and faculty at step 5 did have a higher take rate than those at steps 6 and 7 (even though those at higher steps might be substantially older). In fact, immediately after the VERIP programs ended, an informal count identified very few faculty who retired under VERIP who then took regular full-time employment at other universities. One conclusion that may be drawn from this information is that the most outstanding faculty who would likely be those with other employment possibilities tended not to retire as readily as other faculty, but the correlations were modest.

After Retirement

After retirement, emeritus faculty tend to continue as active members of the university in research, department activities, and/or Academic Senate activities. The faculty who retired under the VERIP programs were no different. Prior to 1991, campuses recalled small numbers of faculty to active service, mainly to teach specific courses. Subsequently, the number of recall appointments increased and continues to remain high to meet the needs of instructional programs. At UCLA, most faculty who retired under VERIP remained active on campus at least immediately after they retired (Kim 1995). Eighty percent were recalled to active service, a few on contract and grant funds, but most were recalled to teach one or more courses, some without salary. Because the hiring of new faculty slowed considerably during the period of budgetary crisis, faculty who retired were often able to retain use of their offices and laboratories whether or not they were recalled to teach. Emeritus faculty remained engaged in research, and this prompted the university to create a special title for faculty who had retired but who wanted to apply for research grants and continued to have active research programs. Immediately following retirement, some faculty took other full or part-time work such as consulting, while only a small number retired completely from professional life. In a follow-up study of VERIP retirees in 1998, almost 70 percent of respondents to their survey of VERIP retirees were still working either full or part time, including 40 percent who continued to work part-time for the University of California (Kim 1998). The VERIP retirees reported a very high degree of satisfaction with their decision to retire and their current activities.

Academic Program Continuity

Because of these incentive programs for retirement, almost 2,000 tenured faculty left their university positions. Many had never planned their retirement. Others were in their late 50s and while they may have thought about retirement, they had not been intending to retire within three months' time, although they ended up doing just that. Departments normally have long notification of impending faculty retirement and can plan an orderly succession, but with the VERIP programs, departments had little or no time to plan. In addition, the timing of retirement for VERIP 2 was especially disruptive to departmental operations. There were 371 faculty who elected VERIP 2 in October 1992 who retired in the middle of the academic year, just as the second term began in January 1993. Faculty and their departments had no time to plan for the upcoming term. A retirement date of July 1 was therefore selected for faculty for VERIP 3, even though continuing budgetary constraints forced the retirement date for staff under VERIP 3 at an earlier date of November 1, 1993.

The disruption following retirement of significant numbers of faculty was ultimately confronted in a variety of ways. Following a break in service, faculty were permitted to be rehired at less than half-time, and many were eager to do so. Many retired faculty were willing to continue to teach on a recall basis or as volunteers. The number of lecturers, adjunct faculty, and visiting faculty showed little change. Almost no classes were canceled. The remaining faculty taught extra classes; some classes were larger when sections were consolidated.

Campuses were concerned that the departure of some of their most prestigious faculty would have an adverse effect on the stature of their departments. However the effect has generally been a positive one: stellar faculty remained active in their departments following the retirement, and the sudden retirement of so many faculty provided a unique opportunity to examine long-range academic planning and organization goals. Several campuses made difficult organizational changes in the wake of the VERIP programs. Overtime hiring of new faculty has been an overall benefit, and some older faculty cited the need for their departments to hire new faculty as among their reasons for electing to retire.

In addition, more than 10,000 staff employees retired under VERIP programs. This created problems for faculty as department support staff took advantage of the retirement incentive programs. On the other hand, research support staff is generally funded from extramural sources, and unlike state-supported staff, money was available to replace those retired research support staff.

Although the defined benefit retirement system is no longer as well funded as it was prior to the VERIP programs, faculty and staff who remain continue to make no direct contributions. The nature of the defined benefit plan means that remaining employees will continue to receive the pension to which they are entitled based on the defined benefit formula. In fact, the age factor profile has recently been changed from what it was during the VERIP programs (see Figure 1) to provide a more generous age factor for those from age 55 to 59, to "smooth" out the discontinuity in the age factor that existed between age 59 and 60. Remaining employees are not faced with the possibility of a reduced pension benefit even though the retirement system was able to fund all aspects of the VERIP program. Another complication has been the cost of replacing faculty.

As seen in Figure 10, as the budget crisis eased, faculty hiring has resumed to replace those faculty who retired with permanent new faculty. Even though the salaries of incoming faculty are normally lower than the faculty who retired, in many fields the cost of recruitment and start-up is high. In fact in some fields, such as business and economics, the salaries of new faculty may be even higher than initially forecasted.

Conclusion

From many points of view, the VERIP programs sponsored by the University of California were clearly successful. These programs reduced the university's payroll through voluntary retirement rather than through layoff or termination, mitigating the possibility of litigation. Generally, those who retired under these programs felt that they made the right decision. No one was forced to retire, and the incentives were generous. The resulting payroll reduction was sufficient to deal with severe cuts in state funding from

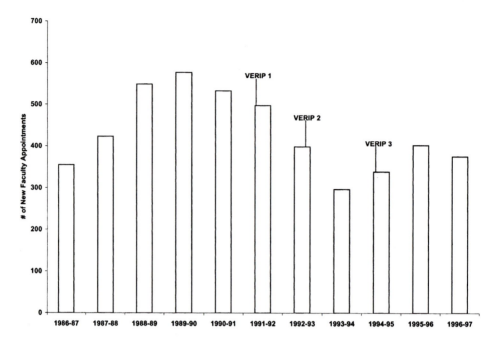

Figure 10. New appointments of ladder rank faculty. Source: University of California, Office of the President, Academic Affairs.

1991 to 1996. The university's retirement system was able to finance all aspects of the incentive programs and the VERIP programs made it possible to realize substantial savings in salary and benefits. In addition, sufficient resources remained in the pension fund to guarantee future defined benefits for remaining employees. By contrast, other universities must sometimes finance early retirement programs from university operating funds, and this can create serious funding problems in a budget crisis.

The University of California's academic program weathered the temporary reduction in faculty and support staff in a variety of ways. A major factor was the willingness of many retired faculty to remain part of the university community, to teach courses on a recall basis at low salaries or as volunteers, and to maintain laboratories and research projects as emeriti while continuing to attract research grants and superb graduate students. Remaining faculty took on additional teaching and service responsibilities, and had reduced staff support. In addition, the mass retirement of so many faculty in a short time provided a unique opportunity for campuses to consider major organizational changes in academic programs. Positions vacated are now being refilled with new faculty with fresh perspectives and in emerging areas. The quality of the University of California's academic programs today seems to be as high or higher than it was at the beginning of the decade.

Each time a new VERIP program was offered, the administration assured faculty and staff that it did not envision future programs. Although that was indeed the expectation at the time each of the programs offered, the continuing budgetary crisis necessitated three such programs. Were expectations raised of continued retirement incentive programs? Did faculty and staff defer their decision to retire in the expectation that something better would come along? It is impossible to answer those questions. However many faculty and staff continue to inquire about the possibility of a new retirement incentive, though another one seems remote. The extreme budgetary circumstances that gave rise to the VERIP programs early in the decade of the 1990s no longer exist.

In order to justify use of retirement system funds for a retirement incentive program, a surplus must exist, and the university would need to demonstrate a business necessity such as the one that arose in the early 1990s. University employees have made no retirement contribution to the defined benefit plan since 1990, but some time in the future, contributions will once again be required. Without a dramatic and looming catastrophe, both active employees and university administrators would be very displeased if retirement system funds were used for a retirement incentive, because that would hasten the day when the employer and employees would again have to make contributions to the defined benefit plan.

Additionally, the University of California is projecting an additional 63,000 students in the next 12 years, a 40 percent increase in the student body. A program to encourage wholesale retirements of faculty and staff at this point would be contrary to anticipated staffing needs for this massive enrollment increase. An employee benefits update in the summer of 1999 carried the following sidebar: "So here's the official word: No more VERIPs are anticipated at this time" (HR/Benefits Review 1999).

References

HR/Benefits Review. 1999. *California Human Resources and Benefits.* University of California, Summer.

Kim, Seongsu. 1995. "Early Retirement Incentives in a Restructuring Organization: The Case of University Professors." Ph.D. thesis, UCLA.

———. 1998. Seoul National University. Private communication, October.

Pencavel, John. 1997. "The Response of Employees to Severance Pay Incentives: Faculty of the University of California." Working Paper, Stanford University.

Chapter 7
Ending Mandatory Retirement in Two State Universities

Robert M. O'Neil

Elimination of mandatory retirement in some states and institutions began well in advance of national legislation affecting all higher education. In fact during the 1980s, I served as president of two major research universities that were forced by state law to eliminate any mandatory age for faculty retirement. The experiences in the two states (Wisconsin and Virginia) where I most closely observed "uncapping" were strikingly different. Wisconsin uncapped faculty retirement in 1983 by amending its age discrimination laws. As a result, the cap was lifted not only for University of Wisconsin faculty, but also for faculty at Beloit, Lawrence, Marquette, and the state's other private institutions (whose administrators were probably unaware of the change until well after it occurred). Maine and Florida were the only other states in which such comprehensive uncapping occurred.

On the fateful day that Wisconsin's legislature addressed this issue, I had asked for a chance to appear before the relevant state senate committee. Having been invited—more accurately, permitted, after an urgent plea—to testify against the proposed uncapping, I was hardly surprised to find the hearing room filled with senior citizens adamantly opposed to continued forced retirement. In such a setting, it would have been futile (indeed, counterproductive in terms of other university needs and priorities) to have flatly opposed a measure that was certain to pass. Instead, the university asked for two things that were later to be a focus both in Virginia and at the federal level: time for transition and authority to offer age-based retirement incentives. The Wisconsin lawmakers did give a brief grace period before the law became effective, but left the university on its own with regard to incentives.

The Virginia experience was different in every respect. There was no chance to testify; uncapping was done quietly in the budget bill; and the university presidents were simply informed as a courtesy on the eve of passage. The issue there was public employment, so the uncapping spared Washington and Lee, Richmond, Hampton, and other private peers. This time there was no grace period; in fact, the effective date was made retroactive as an "emergency" bill. University administrators thus faced the very delicate issue of how to treat senior colleagues who were about to reach 70 and had completed filing their retirement papers before the enactment but after the effective date of the uncapping. In one instance the story had a happy ending. One of our most productive scholars—he still is so to this day—asked to stay and the university was only too delighted to rescind his retirement. For a few other late sexagenarians whose papers had been processed before the effective date of the uncapping, there was no such reprieve.

What the Virginia legislature denied in time they more than made up in authorization of incentives. While the scope of the authority was quite limited—1½ percent of the tenured faculty in any given year—the institutions were given substantial flexibility in designing plans. The University of Virginia was able to base judgments about eligibility not only on the obvious factors of age and length of service, but also on an individualized assessment of relative institutional need by discipline and academic unit. Thus a professor of curriculum and instruction in the Education School might be favored for incentive retirement over a demographically comparable colleague in a higher demand field such as computer science. Though some initially raised concerns about the legality of such a subjective element in the equation, it seems to have stood the test of time and has expanded the utility of an otherwise rather limited incentive program. Any incentive plan that does not take some account of relative need is likely to overshoot the mark.

The federal experience followed close upon Virginia's uncapping. National uncapping was legislated in 1986, but it was delayed pending the outcome of a National Research Council (NRC) committee study of which I was a member. Committee membership had a Noah's Ark quality—one person from a senior private institution, one from a community college, one from the health sciences, and a few of us less easily typed. The only standard I could perceive was that each member had to be acceptable to so many organizations—Association of American Universities (AAU), American Council on Education (ACE), American Association of University Professors (AAUP), American Association of Retired Persons (AARP), and many others—that only the bland or the omnicompetent could have survived. Yet the group functioned effectively and well, produced a report on time, said what it needed to say, and dissolved.

Some may still feel the committee was unduly compliant—that it should have fought for an extension of the cap. The committee proceeded on the assumption that it did have a choice, whether or not Congress would have acceded had it reached a different conclusion. In the end, the committee recommended letting the cap expire because we believed that was the right thing to do. Several factors shaped this conclusion. We were genuinely concerned about prolonging the appearance of special pleading by the professorate, at a time when academics could not be said to be universally popular. We were also persuaded that fears expressed in some quarters about the impact of uncapping had been exaggerated.

While a few institutions might suffer genuine hardship during the period of transition, the experience of uncapped states—Wisconsin being high on the list—suggested that most institutions could cope better than the skeptics and doomsayers had warned. In fact, at only one university—Yale—did more than 75 percent of the tenured faculty remain active until their 70th year, and thus might be presumed to have been involuntarily retired prior to the uncapping (National Research Council 1991). Even at such prestigious places as Michigan and Berkeley these percentages were under 40 percent (National Research Council 1991). In fact, one oddity in the data was the striking similarity of actual retirement patterns at comparable institutions with pension plans as disparate as those at Berkeley (defined benefit) and Michigan (defined contribution). There seemed to be no principled way in which to create an exception or dispensation for a small number of private universities that the NRC committee believed would experience transitional hardship. Also the committee saw no solid reason why universities and their tenured professors should not be treated roughly the same as the rest of society. The group looked closely at data that correlated productivity and age in academe, and found striking differences by discipline. People in the sciences do tend to peak early in publications and discoveries—though it would be quite unfair to infer that even a physicist is no longer useful after 50. The humanities showed a steady rise in published scholarship, into and even beyond their 60s, with some striking evidence of late blooming. In the social sciences, a third and again different pattern appeared: a sort of bimodality, with productivity peaking in the late 20s and 30s and reviving again in the mid- to late 50s, with a slump in early middle age.

In any event, these data suggested the fallacy of the claim that academic institutions needed to send their elder members out to pasture at a predetermined age. So long as there remained ways in which to address special cases —including medical disability as a valid basis for terminating even a tenured appointment, which it has always been—the need for a continued cap simply could not be shown. And while a transitional period might have been helpful to the few most severely impacted institutions, uncapping would surely eventually have come to pass. The most the committee could possibly have done would be to stick a finger in the dike—a step that seemed unwise and unwarranted.

There was one other premise to the committee's conclusion, and here the group may have been naïve. The committee pleaded for Congress to grant flexibility in offering age-based retirement incentives. It noted the precarious uncertainty of the situation with respect to defined contribution plans—even though defined benefit plans seemed to be exempt from age discrimination claims for the offering to their faculties of such creative inducements. It assumed Congress would view this request as a kind of trade-off; in effect, the commission could fully support uncapping if—but only if—it anticipated greater flexibility than a narrow reading of the age discrimination laws then afforded. The subsequent delay in responding to this request was understandable. Congress took the bait and—for a time—left higher education in the trap. But as David Raish (this volume) shows, Congress has now acted to make it easier for faculty and administrators in higher education to design cost-effective retirement incentives.

Another relevant datum here was actual institutional experience. The longest uncapped senior institution, the University of Florida experienced no change in the aggregate or average age of retirement. Also there were two trends among those taking advantage of uncapping: a very small number of people stayed on for a very long time, and a much larger number stayed for a brief time beyond 70—brief in part because they could then say they had made a wholly voluntary choice of retirement date, and in part because of the minimum distribution pension requirements which made that choice less than completely voluntary. Of course, in 1997 Congress changed the minimum distribution requirements, too, so that those who now choose to continue working at the same institution are not required to draw down their retirement savings. To test the possibility that climate and quality of life might have skewed the sample, it was important to turn again to Wisconsin, where by 1991 uncapping had been around for seven years. Happily, the patterns varied little between Madison and Gainesville; similarities among the types of faculties seemed to transcend not only geography, but also dramatic differences in pension plans. On the basis of such admittedly incomplete data as these, it appeared that the sky had not yet fallen where uncapping had been in effect for some time, and that it probably would not fall elsewhere after uncapping.

Some institutions may well have quite different experiences. Some may also be naïve.

There is a related issue, namely that tenure and retirement are linked. Tenure will make implementation of uncapping more difficult for some universities. Even here, it is hard to imagine that a responsible institution without tenure (Hampshire, for example) would be completely free of those constraints. Would the presence of tenure create serious enough problems to justify a continued cap? The NRC Committee, which was composed of administration as well as faculty, was unanimous in its negative response: whatever the complications of tenure, they did not warrant continued mandatory retirement. That is, the committee believed that tenure was not the cause of the problem, nor would its curtailment provide a solution. Rather, it recognized the importance of more rigorous standards in the initial granting of tenure—something we should have been imposing anyway. The committee also acknowledged the value of periodic review for all faculty, tenured or not, though it warned against the abuse of such reviews as a subterfuge for discrimination on the basis of age or viewpoint. And AAUP standards do not preclude dismissal of tenure faculty for cause, for proven medical disability, or on the basis of demonstrated financial exigency or the bond fide discontinuance of a program or department for educational reasons. Given those recognized alternatives and experience, it seemed that institutions would be able to adapt to the change.

Retirement incentives, valuable though they surely are, should not be viewed as a panacea, but rather as one element in personnel and policy planning. Lawyers are already likely to share this view. The audience for whom this caution should be stressed includes personnel directors, human resource experts, and academic administrators of a more general background. There is a belief that incentives are the cure for whatever problems the ending of mandatory retirement may create. The intervening years have taught us some of the limitations in that assumption. For one, the people we might most hope to encourage to retire are, because of their typically modest salaries, least likely to be induced by such an opportunity. They are also least likely to be able to find supplemental or successor employment prospects to mitigate the loss of income even under a generous incentive program. The professors who find such an option most attractive—indeed, for whom it may be an offer they can't refuse—tend to be the most respected of our colleagues, whom we would least wish to lose.

In this sense, several institutions—perhaps most poignantly the University of California during the final voluntary early retirement program (VERIP) cycles—set out a breakfast for the canary, only to have the cat steal it and then found themselves without cats enough to combat the next invasion of rats and mice. Such experiences heightened the need for creative programs that will in effect create separate feeding stations for the canaries, while the cats keep doing what we want them to do. One attractive approach is the institutional and unit need that was an important part of the University of Virginia retirement incentive program. That one factor, among several, helped to make the incentive program far more efficient than it would otherwise have been. The sole negative effect of Virginia's program was dissatisfaction on the part of a few prospective retirees who were in "low-need" disciplines, and thus could not claim an incentive even though they met the other criteria and would like to have retired early. But that was a small price to pay for being largely spared the agonies of wholesale early exodus of the best and still brightest that many of our sister institutions have encountered. This is but one possible way of tailoring the program better and more precisely to suite the university's need and overall personnel goals.

Conclusion

Uncapping has been very much a part of the higher education vocabulary for at least a decade and a half. Many dreaded it, yet knew it would eventually occur. We have begun to come to terms with it, more easily in some cases, less easily in others—and with great difficulty in certain instances. In sum, we have sought to do our level best to help mitigate the worst effects of what is for some institutions a dramatically changed environment. Lessons from Wisconsin, Virginia, Florida, and other early uncappers have helped us find solutions to these challenges.

References

National Research Council, Committee on Ending Mandatory Retirement in Higher Education. 1991. *Ending Mandatory Retirement for Tenured Faculty: The Consequences for Higher Education*, ed. P. Brett Hammond and Harriet P. Morgan. Washington, D.C.: National Academy Press.

Chapter 8
Intangible and Tangible Retirement Incentives

John Keefe

A large number of colleges and universities have designed programs that provide incentives for faculty to retire earlier than they might otherwise choose. Other chapters in this volume offer surveys and case studies of retirement plan features and behavior, including how they were developed as well as statistics on faculty acceptance. This chapter takes a different tack by examining the early retirement decision primarily from the employee's perspective — that is, how an individual might weigh the choice between full-time professorship and part-time work or full retirement. We find that in designing retirement incentive programs, administrators and faculty should place an equal emphasis on how the intangible aspects of retirement will compare to the accomplishment and collegiality of teaching life. The importance of these intangibles varies from person to person and will likely be different from institution to institution. Nonmonetary factors are difficult to sort out, and may require more flexible offerings than administrators are accustomed to making. Nevertheless, the lifestyle and self-esteem factors are often as important to a plan's success as are the cash incentives.

The process of identifying the relevant nonmonetary variables, and then measuring the value or level of utility they provide to different individuals, is problematic. Consider, for instance, differences in lifestyle preferences and other factors expressed in national retirement statistics. Americans are retiring, on average, at younger and younger ages. As Dora Costa points out in her important work on the history of retirement, people no doubt have monetary justifications for retiring sooner, but, monetary factors being equal, nonmonetary factors help explain why some people retire sooner than others (Costa 1998).

The Decision of the Early Retiree

One approach is to think about how a faculty member might evaluate his or her own well being. Typical early retirement offers result in a mix of factors that are both monetary (such as the value of a lump sum incentive payment for early retirement, part-time salary, or ongoing health insurance) and non-monetary (such as the rewards of pursuing hobbies or travel earlier than would otherwise be the case). The retiree's challenge is to weigh the prospective value of the mix of the new options against the expected value of full-time employment.

Predicting how an employee will react to an early retirement offer is complicated. Individuals have different economic situations, lifestyle preferences, and views of the future. To an individual who has saved enough to fund a comfortable retirement, the monetary options of early retirement — or even a continuing salary from full-time employment — may have less influence on the retirement decision than the nonmonetary options. For a person for whom working is a hardship, due perhaps to illness, the non-monetary value of continuing to work full time may be relatively small, or even negative. On the other hand, a person who has few interests outside academia, or who has particularly strong attachments to the university, may place a relatively low value on the nonmonetary aspects of retired life.

Not only will the estimate of the future value of an early retirement choice vary across individuals, but also a given individual's view of the decision to retire early may change over time. Between the ages of 60 and 70, the relative importance of salary, collegiality, and career achievement can vary substantially. Moreover, there is great uncertainty surrounding the retirement decision. Most people can only guess at how well they will adapt to leaving their institutions, whether they will enjoy the sudden abundance of free time, and what standard of living their retirement income will provide over the long run.

A Complete Example: Incentive Payment

To consider a hypothetical example, assume that a professor age 62 years and who has planned to retire at 65, is offered a lump sum cash incentive to retire early. How can she determine her "best" alternative?

By simplifying what is almost always a complex personal decision, we can examine the question in a more rigorous way. The pertinent period of time is only the three years subject to early retirement; our professor had planned to retire at 65 anyway. Therefore, during the prospective early retirement years of 62 to 64, how can the professor estimate the future value of continuing to work, versus taking the early retirement package?

Her first option is staying in her job full time for three more years, earn-

Table 1. Retirement Versus Continued Work

	Full-time work	*Retirement*
Primary income	Salary Saving for retirement	Lump-sum payment
Secondary income	Consulting	Consulting
Work life	Teaching and research	Postuniversity study
Nonwork life	"Being a professor at the university" Community Prestige	Time with spouse and family Travel, hobbies, etc.

Source: See text.

ing the monetary value of salary and retirement contributions from the university, plus any consulting or other nonteaching income, and enjoying the personal satisfaction of teaching, research, and service to the faculty and students. Her alternative is to accept the university's early retirement offer and retire immediately. In so doing she would collect the lump sum retirement incentive and gain the nonmonetary value of increased leisure time. However, she would forgo the salary to be earned until 65, and her pension account would be smaller, having missed three years of contributions (a possible indirect effect is that consulting and other outside income might drop off if she were no longer affiliated with her institution). She would also give up the nonmoney benefits of teaching and research. Table 1 details the monetary and nonmonetary options of this example.

A little more background is needed to evaluate such a decision. First, we have to know the standing of the professor's retirement account, to determine whether retirement is even a realistic choice. Can she retire at 62—living on the lump sum plus savings until 65—and then have an adequate income for the rest of her life? If not, her decision is straightforward. She needs to keep working until 65, and perhaps beyond.

Let's assume that the professor does have sufficient savings and retirement funds. The relative values of factors she has to trade off are her salary versus the lump sum, and the value of work versus retirement. To express the point more formally, we can hypothesize that the professor will accept early retirement when the total estimated future value from early retirement in the years 62 through 64 is greater than the value of being a full-time professor. We then decide by comparing the monetary and nonmonetary aspects of working and retirement, as illustrated in Tables 2 and 3.

During the years of age 62 to 64, the professor would receive after-tax payments worth $180,000 were she to continue working, and $75,000 were she to accept the early retirement offer. The nonmonetary value of working

Table 2. Value of Working Until 65

Monetary assumptions:	
Three years salary	$250,000 before taxes
	$150,000 after taxes
Three years of institution's retirement contributions	$ 30,000 after taxes
Total monetary value	$180,000 after taxes
Nonmonetary assumptions: value of teaching, scholarship, service = $3W$	

Source: See text.
W = nonmonetary value of working.

Table 3. Value of Early Retirement, 62–64

Monetary assumptions:	
Early retirement lump sum	$80,000 before taxes
	$50,000 after taxes
Medical insurance	$25,000 after taxes
Total monetary value	$75,000 after taxes
Nonmonetary Assumptions:	
Value of retirement activities = $3R$	
Uncertainty of benefits of retirement = ε	

Source: See text.
R = nonmonetary value of retiring.

for one year is represented by W, and the nonmonetary value of retiring is represented by R.

In addition to creating variables to represent the nonmonetary values of work and retirement, we have introduced an uncertainty factor, ε, to represent the uncertainty of the benefits of retirement. Although this uncertainty cannot be quantified and varies from person to person, it is important to recognize. Retirement is a decision a person makes only once, and the cost of a bad choice is very high. The value of ε is negative in many cases, but because it is not quantifiable, we have assigned it a zero value and left the variable in the expressions simply as a reminder of its importance.

Two additional monetary variables might be considered in the case of early retirement. First, our professor might be able start drawing social security payments at age 62, and thus receive an additional monetary benefit for retirement in the years 62 through 64. We have ignored this income for the sake of simplicity, but we note that in many cases it might be an important cash flow to the early retiree, and thus tilt the analysis in favor of selecting early retirement. Second, we have ignored the value of a retirement account or other savings on which she might draw before age 65. In drawing down a retirement account she would be better off by the amount of the income, but worse off by the amount of the reduced savings, so again for simplicity we omit this from the analysis.

Should our professor accept the offer? The arithmetic says that she should retire early if

$$3R + \$75,000 + \varepsilon > 3W + \$180,000.$$

That is, the prospective retiree should accept this offer if the intangible value of being retired for three years, $3R$, discounted for uncertainty, ε, is worth \$105,000 or more than the intangible value of continuing to work for three years. Looking at the expression in terms of one year gives this relationship:

$$\text{Intangibles of Retirement} = \text{Intangibles of Work} + \$35,000.$$

Thus the structure of this offer puts a very high implicit cash value on retiring. Our example professor should accept only under unusual circumstances. One case is where the value of retirement is especially high to her, for instance, if an attractive job offer has happened to come along at the same time as the early retirement offer. Similarly, she should accept if, for some reason, the value of hobbies or travel in those three years is especially high (in most cases, however, she would be able to hike the Appalachians or collect snails at age 65, and come out ahead financially through continuing to work). Another case where she should accept the early retirement offer is where the value of work is especially low, or even negative. This offer might prevail where the professor or her spouse is suffering an illness, or where the professor has completely lost her taste for teaching.

The arithmetic tells us that to make the offer of early retirement as attractive as continuing to work, the school's lump sum payment has to make up for (1) the lost salary and pension contribution in years 62 to 64; (2) the difference, if any, between the intangibles of work and the intangibles of retirement; and (3) the uncertainty of retiring three years early. (A professor who thinks in plain English might express the offer this way: "They are asking me to give up the work I like and have done well for thirty years, and to start a retirement I am not sure I am ready for. Maybe I'm better off working for the three years and earning the extra \$100,000.")

Adding a Phased Retirement Option

We now examine the decision to accept or reject a "phased retirement" offer. Instead of the lump sum incentive offer, let's assume the same professor receives an offer where she would work half-time for the years 62 to 64 and receive 50 percent of her salary. Pension contributions would be made on the reduced salary, and she would retain health benefits at the same cost as under full-time employment.

Table 4. Phased Retirement Until 65

Monetary assumptions:	
Three years salary	$125,000 before taxes
	$ 75,000 after taxes
Three years retirement contributions	$ 15,000 after taxes
Total monetary value of phased retirement	$ 90,000
Nonmonetary assumptions:	
Value of teaching, scholarship and service	$= (3 \times 0.5W) = 1.5W$
Value of retirement activities	$= (3 \times 0.5R) = 1.5R$
Uncertainty of retiring	$= 0.5 \times \varepsilon$

Source: See text.
R = nonmonetary value of retiring.
W = nonmonetary value of working.

In this case, our professor is enjoying a portion of the nonmonetary benefits of both working and retired life, and she faces only part of the uncertainty of retirement. (For the moment we have assumed that each factor is reduced by half, but we will demonstrate later that the proportions of work, salary and retirement are crucial to the analysis). Table 4 summarizes the assumptions.

Under these assumptions the decision-making expression becomes:

$$1.5W + 1.5R + \$90,000 + (0.5 \times \varepsilon) > 3W + \$180,000.$$

That is, if the sum of the nonmonetary attributes of a half-working and half-retired life, plus the $90,000 to be received from working part time, are greater than the value of working plus salary, then our professor should accept phased retirement. Working through the arithmetic gives this result in terms of one year's worth of retirement:

$$\text{intangibles of retirement} = \text{intangibles of work} + \$60,000.$$

Assuming these proportions, this offer is *less* attractive than the previous lump sum example by the amount of the incentive payment. That is, to a person who accepts this offer, the implicit cash value of retiring is $60,000 over the value of working. However, if the assumptions are altered so that (1) the arrangement calls for 50 percent of full-time pay for 33 percent of full-time teaching, and that (2) the balance between the intangible benefits is changed—so that we assume that our professor manages to give up *less* of the value of work and get *more* benefit from retirement—the decision equation becomes:

$$2W + 2R + \$120,000 + (0.5 \times E) > 3W + \$180,000.$$

In terms of one year, this expression becomes:

$$\text{intangibles of retirement} > 0.5(\text{intangibles of work}) + 30{,}000.$$

Under the assumption that the phased retiree can keep more of the benefits of work (perhaps due to participation in a special senior faculty advisor program, or other measures that place an emphasis on the contributions of retiring professors) and at the same time add more of the benefits of retirement (due to a lighter teaching load), the option of early retirement becomes more attractive. Accepting early retirement is twice as valuable in the second phased example as in the first, and more than twice as valuable as the incentive payment example.

Prospective Retiree "Types"

We can categorize the decisionmakers according to their preferences — grouping them into "types" — and thus account for the consequent range of decisions (Harsanyi 1967, 1968). Four different types within the population of prospective academic retirees may be identified, according to individuals' utility for the nonmonetary aspects of work life and retired life. Prospective retirees who assign a high value (or low value) to teaching, research, school service and collegiality are ranked "high W" (or "low W"). Prospects who place a high value (or low value) on travel, hobbies or time spent with family are ranked "high R" (or "low R"). Other determinants of a potential retiree's R status, as noted earlier, would be his or her employment options outside the university, or a personal or spouse health limitation that would make working full-time less attractive.

Table 5 lays out the four types in this analysis. A person who is satisfied with working full time and has little interest in travel or hobbies — at least during the years 62 to 64, the time subject to consideration for early retirement — would be ranked "high W, low R." A professor with both a high level of current job satisfaction and excellent work prospects outside the university would be ranked "high W, high R." As mentioned earlier, the shifting of a person's preferences over time could mean that an individual's type could change as well.

In general, prospective retirees with low W values would probably be attracted to incentive payment plans, as they are giving up little job satisfaction. Those with high W values, on the other hand, would likely want to keep a hand in teaching or research, and might thus be more attracted to offers involving part-time teaching assignments. People with high R values are more likely to accept early retirement offers than those with low values.

Two analyses examining the early retirement offerings made to professors in the University of California (UC) system have used a similar typology:

Table 5. "Types" of Faculty by Nonmonetary Values

	Low W	*High* W
Low *R*	Low value to working	High value to working
	Low value to retirement	Low value to retirement
High *R*	Low value to working	High value to retirement
	High value to working	High value to retirement

Source: See text.
W = the nonmonetary value of working.

Switkes (this volume) and Pencavel (1997). From personnel dossiers of faculty eligible for three waves of early retirement incentive offers, Pencavel developed profiles on those likely to participate in UC's early retirement programs. He found that individuals who accepted the offers tended to be older and earned lower salaries. Both Pencavel and Switkes indicate that the UC plans hit their mark, by encouraging retirement by less productive faculty while not causing the more productive faculty to leave. In particular, in one wave of offers, only 6 percent of faculty in their late 50s accepted, versus nearly 60 percent of those in their late 60s. They also found that individuals turning down early retirement offers tended to earn much higher salaries than those who accepted, suggesting that the more accomplished and active scholars (the high *W* group) stayed while their less productive colleagues (the low *W* group) chose to retire. Last, faculty rejecting the early retirement incentives were entitled to pensions averaging only 62 percent of final salary, while those accepting were slated for a replacement rate of 75 percent. A higher replacement rate would reduce some of the financial uncertainty surrounding retirement (the ε term in the expressions above).

When an institution is designing an early retirement plan, identifying types among the targeted faculty is crucial. Once the needs and preferences of the targets are understood, administrators can then create incentives that will encourage the redundant professors to leave or cut back, while reducing the risk of adverse selection (that is, losing key senior faculty as a result of offering the wrong incentives).

What Does All This Mean?

Our analysis suggests three conclusions that may be useful to administrators in the real world:

- The size of incentive payments is *not* the most important variable in an early retirement decision.
- The most important variables are the prospective retiree's intangible re-

wards from work and retirement. In most circumstances, these factors are not under the administrator's control.

- Early retirement is not an effective form of performance management.

Money by itself—at least, in amounts affordable to most institutions—will likely have little impact on the early retirement decision. If a tenured professor is unwilling to retire because he needs the money, then an institution probably will have to pay the professor at least as much as his salary to leave. If he has already provided for retirement, but cannot imagine a life without teaching, the institution will be at a disadvantage in encouraging his retirement if its only tool is a payment incentive.

While it is difficult to place dollar values on the intangibles of work, it is clear from the low acceptance rates of most programs that faculty value these as highly as cash. Thus if an institution can meaningfully enhance the status of retired professors, design an appealing part-time program, or otherwise make retirement into a "win–win" situation for both the professor and the institution, a greater acceptance rate may result.

Some institutions have undertaken unconventional strategies to encourage early retirement, with the goal of reducing the nonmonetary value of professorship, including enforcing tenure review, appropriating office space, and otherwise making life difficult for prospective retiree. We would not recommend these approaches, however, as they are harsh for the employee and may send undesired signals to the next generation of senior faculty. Another option—one requiring a long-term view on the university's part—would be to carefully study professor demographics, share the information and the university's goals with the faculty, and encourage them to contemplate retirement or part-time teaching well before any bottlenecks occur. With a better understanding of the university's reasons for the early retirement transaction, and a clearer vision of the retired life five or ten years in advance, academics would suffer less uncertainty and might possibly welcome early retirement offers.

Conclusion

In designing a retirement plan, administrators must place an equal emphasis on how the intangible aspects of retirement will compare to the attractions of teaching life. In developing retirement offers, administrators should take into account what factors will appeal to different groups, or "types," within the population of prospective retirees. Nonmonetary factors are difficult to sort out, and may require more flexible offerings than administrators are accustomed to making, but the lifestyle and self-esteem factors are as important to a plan's success as the cash incentives.

By their nature, however, these techniques have limitations, and they must be developed and applied carefully. It is difficult for administrators to assess an objective value for the nonmonetary factors embedded in an offer, or predict how employees will react to them. Nonetheless, the intangibles are an important part of each person's retirement decision, and should be considered alongside retirement income and incentive payments.

Dr. Yaw Nyarko of New York University contributed to the game theory analysis in this essay.

References

Costa, Dora L. 1998. *The Evolution of Retirement: An American Economic History, 1880–1990.* Chicago: University of Chicago Press.

Harsanyi, J. C. 1967, 1968. "Games with Incomplete Information Played by Bayesian Players." Parts I, II, III. *Management Science* 3, 5, 7, 14.

Pencavel, John. 1997. "The Response of Employees to Severance Pay Incentives: Faculty of the University of California, 1991–1994." Working paper, Stanford University, July.

Switkes, Ellen. This volume. "The University of California Voluntary Early Retirement Incentive Programs."

U.S. Department of Education, National Center for Education Statistics. 1997a. *Digest of Education Statistics, 1997.* NCES 98-015. Washington, D.C.: NCES.

———. 1997b. *Retirement Plans and Other Departure Plans of Instructional Faculty and Staff in Higher Education Institutions.* NCES 98-254. Washington, D.C.: NCES.

Von Neumann, John and Oscar Morgenstern. 1947. *Theory of Games and Economic Behavior.* 2nd ed. Princeton, N.J.: Princeton University Press.

1998 Higher Education Directory. 1998. Falls Church Va.: Higher Education Publishers.

Chapter 9
Faculty Retirement: Reflections on Experience in an Uncapped Environment

Sharon P. Smith

In 1986 Congress passed the Amendments to the Age Discrimination in Employment Act of 1967 (ADEA) and abolished mandatory retirement[1]; subsequently these legislative amendments went into effect for tenured faculty. The 1986 amendments had allowed seven years for study of their potential impact, so that a permanent exemption could be sought if analysis suggested that uncapping of mandatory retirement for tenured faculty would have an adverse impact on the quality of higher education. Two studies undertaken to explore the consequences of these actions for the higher education community concluded that no special exemption was warranted and that uncapping should commence on January 1, 1994, as legislated.[2] Now, after more than five years of actual experience with uncapping, it is timely to consider whether these judgments still stand.

As we shall show, available evidence so far suggests little change in the principal conclusions from the earlier analyses. Uncapping itself should cause little concern for the quality of higher education where institutions have reliable processes to ensure that tenured faculty maintain a record of good performance. If, however, mandatory retirement was used as a substitute for facing the need to create incentives to maintain effectiveness and monitor performance, then under these conditions, uncapping may prolong problems of poor performance that probably began ten or more years before age 70. Uncapping does raise some concern with respect to increases in the cost of higher education. The principal source of alarm here is not anticipated lower levels of replacement (senior faculty who are assumed to be relatively highly paid being replaced by newly minted faculty at lower rates). Rather, a much more serious concern is that institutions will unnecessarily introduce costly retirement incentive plans that become entitlements and escalate faculty compensation costs.

Uncapping: Origin and Implications

Although the legislative effort to eliminate age discrimination in employment was launched at the 1961 White House Conference on Aging, it was not until 1967 that the ADEA was enacted, thus providing federal protection against age-related employment practices for those between the ages of 40 and 65.[3] However, mandatory retirement below age 65 was still allowable in the initial legislation provided this requirement was part of a bona fide pension plan. These protections were expanded in subsequent amendments in 1978 — raising the upper end of the covered group from 65 to 70 — and in 1986 — eliminating the upper end entirely. Advocates for the elderly cheered what they saw as a twofold legislative contribution that benefited individuals and the economy by protecting the rights of the elderly to work and in allocating these resources to their highest valued uses by enabling what is presumably the most productive contribution of those elderly who are willing and able to do so.

It is important to recognize that age discrimination is distinct in that it is directed against individuals who may have been highly valued at younger ages. Indeed it is not directed against the employee "because of who the worker *is*" but rather affects individuals because of "what they *have become*" (DiGiovanni 1989: 2). Thus, the rationale behind age discrimination is that age is inevitably accompanied by a decline in performance and effectiveness. Implicit in the concern over faculty effectiveness is the recognition that individual and institutional vitality are strongly correlated. Age becomes an instrument to identify effectiveness. The elimination of mandatory retirement, in contrast, is a triumph for what Berkowitz (1985, p. 113) terms an "article of faith" among gerontologists: that chronological age is irrelevant. However, as Berkowitz further observes:

That sword cuts both ways. Some older people are competent past the age of retirement and some younger people are incompetent prior to the age of retirement. Eliminating the compulsory retirement age means that we have to get serious about tests of performance for younger workers. (133–34)

The original ADEA had little impact on retirement rules in higher education, as almost all institutions of higher education had mandatory retirement ages of 65 or higher. Beginning with the 1978 amendments, the legislation had treated tenured faculty as a special category. When the upper end of the protected class was lifted to 70 in 1978, representatives of higher education raised concerns that a shortage of jobs for young scholars would result. Accordingly, the effective date for this change for tenured faculty was delayed until July 1, 1982, to allow time for study and a request for a permanent exemption. Many institutions raised their age of mandatory retirement to 70 before that date; others waited until required to do so.

Clark and Hammond (this volume) observe that with the elimination of mandatory retirement individual tenured faculty have, in effect, been granted an additional contractual benefit. Tenure becomes a life contract and all retirement is voluntary. The American Association of University Professors (1989) has suggested that tenure in an uncapped environment

means that faculty members have tenure until *they* choose to retire, absent cause for dismissal or financial exigency. But it means, moreover, that by law their terms and conditions of employment cannot be different, because of their age, from those of their younger colleagues.

In the capped environment, mandatory retirement was viewed by many as a "civilized" way to handle certain older faculty after many years of service, to "carry the obsolescent or somnolent (but not incompetent) faculty member along for a period of years, so long as the prospect of a definite date of separation looms ever on the horizon and ever closer" (Finkin 1989: 98). Hansen has suggested that the ultimate downside implication of uncapping is that all tenured faculty would have the opportunity "to continue teaching until the infirmities of old age caught up with them or they died with the chalk still clutched in their fingers (1985: 28). This possibility raised grave concerns throughout higher education. Rosovsky most clearly articulated the extent of that distress:

No institution interested in preserving quality can tolerate a growing gerontocracy that necessarily brings with it declining productivity. The disastrous effect on young scholars surely needs no elaboration. If ever mandatory university retirement is deemed to be age discrimination, an alternative mechanism will have to be found to accomplish the same purpose. . . . Older professors could increasingly keep out the young, and that is bad. Lesser opportunities could lead the young to be ever less interested in academic careers—a sad picture. (1990: 211–12)

These concerns have several dimensions. The central question is, of course, when all retirement is voluntary, will any faculty volunteer? If the answer to this question is no, then there may be important implications for: job opportunities for new faculty—either "new" to the profession or "new" to the particular institution in question; the success of affirmative action initiatives intended to make a faculty population that historically had been predominantly white male more representative of the population at large; the cost of higher education[4]; and the quality of higher education. Put in simplistic terms, the questions are:

• If faculty do not have to retire, will they?
• If faculty do not retire, does it matter and why?

Estimates of the Impacts of Uncapping: Ex Ante

Two studies of uncapping were completed during the period from 1986 until 1994. The first to be initiated, the Project on Faculty Retirement (PFR), was not intended to address the potential implications of uncapping for all higher education in the United States. Instead, to keep the study manageable (and based on the principal interest of its leading source of funding — the Andrew W. Mellon Foundation), the focus was restricted to research and doctorate-granting universities and selective liberal arts colleges.[5] Because a number of states had already eliminated mandatory retirement by state law, it was possible to include both capped and uncapped institutions in public research universities and liberal arts colleges in the data sample collected. The second study, initiated by the National Research Council's Committee on Mandatory Retirement in Higher Education (NRC), was mandated by law to address the potential effects of uncapping on *all* colleges and universities and faculty members. Both the PFR and the NRC reached the same conclusions:

- There is little basis for concern about the impact of uncapping, as very few faculty will choose to remain beyond age 70.
- At some research universities a substantial proportion of faculty will choose to remain beyond age 70, but the majority of those who do stay on will be vital contributors to the educational process.

Moreover, these institutions tend to have large endowments and thus have the means to offer selective retirement incentive programs to targeted areas, when turnover is needed.

The data clearly indicated that the existence of a mandatory retirement law did not prevent the presence of active faculty beyond the mandatory retirement age nor does the absence of a mandatory retirement law eliminate retirement of faculty at or before what had been the mandatory retirement age. The difference is that in a capped environment, the decision to remain beyond the mandatory retirement age rests with the institution, whereas in an uncapped environment, the decision to retire or remain rests with the individual faculty member.

The PFR data on flows into and out of tenure showed characteristic differences by type of institution. At liberal arts colleges, most faculty arrive early in their careers without tenure and, if subsequently tenured, they remain at that institution until retirement. At private universities, in contrast, faculty are nearly as likely to be appointed with tenure as to be promoted to tenure. At public universities, the pattern falls between these two. On average, hires with tenure take place at a later age (early 40s) than promotions to tenure (mid to late 30s), though the dispersion is such that the differences would not be judged statistically significant. Many of the hires with tenure take place at much later ages: 20 percent of these hires in private universities were at age 50 or older. These observations call into question the widely assumed replacement effect—that is, the expectation that relatively highly paid retiring faculty would be replaced by newly minted, untenured, and relatively lowly paid assistant professors. Instead, the retiree might be replaced by a newly hired but senior and possibly more distinguished and more highly paid faculty member. Even in cases where the new hire is newly minted, in many disciplines the market rate for the new hire may exceed the salary of a long-term faculty member.[6]

The PFR studies also found characteristic differences in mean retirement ages by type of institution: the age was highest in private universities and lowest in liberal arts colleges, with the age in public universities between these two. In both liberal arts colleges and public universities, mean retirement age tended to be lower in uncapped institutions. Regression analysis suggested that tenured faculty retire later (that is, at age 70 or later) when their positions are largely research, they have relatively light teaching loads, and they teach good students.

The proportion of faculty over age 70 depends largely on decisions made at earlier ages. An examination of the PFR's findings suggests that the proportion who will have the opportunity to choose to remain active beyond age 70 is likely to be quite small because the majority of faculty will have chosen to retire before that age. Indeed the retention rate in each age cohort was observed to drop sharply after age 65 in all institutional categories.[7] Using a Markov model, it was possible to simulate the size and age structure of tenured faculty into the future under a variety of assumptions with respect to faculty retirement behavior and overall demand for faculty. This is a powerful form of analysis in which scenario design can sometimes substitute for complete information on actual behavior and thus is ideal for simulating the impact of uncapping ex ante. Even under the most extreme scenario that might result from conservative assumptions with respect to overall faculty growth—zero growth in tenured faculty—and a strong pattern of sharp aging in the ranks of the existing faculty (large increases in retention beyond the mandatory age)—a retention rate in the oldest cohort 50 percent higher than that observed historically in uncapped institutions—the PFR found little basis for concern in lost opportunities for new and/or minority faculty. Moreover even with these assumptions of severe aging of faculty, the model projections suggested that the proportion of faculty age 40 or less would be larger in 2004 than in 1989 and that the proportion of faculty over age 70 would be at most 1.9 percent.[8]

The PFR review of surveys of faculty attitudes toward retirement provides further encouragement concerning the impact of uncapping. Retired faculty report high levels of satisfaction with retirement. Although the retirement decision is influenced by a number of different factors, the fact that faculty identified their ability to perform their job up to their own expectations as an important influence on their retirement decisions suggests that relatively few faculty with declining vitality will cling to their jobs. The responses of two early retirees surveyed vividly illustrate this point:

In the last two or three years . . . I was not as satisfied with the intellectual exchange with students . . . I wasn't learning much.

I originally thought I would retire at the mandatory age, but two or three years before I felt my energies decrease, so I decided to stop. (Rees and Smith 1991: 87)

In a world in which all retirement is voluntary, it is reassuring that faculty choose to retire when they no longer feel they can command the respect of their peers and their students. Nevertheless, the question remains whether such self-assessment is accurate. The findings of numerous studies of the relationship between chronological age and cognitive abilities, teaching effectiveness, and research activity confirmed that faculty can continue to perform and contribute well past the age of 70.[9] Competition in the academic environment is such that the activity of some members of a department can and will stimulate activity among the remaining faculty. There is the question whether the contribution of such faculty provides sufficient incentive for the overall performance of each group of faculty. The comments of one of the administrators interviewed in the NRC study are encouraging in this regard:

I have found older professors very capable of stimulating younger faculty members. The older generation can contribute much to the development of the younger generation of professors. (college president in National Research Council 1991: 58)

Estimates of the Impacts of Uncapping: Ex Post

With experience under full federal uncapping, a number of analysts have begun to ask whether the ex ante expectations have been fulfilled. Many of the findings are still preliminary.[10] Moreover, several of these studies focus on individual institutions and thus their findings are not directly comparable to the earlier analyses. Two address national data. The U.S. Department of Education (1997) analysis by Chronister, Baldwin, and Conley of data from the 1993 Survey of Postsecondary Faculty reports the retirement plans of faculty and staff in fall 1992, which is before uncapping took effect. Nevertheless their observations can be extrapolated to an uncapped environment, as over 95 percent of those surveyed were less than 65 years of age and would thus be uncapped. This extrapolation offers some confirmation for the ex ante expectations of the NRC and the PFR: Only 4.8 percent of the tenured faculty surveyed in 1992 report that they plan to work beyond age 70. However, there is also substantial uncertainty in this population: 19.1 percent indicate that they do not know at what age they plan to retire.

Ashenfelter and Card (1998) offer a preliminary analysis of an early wave of data from an exciting new database, the Princeton Retirement Survey. This survey will eventually provide a "retrospective panel," merging administrative payroll data from a representative sample of individual colleges and universities with pension data from the TIAA-CREF system. These authors' preliminary observations suggest some noticeable changes in behavior: a sharp decrease in the retirement rate of faculty who reach age 70 and a rise in the retirement rate of faculty at younger ages. Nevertheless, these findings do not raise concerns with respect to uncapping. The strong decrease in the retirement rate which Ashenfelter and Card report—whereas prior to 1994 they observed that two thirds of the faculty who reached the age of 70 would leave teaching within the next year, after 1994, they found that this proportion had fallen to less than one third—is analogous to the "sharp aging" scenario which the PFR simulated in a Markov model. Even with the assumptions of that scenario, the proportion of faculty over age 70 was still less than 2 percent. Moreover, the impact of this observed decrease in the retirement rate at age 70 is further diminished by Ashenfelter and Card's finding of an increase in the retirement rate at younger ages: a smaller number of faculty remain to be able to make a decision to work beyond age 70.

Conclusion

It appears, then, that the data available so far for over five years of national uncapping suggest little change in the principal conclusions from earlier analyses. Uncapping itself does provide an additional benefit to the tenure contract but should not cause concern for the quality of higher education so long as institutions have reliable incentive and monitoring processes to ensure that tenured faculty maintain a record of good performance. The central issue is not whether faculty choose to remain beyond age 70 but rather how effective are faculty, regardless of age. In most institutions, these initial studies and what is known since suggest that relatively few faculty will choose to remain beyond age 70. The majority of those who do stay on will be vital contributors to the educational process. If, however, mandatory retirement was used in the past as a "civilized" substitute for such processes, uncapping may prolong problems of poor performance that probably began ten or more years before age 70.

It is likely that more faculty will remain beyond age 70 in premier research institutions where teaching loads are relatively light. Hence the important question is not how many faculty remain, but how effective are the faculty who do continue? Nevertheless uncapping does raise some concern with respect to increases in the cost of higher education. The principal alarm here is not a low replacement effect. Instead, it is the possibility that colleges and universities will introduce costly retirement incentive plans that soon become entitlements. Such plans can be highly effective in encouraging retirement, but they are also very expensive. They should be used very sparingly for specific target groups.

I am grateful for comments and suggestions from V. Kerry Smith. The views expressed here are the author's and should not be attributed to the University as an institution. The author takes responsibility for all errors and omissions.

Notes

1. Exceptions were made to allow mandatory retirement in the case of the bona fide executive or high policymaker and in the case where age is a bona fide occupational qualification.

2. As part of the 1986 amendments to the ADEA, Congress called for the U.S. Equal Employment Opportunity Commission to ask the National Academy of Sciences to form a committee to conduct such a study. The committee's findings were reported through the National Research Council in 1991 (National Research Council 1991). Because there was substantial delay in the provision of funding for the National Academy study, the Project on Faculty Retirement was formed through generous grants from the Andrew W. Mellon Foundation, the Carnegie Corporation of New York, and the William and Flora Hewlett Foundation. The late Albert Rees was director of the project and I was the associate director. Its work was guided by an advisory committee chosen by the American Association of University Professors, the Association of American Universities, the Consortium on Financing Higher Education, and the National Association of State Universities and Land Grant Colleges. Its findings were reported in Rees and Smith (1991).

3. For a more complete discussion of this legislative history, see Pratt (1989: 15–31).

4. The implicit assumption here is that senior faculty are relatively highly paid. With recent mounting national anxiety over the rising costs of higher education, the question of whether "uncapping" will exacerbate these costs has increased significance.

5. In particular, these choices were based on the institutions where the advisory committee anticipated that faculty would most likely postpone retirement—research institutions where teaching loads are relatively light and the research benefits of institutional attachment are relatively heavy—or where a decline in the vitality of any one individual faculty member has a relatively large impact on the overall quality of education at the institution—selective liberal arts colleges where the size of the faculty is small.

6. The comparison in the cost of the two different faculty members should be made on a per course or per student basis and should take account of any signing bonuses, as well as the value of reduced teaching loads and committee service. Moreover, the comparison may be compounded if the retiree provided regular offset to institutional overhead through outside grants and the new hire does not.

7. Retention rates were estimated for age cohorts in five-year intervals from data on five years of flows into and out of tenure in the sample institutions. The retention rate, which is net of inflows, was defined as one minus the outflow rate, that is, the outflows from the age cohort during a five-year period from all sources (resignation, retirement, death) as a percentage of the total population in the age cohort at the beginning of the period.

8. As noted, the PFR data are not a representative sample of all faculty in the

United States but rather are drawn from a sample of tenured faculty in research and doctorate-granting universities and selective liberal arts colleges. Nevertheless, data reported in "The American College Teacher" based on the 1998–99 Higher Education Research Institute (HERI) Faculty Survey are consistent with the PFR projections. These data are based on a survey of 33,785 faculty members at 378 colleges and universities (both tenured and nontenured) and have somewhat different age intervals than in the PFR study. The HERI data indicate that the proportion of faculty under age 40 is 19.5 percent—while the PFR projection for 1999 for faculty age 40 and under was 22 percent—and the proportion age 70 and over is 1.3 percent—while the PFR projection for 1999 for faculty over age 70 was 0.7 percent. The upper age interval of the HERI data includes individuals who would retire at age 70, a common age of retirement. These data thus give no indication that a large proportion of faculty is remaining beyond age 70.

9. See National Research Council (1991: 49–66) and Rees and Smith (1991: 53–78).

10. See, e.g., Ashenfelter and Card (1998); Clark, Ghent, and Kreps (this volume); U.S. Department of Education (1997); and Ehrenberg, Matier, and Fontanella (this volume).

References

American Association of University Professors, Committee A on Academic Freedom and Tenure. 1989. "Faculty Tenure and the End of Mandatory Retirement." *Academe* 48 (September/October).

"The American College Teacher: National Norms for the 1998–99 H.E.R.I. Faculty Survey." 1999. University of California at Los Angeles Higher Education Research Institute. Cited by Debra K. Manger, "The Graying Professoriate," *Chronicle of Higher Education*, September 3: A18-A21.

Ashenfelter, Orley and David Card. 1998. "Faculty Retirement in the Post-Mandatory Era: New Evidence from the Princeton Retirement Survey." Paper presewnted at TIAA-Cref and NC State University conference, "Examining Life After the End of Mandatory Retirement," Washington, D.C.: May 18.

Berkowitz, Monroe. 1985. "Over the Hill and Under the Weather: Age v. Health." In *The Economics of Aging*, ed. Myron H. Ross. Kalamazoo, Mich.: Upjohn Institute. 113–38.

Clark, Robert L., Linda S. Ghent, and Juanita Kreps. This volume. "Faculty Retirement at Three North Carolina Universities."

Clark, Robert L. and P. Brett Hammond. This volume "Introduction: Changing Retirement Policies and Patterns in Higher Education.

DiGiovanni, Nicholas, Jr. 1989. *Age Discrimination: An Administrator's Guide.* Washington, D.C.: College and University Personnel Association.

Ehrenberg, Ronald G., Michael W. Matier, and David Fontanella. This volume. "Cornell University Confronts the End of Mandatory Retirement."

Finkin, Matthew W. 1989. "Tenure After the ADEA Amendments: A Different View." In *The End of Mandatory Retirement: Effects on Higher Education*, ed. Karen C. Holden and W. Lee Hansen, pp. 97–111. New Directions for Higher Education, 65. San Francisco, Calif.: Jossey-Bass. 97-111.

Hansen, W. Lee. 1985. "Changing Demography of Faculty in Higher Education." In *Faculty Vitality and Institutional Productivity: Critical Perspectives for Higher Education*, ed. Shirley M. Clark and Darrell R. Lewis. New York: Teachers College Press. 27–54.

National Research Council, Committee on Ending Mandatory Retirement in Higher Education. 1991. *Ending Mandatory Retirement for Tenured Faculty: The Consequences for Higher Education,* ed. P. Brett Hammond and Harriet P. Morgan. Washington, D.C.: National Academy Press.

Pratt, Henry J. 1989."Uncapping Mandatory Retirement: The Lobbyists' Influence." In *The End of Mandatory Retirement: Effects on Higher Education,* ed. Karen C. Holden and W. Lee Hansen. New Directions for Higher Education 65. San Francisco, Calif.: Jossey-Bass. 15–31.

Rees, Albert and Sharon P. Smith 1991. *Faculty Retirement in the Arts and Sciences.* Princeton, N.J.: Princeton University Press.

Rosovsky, Henry. 1990. *The University: An Owner's Manual.* New York: W. W. Norton.

U. S. Department of Education, National Center for Education Statistics. 1997. *Retirement and Other Departure Plans of Instructional Faculty and Staff in Higher Education Institutions.* NCES 98-254. Washington, D.C.: NCES.

Chapter 10
Reflections on an Earlier Study of Mandatory Retirement: What Came True and What We Can Still Learn

Karen C. Holden and W. Lee Hansen

When the federal government eliminated age-based mandatory retirement in 1994, almost two decades of uncertainty ended regarding mandatory retirement age (MRA) policies in higher education. During those years, academe faced periods of high inflation that threatened to erode the real value of faculty salaries and pensions and thus, perhaps, delayed retirements and constrained operating budgets. This in turn limited the ability of institutions to expand and develop new programs by hiring new faculty. At the same time, the age distribution of faculty in higher education meant a rise in their mean age even without any change in retirement age policies. The prospect of uncapping was viewed with the same fears by academic institutions, as was the earlier rise (in 1982) in the MRA from 65 to 70.

Predictions about the dire effects on colleges and universities of raising the minimum MRA from age 65 to 70 in the early 1980s, and of subsequently uncapping the MRA in 1994, failed to materialize (see Smith, this volume). Yet, as evidenced elsewhere in this volume, colleges and universities continue to express concern about faculty retirement issues: too many highly paid (but less productive) professors will continue teaching well into their 70s; early retirement programs developed to help prevent this from occurring will be costly; and the age-bunching of faculty hires from the 1960s will make the retirement problem even more acute in the coming decade.

This chapter describes and assesses the only nationally representative study of retirement policies and practices and of retirement behavior in higher education. We address three questions:

- What are the institutional policies and individual characteristics that shape retirement timing?
- What bearing do the findings from our earlier study on raising the mini-

mum allowed MRA from 65 to 70 have on understanding how institutions and individuals may respond to uncapping mandatory retirement? and

• What will the likely pattern be of faculty retirements over the coming decade?

Lessons Learned from Prior Research: The 1978 Amendments

Background. The 1978 Amendments to the Age Discrimination in Employment Act (ADEA) raised the minimum allowed age of mandatory retirement from 65 to 70 for all Americans but granted a four-year exemption (until July 1, 1982) for faculty members with indefinite (i.e., tenured) appointments in institutions of higher education. In the meantime, colleges and universities could continue to retire faculty forcibly as early as age 65 for reasons of age alone, unless Congress made the exemption permanent, something it did not do. The subsequent 1986 ADEA eliminated mandatory retirement at any age, although once again faculty members in higher education were exempt, this time through January 1, 1994.

The 1978 and 1986 exemptions for faculty were granted in response to strong opposition from academe to the loss of what was viewed as an essential human resource tool. The principal arguments rested on the academic enterprise's unique mission to educate the next generation of workers and scholars and to nurture intellectual and scientific advances. Thus, it was argued, orderly and predictable retirements were essential to creating opportunities to hire recently trained new faculty who would further this mission. In the absence of this means of compelling older faculty to retire, the intellectual atmosphere and rewards and the nonphysically demanding nature of the job would lead to unacceptable delays in retirement. In addition, it was generally accepted wisdom that the defined contribution plans covering faculty in private institutions, in contrast to the defined benefit plans in public institutions and private industry, provided a financial incentive to delay retirement well past the plan's "normal" retirement age.

Because so little was known about the actual effect of MRA policies on retirement behavior even for the general workforce, a provision of the 1978 legislation called for the U.S. Department of Labor to carry out a study of the effect of raising the MRA to 70, including a separate study specifically on its impact for higher education. In 1979 we were commissioned to undertake the study of ending the 1978 exemption for tenured faculty.

Our study addressed four major questions: (1) What MRA policies prevailed in higher education? (2) What effect did these and other personnel policies have on the age of retirement of faculty members? (3) What would be the likely, first-round effects of raising the MRA from 65 to 70? (4) What adaptations in behavior both by higher education institutions and faculty would be triggered by such a change? These were not easily answered questions since an MRA is just one factor influencing retirement. Personal characteristics of faculty members, institutional characteristics, job histories and current responsibilities, and fringe benefit and other personnel policies also influence when faculty members retire. Thus, understanding mandatory retirement policy effects required collecting and analyzing data so that we could distinguish the influence of other important factors from that of mandatory retirement rules. There were no national data on retirement policies and faculty characteristics across universities and colleges, so we collected data from a sample of institutions and from their tenured faculty members. This matched institutional-faculty data set still remains the only nationally representative study of retirement policies, pensions, and retirement timing in academe (Hansen and Holden 1981b; U.S. House of Representatives Select Committee on Aging 1982; Holden and Hansen 1989).

Although the surveys were conducted in 1979–80 and the study was completed in 1981, the findings on the determinants of retirement timing remain relevant to the current debate over the consequences of finally eliminating mandatory retirement in higher education. This claim stems from the following observations: (1) the underlying factors shaping retirement behavior have not changed to any substantial degree; (2) TIAA-CREF and state plans continue to be the principal retirement plans for the vast majority of faculty members and thus shape retirement options despite somewhat greater flexibility since then in benefit structure and supplemental annuity options; (3) evidence on retirement rates from those few institutions that in 1979–80 had no age of mandatory retirement both anticipated and are suggestive of the effects of raising the MRA to 70 and eventually uncapping it in 1994. Further, the chapters in this volume that describe primarily an uncapped world confirm many of our study's conclusions and predictions about retirement behavior in general and MRA effects specifically.

Retirement timing determinants. The lessons from our study that are most relevant to understanding the current and future patterns of faculty retirement include the following: (1) The absence of a comprehensive database severely limits the ability of higher education to plan for externally mandated personnel policy changes and is essential for understanding current and future retirement behavior; (2) although private institutions were more likely than public institutions to have an MRA of 65, they coupled this with liberal extension policies that resulted in similar retirement age patterns on average between public and private institutions; (3) although public and private institutions were generally covered by different types of plans, type of plan did not matter in explaining retirement patterns; (4) the average expected age of retirement is different for faculty members in public and private institutions, but this difference cannot be attributed to MRA policies; (5) other institutional policies matter and have an important influence on retirement timing in higher education; and (6) although eliminating the MRA would lead to some faculty continuing longer than they otherwise would be able to, it is the more productive faculty members who tend to retire later.

The matched faculty-institutional data. We developed two surveys, one for a nationally representative sample of colleges and universities and another for a sample of faculty members at the responding institutions.[1] Information came from a sample of institutions drawn to reflect the population of degree-granting institutions with 250 or more students, including two-year community colleges, four-year colleges, and research universities. We then surveyed faculty at responding institutions; responses came from more than 6,000 associate and full professors at the 298 responding institutions. We matched the individual faculty data with that from the specific institution in which they were employed.

From institutions we obtained data on institutional characteristics, faculty numbers, and retirement-related policies. This included information on retirement age policies (mandatory, normal, and early ages of retirement) both at the time of the survey and just prior to the 1978 amendments, on the age distributions of their current faculty and of faculty retirements over the previous two years (1978–79, 1979–80), on benefit formulas for those covered by defined benefit plans, on contribution schedules for those covered by defined contribution plans, on reductions in pension benefits for early retirement, and on any post-MRA employment restrictions. We asked each faculty member for their expected age of retirement as well as demographic characteristics, work histories, professional accomplishments, health conditions, accumulations in defined contribution plans (most often TIAA-CREF), years covered by their current retirement plan, and their current institutional salary. We also obtained information on any other type of retirement benefits they expected to receive, including Social Security and pensions from former jobs. In addition, respondents provided detailed information on all sources of current income (institutional salary as well as income from, for example, consulting fees) and expected sources of income after retirement. To help understand the impact of other fringe benefits we obtained from each institution information on the availability and continuation into retirement of life insurance and health insurance policies, since the loss of this coverage would be a real economic loss on retirement. The linking of the two surveys enabled us to calculate the pension amounts — whether from a defined benefit or defined contribution plan — for which a faculty member would be eligible at different retirement ages. We could thus estimate, in combination with individual faculty service and salary characteristics, the incentives built into each pension for retirement at alternative ages. Our analysis focused on faculty members who were age 56–64, the group we expected to be most aware of and affected by the MRA provisions and the subsequent expiration of the faculty exemption.[2]

Distribution and enforcement of MRA policies. Our study found that MRA policies were neither universal nor strictly enforced during the period when

Table 1. Distribution of Full-Time Faculty by Mandatory Retirement Age and
by Type of Institution, 1980

	Percent of all faculty		Percent of full-time faculty with MRA of age		
Type of institution	With no MRA	With MRA-total	65	66–68	70+
Private	1.2	21.9	13.0	1.4	7.5
2-year	0.3	0.5	0.2	0.0	0.3
4-year	0.9	14.5	8.3	0.6	5.6
University	0.0	7.0	4.5	0.8	1.7
Public	11.1	65.7	19.4	2.6	43.7
2-year	6.2	19.7	10.9	0.0	8.8
4-year	3.7	25.8	5.2	0.0	20.6
University	1.2	20.2	3.3	2.6	14.3
Total	12.4	87.6	32.3	4.0	51.3

Source: Holden and Hansen (1981b)
Cells are percentage of all faculty in that group.

they existed. This meant their potential impact on retirement timing varied
across institutions and that the impact of eliminating the MRA was moder-
ated. Just prior to passage of the 1978 ADEA, 84 percent of all responding
institutions had some age of mandatory retirement with the majority (73
percent) setting this age at 65, 20 percent at 70, and the remainder having no
MRA. A sharp contrast was evident between public and private institutions,
with fewer than half the public universities (46 percent) and public four-year
colleges (47 percent) having an age of 65 as compared to 81 percent and 67
percent of private colleges and universities, respectively. Because public institutions are on average larger, even at the time the 1978 ADEA was passed
only about half of all full-time faculty members were covered by an MRA of
65. Another 15 percent were subject to an MRA of 66–68.

By the time of our survey—in 1980, about two years before the expiration of the exemption—only one third of all full-time faculty members were
employed in institutions with an MRA of 65; another half were covered by
an MRA of 70, while the remaining 12 percent were subject to no MRA
(Table 1). Public institutions had moved most rapidly after 1978 to raise their
MRA; 56 percent of public institutions with an MRA below 70 had raised
or eliminated their MRA in contrast to only 25 percent of private institutions. As a result, among institutions with an MRA in 1980, only 26 percent of
public universities and 34 percent of public four-year colleges had an MRA
of 65 in 1980 as compared to 64 percent and 61 percent, respectively, for
comparable private institutions.

Mandatory retirement does not require total separation from academic
employment, and institutions reported considerable flexibility in its appli-

Table 2. Average Expected Retirement Age and Percentage of Faculty Expecting
to Retire Before Age 67 and 70, by Mandatory Retirement Age, by Age
and Control of Institution

Current age 63–64, and Type of Institution	Expected retirement age		Percent expecting to before age 67		Percent expecting to retire before age 70	
	MRA 65	MRA 70	MRA 65	MRA 70	MRA 65	MRA 70
All	66.3*	67.2	69.8*	52.6	81.1	69.2
Public	65.6*	66.8	90.5***	57.8	90.5	78.1
Private	66.8**	69.0	56.2*	28.6	75.0***	28.6

Source: Holden and Hansen (1981b).
Different from retirement probability with MRA of 70:
*Significant at .01; **significant at .05; ***significant at .1.

cation. Only a small fraction—13 percent—of all institutions in our survey
that reported an MRA of 65 responded that retirement was in fact required
at that age. Extensions beyond that date were standard, with most institutions reporting no age limit for extensions, while others granted extensions
for one to five years. In effect, the MRA in higher education signaled the end
of a tenure contract at which time some faculty members who could continue their teaching and research, perhaps after a review by colleagues or
administrators on their ability to continue to perform effectively. The ability
to extend service beyond the formal MRA meant the exemption's expiration
promised to have a smaller impact on retirement timing than might have
been expected although its expiration would clearly alter the nature of the
post-65 employment contract.

Expected and actual retirement ages. Few faculty members plan a complete
cessation of academic work after their expected age of retirement. In this
study, we defined retirement as that age at which a person ceased employment at the institution at which he or she held a full-time, tenured job at
the time of our survey. It is this institution-based job change that is the issue
in estimating MRA effects on institutional retirement patterns and budgets.
Thus, our data on retirement patterns refer to the age at which faculty separate from the institution at which they are employed, regardless of whether
they seek a postretirement teaching assignment elsewhere.

The reported prevalence of service extensions beyond the official MRA
in part explains why the average actual retirement age for faculty—even at
schools with a 65 MRA—was higher than that. The average expected retirement age among faculty who would reach age an MRA of 65 before the exemption expired was also above 65. We examined differences in expected
retirement age by age of MRA prevailing at the institution. In Table 2 we
show differences for faculty who were age 63–64, a group that would still

have been covered by the 1978 ADEA exemption when they reached age 65. Although faculty members employed in institutions with an MRA of 65 had a somewhat lower expected retirement age (66.3 years vs. 67.2), the striking difference is between retirement ages in private and public institutions. Indeed, the average expected retirement age at public institutions with an MRA of 70 is identical to that at private institutions with an MRA of 65. Expected retirement from public institutions was significantly earlier than from private institutions, regardless of the MRA in effect (i.e., whether it is age 65 or 70).[3]

Type and value of retirement benefit plans. Because virtually all institutions offer their faculty members some kind of pension plan, the question for colleges and universities is not whether having a pension makes a difference to retirement timing, but rather the influence of different plans on retirement timing of individual faculty members. Faculty in our survey who were employed in private institutions were covered primarily by TIAA-CREF while those at public institutions were covered by a state retirement plan. Thus, to some extent perceptions of and empirical estimates of MRA effects are confounded by systematic differences between public and private institutions in both MRA and plan type (see also Clark et al., this volume). The gains to postponing retirement for a faculty member covered by a defined contribution plan will depend primarily on the expected investment earnings on accumulations. For faculty covered by a defined benefit plan the gain will depend primarily on expected increases in salary, which raises the salary average in the formula, and the contribution of the additional year of service. What type of plan is most likely to encourage delayed retirement depends on how expected gains in market earnings compare to salary (and formula) increases. We estimated these gains for faculty in our sample using 1981 prevailing interest and earnings gain expectations.[4]

For each institution we estimated the pension for which a faculty member with an identical service and salary profile would be eligible at age 65 and at 66. The benefit at age 65 and the gain in pension on delaying retirement by one year was almost identical on average for faculty in TIAA-CREF and in public plans. This indicated that, contrary to the then prevailing wisdom, on average the benefit gained by including one more year and a higher salary was equivalent to the then-actuarial gain and additional dividends provided by TIAA-CREF. One explanation is the short salary-averaging period (typically three years) in defined benefit plans in higher education, which in combination with additional years of service lead to relatively high gains from continued work if salary increases are generous. Although other relative salary gain and investment earning scenarios would alter these comparative estimates, our pension simulations showed that relative market and compensation conditions, not basic plan types, determine the gains to postponed retirements. These similar averages between the two types of plans, however, obscure enormous variations within each type of plan. For example, the most generous public pension offered a benefit 2.5 times that offered by the least generous state plan to an identically positioned faculty member.

Identifying the separate effects of an MRA and other factors. We assessed the separate effect on average retirement age of an MRA by estimating a retirement model built around the assumption that faculty members are influenced by the relative rewards of retirement versus those of continuing to be employed in their current positions (see Appendix A and Keefe, this volume). Two approaches were taken. In the first approach we estimated the effect of an MRA on the actual retirement probabilities reported by institutions, controlling for institutional characteristics (public, private, and size), postretirement fringe benefit continuation (health insurance, and life insurance), and pension wealth (estimated for a hypothetical faculty under each institution's pension plan but with identical personal characteristics across institutions). In the other, which was the main focus of our study, we used the matched institutional-faculty data to examine determinants of expected retirement age, controlling for the same institutional characteristics as in the first analysis, plus individual-specific pension wealth and other financial characteristics. Because of the absence of any prior data on retirement behavior, our study relied on comparison of retirement behavior of faculty subject to different (including no) MRA rules to infer how changing the MRA would influence retirement timing.

In analyzing retirement probabilities at the institutional level, we estimated the effect of an MRA on the probabilities of retiring over a one-year period between ages 60 and 65 and between ages 60 and 69, using institutionally provided data on actual retirements. Three main conclusions emerged. First, an MRA (of 65) appears to have a relatively small effect on retirements, raising the probability among faculty 60–69 of retiring before age 65 by about 12 percentage points and before 70 by about 22 percentage points. At the mean an MRA of 70 (versus an MRA of 65) raises the average age of retirement from 65.6 to 67.0 years even when controlling for the retirement effects of institutionally provided benefits and the change in present value of the institution's primary pension plan if benefits were postponed from age 65 to 66. Second, private institutions, even after adjusting for average annuity wealth offers, could still expect to experience lower rates of retirement—by about 12 percentage points before age 65 and by about 15 percent before age 70. Third, the continuation of other fringe benefits into retirement has an equal or larger impact on retirement timing. Health insurance continuation offers raise the probability of retirement before age 65 by about 14 percentage points. Somewhat surprising, pension wealth had no effect on the actual retirement probabilities, a result perhaps of having to use a value for a hypothetical faculty member whose characteristics are identical across institutions. This is consistent with our earlier conclusion that it is not broad pension type that matters, but how pension policy interacts with institution-specific hiring and salary policies.

We estimated a second retirement model, this time of retirement age expectations of individual faculty members. The matched faculty-institution data enabled us to incorporate the richer matched data including that on other financial assets held by the individual. The pension wealth variable was based on individual salary-service and contribution profiles. Results are presented in Appendix A, Table A1, with separate estimates for faculty aged 56–61, the group who could anticipate being subject to a minimum MRA of 70, and for those aged 62–64, who would have been subject to the ADEA exemption. The major conclusions we draw from this analysis follow.

Among the older group, the presence of an MRA of 65 accelerated retirement by about 1.1 years. This contrasts with the separate effect of employment in a private institution that alone raised the retirement age by even more — 1.5 years later than faculty at public universities. Not surprisingly, an MRA of 65 had no effect on the retirement plans of younger faculty since they knew then they would be able to work up to age 70. For the younger faculty, however, the further they were from age 65, the younger they expected to retire.

We were surprised to find that the *level* of pension wealth did not affect retirement timing for the older faculty, although for younger faculty, the additional gains anticipated in earnings and pensions had a delaying effect on the expected age of retirement. Perhaps the most relevant finding for predicting uncapping effects was the increased chances of *delaying* retirement as *nonsalary* professional income rose. This is consistent with Switkes's discussion of the experience with the California voluntary early retirement plans (VERIPs) under which those faculty who had other employment opportunities had *lower* early retirement take-up rates and with Keefe's conclusions that it was the more accomplished scholars who delayed retirement (Switkes, this volume; Keefe, this volume).

Our major conclusion was that it was the combination of rewards provided by higher education to continued employment that mattered with an MRA playing a relatively small role. Factors that remain under control of administrators — salary increases, pension benefit gains with continued work, and research support — encourage faculty to plan a relatively late retirement. Indeed, our interpretation of the effect of nonsalary professional income on retirement timing is that faculty engaged in consulting activities depend on an institutional affiliation for the continuation of those activities. While in some occupations opportunities to earn outside a regular job may continue even after (early) retirement, this appears not to be the case in academe where the receipt of outside income may be conditioned on an institutional affiliation and use of institutional facilities. Our conclusion on the importance of ongoing institutional affiliation to the ability of faculty members to continue receiving outside income suggest that Cornell University was right on target in proposing supplements to emeritus status as one tool for encouraging early retirement (Ehrenberg et al., this volume).

Finally, our analysis of both actual and expected retirement timing highlights once again the difference between public and private institutions: at the latter faculty expect to retire later even after controlling for pension and MRA policies. We conclude that the perception that pension plan type matters (with defined contribution plans such as TIAA-CREF encouraging later retirement) is wrong. The public-private variable is picking up some other aspect of retirement policies of the academic environment that encourages earlier retirement.

Faculty productivity and retirement expectations. Because a critical issue in the debate on uncapping MRA is the scholarly productivity of faculty who would otherwise have retired, we asked faculty respondents about the number of articles published in the last three years and over their lifetime, as well as their perceptions of the quality of their research and scholarly output relative to that of other faculty in their field, plus a self-assessment of their teaching effectiveness. The analysis of retirement age expectations (Appendix A) indicated that faculty currently engaged in research expected to retire later—by as much as 1.4 years—than those reporting they were not engaged in research. This result is net of other effects and is consistent with Switkes's report of the California experience in which those with more recent publication retired at lower rates (Switkes, this volume).

Simulating effects on budget costs and new hire. We used our data on faculty age structure and retirement expectations to simulate the effect on budget and new hiring of having an age 65 versus age 70 MRA. Assuming constant faculty size, the higher MRA would raise average budget costs within the first five years by about 2 percentage points. New hires initially drop by about 20 percent below the level prevailing with an MRA of 65 but then begin to slowly rise back to near but not quite up to their old levels. When the simulations are undertaken with different faculty age structures the effects in five years on faculty budget costs ranges between 1.7 and 3.7 percent with a fall in that percentage and a narrowing of the range over time. For new hires as well the largest impact is in the short term but quickly diminishes. For the oldest age distributions hirings are actually greater in some later years than they would have been under a younger MRA.

Early retirement incentives. Because other personnel tools will have to be used in an era of a higher (and uncapped) MRA to manage retirements, we explored the attractiveness of several early retirement incentives (ERI) on expected retirement timing. Faculty respondents were presented with three hypothetical offers: (1) their pension benefit levels would not be reduced if they took early retirement; (2) their pension benefits, though reduced for early retirement, would be fully adjusted for cost of living changes during their entire retired life; and (3) faculty could phase down their workload, with proportionate reductions in their salaries in the years immediately prior to their currently expected retirement age. We asked individuals not only about their interest in each plan but also the age at which they would definitely or possibly take up one of these options.

Among faculty members in our survey (all of whom were age 50 or older) about 25 percent said they would definitely retire earlier if there were no penalty for early retirement. While another 27 percent said they possibly would retire earlier, 41 percent said they definitely would not be interested. The average age at which people said they would retire under such an offer was age 62 compared with their average expected retirement age of 66. Despite then high prevailing rates of inflation, only 22 percent of faculty said that with a fully inflation-indexed pension they would definitely retire earlier and would do so at age 62. The option attractive to the most was the phased retirement offer; 37 percent said they would definitely take such an option although 47 percent expressed absolutely no interest. Postretirement indexing would reduce the average age of retirement by 2.4 years, and the ability to reduce work load would accelerate retirement by 2.9 years.

Faculty age affected the attractiveness of these options, a conclusion that has important implications for the short- and long-term impact of early retirement offers. Faculty members 65–69 expressed no interest in retiring earlier; these individuals had already planned (and acted upon) a delayed retirement or may have been close enough to their expected retirement age that little change in age (even if they took the offer) was possible. These options were also of little interest to the 50–59-year-olds whose expected retirement ages were already relatively early. These options mattered most to the age group 60–64, who on average expected to work another six years. Because an ERI offer appeared to accelerate retirement—and by even more than did an MRA of 65—we conclude that these may be powerful tools for managing retirement timing. Faculty actively engaged in research as well as those who were not were equally likely to accelerate retirement, although the former group made this change from an already later age of retirement. Thus, it appears that with appropriate early retirement incentives, both less productive faculty members, who already plan to retire somewhat earlier, and more productive faculty members can be encouraged to retire earlier than they had expected to retire.

At the time of our survey, few institutions offered ERIs that were anywhere near as attractive as these options. In the institutional survey we tried to obtain data on early retirement benefits that were universally offered to faculty through provisions built into institutional retirement plans as well as those paid fully out of institutional budgets and designed specifically to target early retirees. About 20 percent of all institutions reported some form of early retirement incentives in their pension plan, including 36 percent of private universities and 22 percent of public universities. Closer examination of institutional ERIs revealed that almost half were optional tax deferred annuity (TDA) plans available to faculty members through salary reductions under IRS code, section 403(b). While the responses indicate a realization by administrators that financial incentives are important to retirement timing, these TDAs offered no greater advantage to earlier retirement than would any defined contribution pension plan.

Institutions were also asked about the ability of faculty members to reduce workloads prior to normal retirement age. Overall, about one third allowed this option, with public universities, in particular, most likely to allow faculty to work part time. Unfortunately, because nothing is known about the conditions faculty must meet to take advantage of this option, it is impossible to evaluate the attractiveness of decreased workloads. Only 31 percent of institutions with a 65 MRA offered a part-time teaching option compared with half of those with a 70 MRA. This suggests that institutions with higher MRAs and public institutions have adjusted in part by offering the option of reduced work loads. The survey results reported by Keefe in this volume document additional movement in this direction, although public institutions remain more likely to have such plans.

How Serious Is the Impact of Uncapping?

If an MRA has an effect on any individual's retirement plans, a change in that policy would lead to some increase in the number retiring after age 70. This increase would be smaller for those institutions that had liberally provided for extensions beyond their formerly established MRA. Thus, it is not surprising to see some small number of faculty delaying retirement beyond age 65 with the rise in MRA and beyond age 70 after uncapping (Clark et al., this volume). An opposing effect of uncapping MRA might also be observed as the MRA is removed as a target age of retirement. That is, as faculty must pay more attention to and are educated by their institutions about other retirement benefit provisions, retirement rates may rise among younger faculty. Clark et al. in this volume report higher rates of retirement among some younger people; the stability of mean ages of retirement even as some faculty delay retirement past age 70 imply increases in retirement rates at younger ages.

Whether the observed or anticipated change in retirement rates should be a concern to affected institutions depends on the teaching and research productivity of those who delay retirement. Clearly the academic enterprise is worse off if less productive faculty members continue past age 70, while those who are popular teachers and would otherwise publish and bring in grant money to support the research and teaching enterprise retire early.

Most chapters in this volume address the question of retirement numbers with but few addressing the question of individual retiree characteristics. In part the inability to address productivity effects adequately is a result of the continuing lack of a comprehensive data set on retirement policies and retirement behavior of faculty across all types of institutions of higher education. For example, Clark et al. (this volume) in their modeling of retirement behavior at three North Carolina universities are restricted to data available from institutional records, lacking what turned out to be important in our study—information on other sources of income and activities outside that particular institution.

Although our study was of the effect of changing the MRA from 65 to 70, our findings anticipate many of those of uncapping. The reports of both the National Research Council's Committee on Mandatory Retirement in Higher Education and Project on Faculty Retirement concluded that the *increase* in the number extending beyond 70 would be small; that those who did extend would tend to be the most productive; and that the private research universities whose average age of retirement was highest were most able to afford well targeted early retirement programs (Smith, this volume). The studies in this volume show that a small number have continued past age 70, while most faculty retire well before that age. Indeed both the data on the age distribution at retirement and on the unchanged mean age of retirement after uncapping imply a spreading of retirement age as faculty take other factors into account than the targeted MRA as they plan their retirement. Clark et al. in this volume point out the seeming anomaly of increases in retirement rates for faculty younger than age 70. Recently obtained data from the University of Wisconsin, Madison campus, which had its MRA eliminated during the exempt period (O'Neil, this volume) showed a slight increase in retirement numbers and a decline in average age of retirement from age 66.0 to 65.3 after its uncapping.

Conclusion

The challenge in assessing the effect of changes in one retirement policy on retirement timing, faculty age distributions, hiring options, and salary costs, is separating its effects from other demographic and economic constraints that would have operated even without that policy change to alter the faculty age distribution and raise institutional costs. The strength of our 1980–81 study lies in attempting to understand the interplay between faculty decisions to retire and the institutionally provided benefits they expect to receive. Unfortunately, higher education has never launched a long-term effort to collect data necessary to understand how and why retirement decisions of faculty members have changed over time and in response to political, institutional, and personal factors. Large national data sets provide these data for the general population (e.g., the Health and Retirement Study) but contain only a small number of faculty members. Institutional employment data do not provide the rich individual and social context within which these decisions are made. TIAA-CREF covers the majority of faculty members working in private institutions, and although it covers an increasing number in public institutions, it still excludes that larger group of faculty members. Because private and public institutions differ so substantially, an analysis that is confined to one or the other sector will leave important questions unanswered. As it was, the institutions taking advantage of the exemption were largely private colleges and universities, and private research universities in particular. It may be possible to examine the determinants of faculty retirement in those institutions and even their responses to early retirement incentives, but an important question remains: How different is the experience at these institutions from that of public institutions which for the most part did not take advantage of the MRA exemption? Similarly, looking only at the experience of private research universities, about which there is the greatest concern, one can see only part of the picture. One of our strongest conclusions is that we need better, industrywide data on faculty in higher education.

The measured effects of uncapping are mixed, a result anticipated in the studies of both the 1978 and 1986 ADEA amendments. Although some institutions saw increases in the number of faculty working up to age 70, the numbers were small, and many institutions saw no major change in retirement rates. Our own analysis anticipated what happened—that the major private research institutions were more likely to find their faculty delaying retirements. But these were precisely those institutions in which even prior to 1978 faculty were most likely to delay retirement, and apparently not simply because of defined benefit coverage, but because of some combination of factors that made delayed retirement more attractive to these faculty. This is good news if delayed retirement was and continues to be more likely because of the institutions' well-targeted (even if unintentional) incentives to continue productive teaching and research. Even if the news is not all good for these institutions, broad changes should not be made (eg in pension plans) until it is clear what the factors are leading to delayed retirements and their productivity consequences. Our study does support the development of options that allow faculty to move into part-time assignments that permit them to continue their research and in some cases limited teaching activity.

Several authors suggest that other economic and noneconomic factors are almost certain to dominate the effects of the relatively small numbers of faculty continuing to teach beyond age 70 (Keefe, this volume). We suggest further research on understanding the role and potential impact of these nonpension benefits on retirement behavior. In addition, at the institutional level the impact of other variables is considerable as our simulations show. In particular, enrollment levels and the revenues they produce, whether through tuition or public subsidies, fluctuate considerably from year to year. The number of faculty on the payroll varies from year to year because of unexpected resignations and less than perfect timing in hiring replacements. Research funding that supports faculty salaries also varies. In short, the fiscal and other effects of faculty continuing until age 70 and beyond appear to be relatively small, when compared with the impact of other forces. This conclusion does not suggest that "at the margin" the continuation of faculty beyond age 70 is of no concern. But with unexpected variations on so many margins, this one is hardly critical and should not be used to divert attention of academe from more critical retirement policy issues.

Appendix A

Our estimated model took the form of

$$RA = f(E, \text{WEALTH}_i, \text{DELTAWEALTH}_i, X_i, F_i),$$

where

RA is defined as the relevant retirement age,
E is earnings that would be received from an additional year of work.
WEALTH is the present value of future retirement benefits,
DELTAWEALTH is the change in the present value of retirement benefits if deferred for another year,
X represents personal and institutional characteristics,
F represents participation changes upon retirement in other fringe benefits.

Description of Variables

Dependent Variable: In the retirement estimates based on institutionally provided retirement data, RA is the probability that faculty within a particular age group one year prior to the survey retired during the following year. In the estimates based on faculty provided data, RA is the expected age at which the faculty expected to retire from their institution.

Independent variables:

Pv65   Present value of retirement benefit income stream at age 65 ($1,000); discount rate depends on postretirement inflation adjustments

CHPA   Net gains from postponing retirement from age 65 to 66 ($1,000); equal to the change in present value of the pension between age 65 and 66 plus the earnings during that additional year of work

INCDIFF   Professional income earned in 1979 above basic institutional salary ($1,000)

WEALTH	Total value of assets plus housing equity at age 65 assuming an interest rate of 2.5% between current age and age 65 ($1,000)
NOSS	Dummy variable equal to 1 if institution is covered by social security
CW	Dummy variable equal to 1 if faculty member is currently engaged in scholarly research that is likely to lead to publication or other form of dissemination in the next several years
PUB3	Number of articles in professional journals during the past 3 years
BOOKS3	Number of books authored or coauthored during past 3 years
STEV	Dummy variable equal to 1 if teaching is evaluated as excellent or above average
HINS	Dummy variable equal to I if health insurance coverage continues on retirement
LINS	Dummy variable equal to 1 if life insurance continues for retiree
CONTST	Dummy variable equal to 1 if contributions to retirement plan stop at some age
MR65	Dummy variable equal to 1 if there is a mandatory retirement age of 65
YRS65	65 minus current age
HLTH	Dummy variable equal to 1 if health is excellent or good
MARSTATE	A dummy variable equal to 1 if married
MATY	Spouse's income in 1979 ($1,000)
SEX	Dummy variable equal to 1 if male
UNIV	Dummy variable equal to 1 if employed
TWOYR	Dummy variable equal to 1 if employed at a two-year college
PUBPRV	Dummy variable equal to 1 if employed at a private institution

Table A1. Determinants of Expected Retirement Age Faculty Members 56–61 and 62–64.

	56–61	62–64
Constant	64.6	65.8
Financial variables		
PV65	−.0025	.0063
CHPA	.0897***	.0200
INCDIFF	−.0069	.1038***
WEALTH	−.0028	−.0033*
NOSS	.3988	−1.5482***
Productivity measures		
CW	1.4050***	.6354
PUB3	.0825***	.0843
BOOK3	−.3984*	.1785
STEV	.2024	.3804

Table A1. Continued

	56–61	62–64
Institutional policies		
HINS	.1229	−.0618
LINS	−.0597	−1.0977**
CONTST	.5755	1.0308
MR65	.3889	−1.0874**
Demographic and institutional characteristics		
YRS65	−.3314***	−.2622
HLTH	.7986	1.0061
MARSTAT	−.5966	1.0597
MATY	−.0012	−.0095
SEX	.9576*	−.7856
UNIV	−.1532	.7340
TWOYR	−.7932	1.7141**
PUBPRV	.1517	1.5081**
R^2	.15	.24
F	3.29	1.71
N	405	139

Source: Holden and Hansen, 1981b.
***Significant at .01 level;** significant at .05 level; * significant at .10 level.

Notes

1. The institutional sample was drawn from the U.S. Department of Education's 1978–79 *Directory of Educational Institutions* and the faculty sample matched to these institutions was drawn from 1979 *The Education Directory* compiled and published by an organization with the same name. For more details, see (Holden and Hansen 1981b).The resulting data were weighted to adjust for sampling and response rate differences between public and private institutions and by institutional size.

2. We asked each faculty member to report his or her current expected retirement age and used this age as our measure of retirement timing. Use of information on expectations was unique and controversial at the time but has since been incorporated into the Health and Retirement Survey and widely accepted as a legitimate measure of retirement timing (Ekerdt et al. 1996; Gustman et al. 1995; Honig 1996).

3. The same contrast appears to exist for faculty not subject to any MRA, although the number in our sample who were 63–64 of age is small. All were in public institutions. But on average, these faculty expected to retire 1.7 years earlier than did faculty employed in private institutions and covered by an age 70 MRA.

4. Wealth calculation takes into account both survival probabilities and benefit gains to postponed retirement. We assumed a fixed TIAA-CREF annuity would be taken at the specified retirement age and the dividend rate was 8 percent. We assumed a real discount rate of 5 percent and a then-realistic inflation rate of 10 percent with inflation adjustments in the annuity options modifying the inflation component. If plans were integrated with social security, we included the effect of that integration on the increase in benefits and TIAA-CREF accounts on gains in service and salary.

References

Clark, Robert L., Linda S. Ghent, and Juanita M. Kreps. This volume. "Retirement at Three North Carolina Universities."

Ehrenberg, Ronald G., Michael W. Matier, and David Fontanella. This volume. "Cornell Confronts the End of Mandatory Retirement."

Ekerdt, David J., Stanley DeVineuy, and Karl Kosloski. 1996. "Profiling Plans for Retirement." *Journal of Gerontology: Social Sciences* 51B: S140–S149.

Gustman, Alan L., Olivia S. Mitchell, and Thomas L. Steinmeier. 1995. "Retirement Measures in the Health and Retirement Survey." *Journal of Human Resources* 30 (Supplement 1995): S57-S83.

Hansen, W. Lee and Karen C. Holden. 1981a. "Effect of the Tenured Faculty Exemption in the 1978 ADEA Legislation," in *Abolishing Mandatory Retirement: Implications for America and Social Security of Eliminating Age Discrimination in Employment.* Select Committee on Aging, House of Representatives, 97th Congress, 1st Session, August.

Hansen, W. Lee and Karen C. Holden. 1981b. *Mandatory Retirement in Higher Education.* Department of Economics, University of Wisconsin-Madison. Report submitted to the U. S. Department of Labor, Contract J-9-E-9–0067, October.

Holden, Karen C. and W. Lee Hansen, eds. 1989. *The End of Mandatory Retirement: Effects on Higher Education.* New Directions for Higher Education 65. San Francisco: Jossey-Bass.

Honig, Marjorie. 1996. "Retirement Expectations: Differences by Race, Ethnicity, and Gender." *Gerontologist* 36 (3): 373–82.

O'Neil, Robert. This volume. "Ending Mandatory Retirement in Two State Universities."

Keefe, John. This volume. "Intangible and Tangible Retirement Incentives."

———. This volume. "Survey of Early Retirement Practices in Higher Education."

Smith, Sharon P. This volume. "Faculty Retirement: Reflections on Experiences in an Uncapped Environment."

Switkes, Ellen. This volume. "The University of California Voluntary Early Retirement Incentive Program."

U.S. Department of Labor. 1982. Final Report to Congress on Age Discrimination in Employment Act Studies. Washington, D.C.: U.S. Department of Labor.

U.S. House of Representatives, Select Committee on Aging. 1982. *Abolishing Mandatory Retirement: Implications for America and Social Security of Eliminating Age Discrimination in Employment.* Washington, D.C.: U.S. Government Printing Office 1982.

Contributors

Robert L. Clark is Professor of Business Management and Professor of Economics at North Carolina State University. His research focuses on retirement behavior, company decisions to offer pension plans, the choice between defined benefit and defined contribution plans, the economic well-being of the elderly, and Social Security as well as international pensions. He is a Fellow of the Employee Benefit Research Institute and a member of the National Academy of Social Insurance, the American Economic Association, and the Gerontological Society of America. He earned a B.A. from Millsaps College and a Ph.D. from Duke University.

Ronald G. Ehrenberg is Irving M. Ives Professor of Industrial and Labor Relations and Economics at Cornell University. He is also Director of the Cornell Higher Education Research Institute and Co-director of Cornell's Institute for Labor Market Policies. He is a research associate at the National Bureau of Economic Research and a member of the Executive Committee of the American Economic Association. From 1995 to 1998 he served as Cornell's Vice President for Academic Programs, Planning, and Budgeting. He received a B.A. in mathematics from Harpur College (SUNY Binghamton) and a Ph.D. in economics from Northwestern University.

David Fontanella is Director of the Office of Institutional Research and Planning, and Senior Data Analyst in the Office of Institutional Research and Planning at Cornell University.

Linda S. Ghent teaches economics at Eastern Illinois University. She is a coauthor of several articles concerning retirement, retiree health insurance benefits, and other aging issues; her work has appeared in the *Journal of Gerontology, Economic Development and Cultural Change,* and other academic venues. She received a Ph.D. in economics from North Carolina State University.

P. Brett Hammond is Director of Corporate Projects for Teachers Insurance Annuity Association-College Retirement Equities Fund Investments.

Previously he served as Acting Executive Director of the behavioral and social sciences division at the National Academy of Sciences, Director of Academy Studies at the National Academy of Public Administration, and a faculty member at the University of California (Berkeley and Los Angeles). His research focuses on investments, pension economics, corporate governance, and higher education. He received A.B. degrees in economics and political science from the University of California at Santa Cruz and a Ph.D. in public policy from the Massachusetts Institute of Technology.

W. Lee Hansen is Professor Emeritus of Economics at the University of Wisconsin-Madison. Previously he taught at the University of California-Los Angeles and several European universities, was a Research Fellow at the Brookings Institution, served as a Senior Staff Economist for the President's Council of Economic Advisers, and was a Fulbright scholar. His research explores topics in labor economics, the economics of education, and economic education. He holds undergraduate and master's degrees from the University of Wisconsin-Madison and a Ph.D. in political economy from the Johns Hopkins University.

Karen C. Holden is Professor of Public Affairs and Consumer Science at the University of Wisconsin-Madison, a Fellow of the Gerontological Society of America, a member of the National Academy on Social Insurance, and an Associate of the Fellows program of the Employee Benefit Research Institute. She also sits on the Executive Committee of the Institute for Research on Poverty. Her research focuses on the economic welfare of the aged and explores how lifting the mandatory retirement age under the Age Discrimination in Employment Act of 1967 affected tenured faculty in higher education. She received a B.A. in economics from Barnard College and a Ph.D. in economics from the University of Pennsylvania.

John Keefe is President of Keefe Worldwide Information Services Inc. Previously he worked on Wall Street as an equity research analyst at two large investment banks and at leading public accounting firm. He earned a B.S. in accounting from Villanova University and an M.B.A. from the University of Pennsylvania's Wharton School.

Juanita Kreps is a widely published author on labor and industrial markets, education, and other economic issues. She served as U.S. Secretary of Commerce and has been a board member of several Fortune 500 corporations along with national educational, research, and philanthropic organizations. Previously she taught economics and was Vice President at Duke University. A graduate of Berea College, she holds a Ph.D. in economics from Duke University.

Michael W. Matier is Director of Institutional Research and Planning at Cornell University. Previously he served as a Resource and Policy Analyst in the Planning and Budgeting Office of the University of Illinois. His research examines faculty recruitment and retention, the persistence of undergraduates in science, space planning, and the nature and future of institutional research. He holds a Ph.D. in higher education administration from the University of Oregon.

Robert M. O'Neil is founding director of the Thomas Jefferson Center for the Protection of Free Expression and is on the University of Virginia's law faculty. Previously he was President of the University of Virginia and President of the University of Wisconsin, and taught at the University of California, Indiana University, and the University of Wisconsin. He also served as law clerk to U.S. Supreme Court Justice William J. Brennan, Jr. His teaching and research, including numerous books and articles, focus on constitutional law of free speech and church and state, the first amendment and the arts, and cyberspace. He has chaired Committee A (Academic Freedom and Tenure) of the American Association of University Professors and served on two occasions as general counsel. He holds three degrees from Harvard University.

David L. Raish is the partner in charge of the employee benefits law practice at Ropes & Gray, a Boston-based law firm, where he concentrates on retirement plans, deferred compensation, and other employee benefit matters. His work focuses on tax-exempt employers including universities, health care organizations, and religious groups. He chairs the annual American Law Institute-American Bar Association conference on retirement and other benefit plans of tax-exempt and governmental employers. He is a graduate of Yale University and Harvard Law School.

Sharon P. Smith is Dean of the College of Business Administration at Fordham University. She previously worked as visiting senior research economist at Princeton University and as Vice President of AT&T. Her research focuses on employee compensation as well as higher education. She has written books on equal pay in the public sector and the impact of ending mandatory retirement for faculty in the arts and sciences.

Ellen Switkes is Assistant Vice President for Academic Advancement at the University of California, Office of the President, in Oakland, California, where she oversees academic personnel policy for the University of California's nine campuses. She previously taught at the University of California, Santa Cruz. Her current responsibilities include faculty compensation, health science practice plans, severance compensation, grievance and layoff policies, and policy for academic collective bargaining. She holds a bachelor's degree from Oberlin College and a Ph.D. in inorganic chemistry from the Massachusetts Institute of Technology.

Index

Academic labor market, vii, 1–20, 21–38, 65–80, 81–105, 148–66. *See also* Faculty; Retirement

Age: and retirement incentives, 21–38, 39–64, 65–80, 81–105, 110–21, 124–25, 128–47, 148–66; discrimination, 1, 39–64, 138–47, 148–66; distribution of faculty, 1–20, 21–38, 32–33, 65–80, 81–105. *See also* Faculty; Human resource policies; Productivity; Retirement

Age Discrimination in Employment Act (ADEA), 1, 9, 19, 21, 26, 39–64, 138–47, 149

Aging faculty, vii, 1–20, 65–80, 81–105, 123–27, 148–66. *See also* Age

American Association of Retired Persons (AARP), 92, 123

American Association of University Professors (AAUP), 123, 146

American Council on Education (ACE), 123

Annuities, 19–20

Ashenfelter, Orley, 6–8, 14, 20, 38, 64, 146

Association of American Universities (AAU), 123

Atkinson, Richard C., 5, 20

Baby boomers, 1, 65–80

Berkowitz, Monroe, 139, 146

Biggs, John, vii

Blacks, 32–34. *See also* Minorities; Race

Bowen, William G., 1, 5, 20

Brewer, Dominic J., 1, 20

Burkhauser, Richard, 32, 38

Card, David, 6–8, 14, 20, 38, 64, 91, 105, 146

Carnegie classification system, 71–74, 138–47

Clark, Robert L., 1–20, 21–38, 62, 139, 146, 154, 159–60, 165

Colleges, 1–5; costs, 40–41, 81–105. *See also* Academic labor market; Higher education

Conference Committee Report on the Higher Education Amendments of 1998, 45, 49–51

Cornell University, 12, 20, 81–105. *See also* Window plans

Costa, Dora L., 128, 137

Costs of delaying retirement, 1–20, 88–89, 138–47, 157. *See also* Delayed retirement

Death benefit plan. *See* Employee Retirement Income Security Act

Deferred compensation, 56–57, 95–96

Defined benefit pension, 7–8, 32, 40–42, 81–105, 106–21, 151. *See also* Pension

Defined contribution pension, 7–8, 32, 40–42, 81–105, 151. *See also* Pension

Delayed retirement, vii, 2–3, 29–30. *See also* Academic labor market; Costs of delaying retirement; Early retirement; Employment; Retirement age

Demographic trends, 16–20, 81–105, 138–47. *See also* Aging; Baby boomers

DeVineuy, Stanley, 165

DiGiovanni, Nicholas, Jr., 139, 146

Disability benefit plan, 61–62. *See also* Employee Retirement Income Security Act; Welfare benefit plan

Duke University, vii, 7–8, 12, 21–38

Early retirement, 1–20, 65–80, 81–105, 106–21, 122–27, 129–32, 138–47, 157; window plans, vii, 13–14, 106–21, 81–105. *See also*

Early retirement (*continued*)
  Academic labor market; Employment;
  Retirement; Window plans
Earnings, 31–33, 95–97, 129–32
Ehrenberg, Ronald G., 12, 62, 81–105, 146,
  157, 165
Ekerdt, David J., 164–65
Emeritus faculty, 93
Employee Retirement Income Security Act
  of 1974 (ERISA), 9–11, 53–64, 74
Employment: older faculty, 1–20, 21–38,
  57–61, 65–80, 81–105, 106–21, 122–27,
  138–47; rights, 4–6, 38–64. *See also* Aca-
  demic labor markets; Discrimination;
  Retirement; Work
Endowment, 90–91
Equal Employment Opportunity Commis-
  sion (EEOC), 10, 40–41, 62–64
Expectations about retirement, 79, 148–66

Faculty: age distributions, 1–20, 81–105,
  134–37, 148–66; flow model, 100–103,
  148–66; performance, 3, 21–22, 138–45;
  reactions to retirement incentives, 81–105,
  122–27, 138–47, 148–66; retirement patterns, 1–20, 21–38, 65–80, 81–105. *See also*
  Academic labor markets; Employment;
  Retirement; Tenure
Fair Labor Standards Act, 40–41
Federal income taxes and pensions, 56–57
Financial: impact of retirement programs,
  88–105, 138–47; planning, 13, 88–91,
  148–66; status of educational institutions,
  21–38, 74–75, 88–105, 106–7, 122–27
Finkelstein, Martin J., 1, 5, 20
Finkin, Matthew W., 139, 146
Fontanella, David, 12, 81–105, 146, 165
403(b) plans, 107. *See also* Defined contribu-
  tion; Pension

Gates, Susan M., 1, 20
Gender. *See* Sex
Geographic differences in retirement, 73–74
Ghent, Linda S., 7, 21–38, 62, 146, 165
Goldman, Charles M., 1, 20
Gustman, Alan L., 164–65

Hammond, P. Brett, 1–20, 21–38, 62, 139,
  146
Hansen, W. Lee, 15, 146, 148–65
Harper, Loretta, 38
Harsanyi, J. C., 134, 137

Health, 21; insurance, 41, 53, 61–62, 76–
  77, 107, 155. *See also* Employee Retirement
  Income Security Act
Higher education, 1–20, 65–80, 122–27,
  148–66
Higher Education Act Amendments of 1998,
  4–5, 43–53, 59, 62–64
Highly compensated employees, 54–55.
  See also Employee Retirement Income
  Security Act
Hiring patterns. *See* Employment
Holden, Karen C., 15, 148–65
Honig, Marjorie, 164–65
Human resource policy, vii, 1–20, 34, 65–80,
  81–105, 126–27, 138–47

Incentive plans, 1–20, 65–80, 81–105, 108–
  21, 122–27, 128–37, 138–47, 148–66. *See
  also* Early retirement; Pension; Windows
Insurance. *See* Health insurance; Pension;
  Social security
Internal Revenue Code, 56–57, 111–12

Jobs. *See* Seniority; Tenure

Keefe, John, 10–11, 14, 62, 65–80, 128–37,
  156, 161, 165
Kim, Seongsu, 118, 121
Kosloski, Karl, 165
Kotlikoff, Laurence J., 32, 38
Kreps, Juanita, vii, 7, 21–38, 62, 146, 165
Kreuger, Alan B., 91, 105

Labor force trends, 1–20, 65–80, 81–105,
  122–27, 148–66. *See also* Retirement; Work
Lederman, Douglas, 92, 105
Legal constraints, 8–9, 39–64
Liberal arts. *See* private colleges and univer-
  sities
Life expectancy, 21
Life insurance, 77
Lump sum payments, 11, 46–53, 66–67,
  81–105

Management pensions, 54–56, 148–66.
  See also Employee Retirement Income
  Security Act
Mandatory retirement, vii, 1–20, 21–38,
  39–64, 65–80, 81–105, 122–27, 138–47,
  148–66. *See also* Academic labor market;
  Retirement
Matier, Michael W., 12, 81–105, 146, 165

Medicare, 76
Medigap insurance, 76
Mellon, Andrew J. Foundation, 141
Mitchell, Olivia S., 165
Mobility, 65–80. *See also* Employment;
    Tenure
Morgenstern, Oscar, 147
Mortality, 21. *See also* Life expectancy
Myers, Daniel, 32, 38

National Center for Education Statistics, 65,
    74–75, 79–80
National Commission on the Cost of Higher
    Education, 40, 64
National Research Council, 1–2, 6, 20, 37–
    38, 40, 64, 105, 123, 125, 127, 141, 145–46,
    160–61
Neumark, David, 91, 105
Normal retirement. *See* Employment; Retire-
    ment; Work
North Carolina, 21–38, 160
North Carolina State University, vii, 7–8, 12,
    21–38

Older Workers' Benefit Protection Act, 43
O'Neil, Robert M., 14, 17, 122–27, 165

Palmer, Bruce A., 67, 79
Paths to retirement, 65–80, 81–105, 122–27,
    148–66. *See also* Employment; Retirement;
    Work
Pencavel, John, 13, 20, 70, 79–80, 121,
    134–45, 137
Pension: assets, 7–8; benefits, 7–8, 54–56,
    95–96, 128–47; coverage, 32–33, 54–
    56; early retirement incentives, 65–80,
    81–105, 122–27, 138–47, 157; eligibility,
    68–69; informal versus formal plans,
    69; participation, 32–33; phased retire-
    ment incentives, 66–80, 81–105, 128–47;
    supplemental, 58–59. *See also* Employee
    Retirement Income Security Act; Defined
    benefit; Defined contribution
Pension plan type. *See* Defined benefit;
    Defined contribution
Pension Research Council, vii
Phased retirement, vii, 1–20, 57–61, 66–80,
    81–105, 128–37
Pitts, Melinda, 38
Postretirement activities, 117–18
Pratt, Henry J., 147
Productivity of faculty, 22–24, 123–24

Private colleges and universities, 4–5, 39–
    64, 71, 74, 142–43
Public colleges and universities, 9, 39–64,
    71, 74, 106, 142–43

Quality of educational programs, 121
Quinn, Joseph, 32, 38

Race, 31–33. *See also* Minorities
Raish, David L., 8–9, 39–64, 125, 237
Recall patterns, 117–18
Replacement rate, 7–8, 67
Rees, Albert, 2, 20, 105, 146
Religiously affiliated colleges and univer-
    sities, 53–59. *See also* Private colleges
    and universities; Public colleges and
    universities
Research universities, 2–3, 74–76, 81–105
Retiree health insurance. *See* Health insur-
    ance
Retirement, vii, 1–20, 21–38; ages, 5–20,
    21–38, 65–80, 81–105, 138–47, 152–53;
    decisionmaking, 44–46, 79, 128–30; ex-
    pectations versus realizations, 22–23,
    81–105, 148–66, 152–53; incentives, 1–20,
    39–64, 66–80, 81–105, 106–22, 128–37,
    157; mandatory, 1–20, 39–64, 81–105,
    81–105, 122–27, 148–66; patterns, 1–20,
    21–38, 65–80, 81–105, 122–27; policies,
    1–20, 21–38, 39–64, 65–80, 81–105, 106–
    22, 148–66; wealth, vii, 1–5. *See also* Early
    retirement; Faculty retirement; Pension;
    Tenure; Windows
Review of faculty performance, 5–6
Rosovksy, Henry, 139, 147

Safe harbor: legislation, 10–11, 18, 39–64;
    plans, 50–55. *See also* Age Discrimination
    in Employment Act; Discrimination
Salary, 31–33, 61–62, 95–97, 145. *See also*
    Deferred compensation; Earnings
Schuster, Jack H., 1, 5, 20
Seal, Robert K., 1, 5, 20
Service and pensions, 39–64, 81–105
Severance payments, 10–11, 46–48. *See also*
    Employee Retirement Income Security
    Act
Sex, 31–33
Size of school, 74–75
Smith, Sharon P., 2, 14, 20, 105, 138–47, 165
Social security benefits, 107
Sosa, Julie Ann, 1, 5, 20

State: age discrimination laws, 57–56; colleges and universities, 39–64, 106–22, 122–27
State University of New York, 105
Steinmeier, Thomas L., 165
Stock, 17–18
Supreme Court, 41
Surplus faculty, 1–2, 39–40, 65–80, 122–27. *See also* Academic labor market; Employment; Retirement
Switkes, Ellen, 13, 70, 79–80, 105, 106–21, 134–45, 137, 156, 165

Tax issues, 56–57, 85, 159. *See also* Internal Revenue Code
Teachers Insurance Annuities Association/College Retirement Equities Fund (TIAA-CREF), vii, 65, 84, 104, 150–51, 154, 157, 161, 164; Institute, vii; participants, 7
Temporary retirement incentive. *See* Phased retirement; Lump sum; Window plan
Tenure, 1–20, 39–64, 65–80, 81–105, 122–27. *See also* Aging faculty; Retirement; Seniority; Work
Top hat plans, 54–56. *See also* Employee Retirement Income Security Act

University: staffing patterns, 1–20, 82–105, 122–27. *See also* Financial impact; Higher education; Human resource policy; Retirement; names of individual institutions
University of California, 12, 70, 74, 79, 106–23, 134–35. *See also* Window plans

University of Chicago, 90
University of Florida, 122, 125–27
University of Maine, 122
University of Michigan, 123
University of North Carolina, 7–8, 12, 21–38, 160–61
University of Virginia, 12, 14, 122–27
University of Wisconsin, 12, 14, 122–27
U.S. Congress, 2–5, 91–94, 123, 150, 165
U.S. Court of Appeals, 43
U.S. Department of Education, 64, 80, 71, 137, 143, 146–47, 164
U.S. Department of Labor, 60–61, 149, 165

Voluntary retirement (VERIP) plans, 13–14, 45–46, 51–53, 65–80, 106–22, 126, 128–47, 156
Von Neumann, John, 147

Wascher, William L., 91, 105
Welfare benefit plan, 61–62. *See also* Employee Retirement Income Security Act of 1974
Window plans, 10–11, 39–64, 65–80, 128–47; Cornell University, 12; University of California, 13–14, 107–21
Wise, David A., 32, 38
Women. *See* Sex
Work: at older ages, 1–20, 21–38, 65–80, 107–21; differences by sex, 31–33. *See also* Academic labor market; Employment; Retirement age

Yale University, 90, 124

The Pension Research Council

The Pension Research Council of the Wharton School at the University of Pennsylvania is an organization committed to generating debate on key policy issues affecting pensions and other employee benefits. The Council sponsors interdisciplinary research on the entire range of private and social retirement security and related benefit plans in the United States and around the world. It seeks to broaden understanding of these complex arrangements through basic research into their economic, social, legal, actuarial, and financial foundations. Members of the Advisory Board of the Council, appointed by the Dean of the Wharton School, are leaders in the employee benefits field, and they recognize the essential role of social security and other public sector income maintenance programs while sharing a desire to strengthen private sector approaches to economic security.

Executive Director

Olivia S. Mitchell, *International Foundation of Employee Benefit Plans Professor*, Department of Insurance and Risk Management, The Wharton School, University of Pennsylvania, Philadelphia.

Senior Partners

AARP
Actuarial Sciences Associates, Inc.
Buck Consultants, Inc.
Morgan Stanley Dean Witter & Co.
Mutual of America Life Insurance Co.
PricewaterhouseCoopers
SEI Investments, Inc.
State Street Corporation
The Vanguard Group

Richard Prosten, *Director,* Washington Office, Amalgamated Life Insurance/ Amalgamated Bank of New York, Washington, DC

Anna M. Rappaport, F.S.A., *Managing Director,* William M. Mercer, Inc., Chicago, IL

Jerry S. Rosenbloom, *Frederick H. Ecker Professor of Insurance and Risk Management,* The Wharton School, Philadelphia, PA

Sylvester J. Schieber, *Vice President and Director of Research and Information Center,* The Wyatt Company, Washington, DC

Richard B. Stanger, *National Director,* Employee Benefits Services, Price Waterhouse LLP, New York, NY

Marc M. Twinney, Jr., F.S.A., *Consultant,* Bloomfield Hills, MI

Michael Useem, *Professor of Management and Sociology,* The Wharton School, Philadelphia, PA

Jack L. VanDerhei, *Professor of Risk and Insurance,* Temple University, Philadelphia, PA

Paul H. Wenz, F.S.A., *Second Vice President and Actuary,* The Principal Financial Group, Des Moines, IA

Stephen Zeldes, *Benjamin Rosen Professor of Economics and Finance,* Columbia University, New York, NY

Recent Pension Research Council Publications

Demography and Retirement: The Twenty-First Century. Anna M. Rappaport and Sylvester J. Schieber, eds. 1993.

An Economic Appraisal of Pension Tax Policy in the United States. Richard A. Ippolito. 1991.

The Economics of Pension Insurance. Richard A. Ippolito. 1991.

Forecasting Retirement Needs and Retirement Wealth. Olivia S. Mitchell, P. Brett Hammond, and Anna M. Rappaport. 2000.

Fundamentals of Private Pensions. Dan M. McGill, Kyle N. Brown, John J. Haley and Sylvester Schieber. Seventh edition. 1996.

The Future of Pensions in the United States. Ray Schmitt, ed. 1993.

Inflation and Pensions. Susan M. Wachter. 1991.

Living with Defined Contribution Pensions. Olivia S. Mitchell and Sylvester J. Schieber, eds. 1998

Pension Mathematics with Numerical Illustrations. Howard E. Winklevoss. Second edition. 1993.

Pensions and the Economy: Sources, Uses, and Limitations of Data. Zvi Bodie and Alicia H. Munnell, eds. 1992.

Pensions, Economics and Public Policy. Richard A. Ippolito. 1991.

Positioning Pensions for the Twenty-First Century. Michael S. Gordon, Olivia S. Mitchell, and Marc M. Twinney, eds. 1997.

Prospects for Social Security Reform. Olivia S. Mitchell, Robert J. Myers, and Howard Young, eds. 1999.

Providing Health Care Benefits in Retirement. Judith F. Mazo, Anna M. Rappaport and Sylvester J. Schieber, eds. 1994.

Retirement Systems in Japan. Robert L. Clark. 1991.

Search for a National Retirement Income Policy. Jack L. VanDerhei, ed. 1987.

Securing Employer-Based Pensions: An International Perspective. Zvi Bodie, Olivia S. Mitchell, and John A. Turner. 1996.

Social Investing. Dan M. McGill, ed. 1984.

Social Security. Robert J. Myers. Fourth edition. 1993.

Available from the University of Pennsylvania Press, telephone: 800/445–9880, fax: 410/516–6998.

More information about the Pension Research Council is available at the web site: http://prc.wharton.upenn.edu/prc/prc.html

Printed in the United States
76358LV00003B/4